G000231789

Chelms

Off the Record

The Life and Letters
of a Black Watch Officer

OFF THE RECORD

The Life and Letters
of a Black Watch Officer

by

David Rose

SPELLMOUNT
Staplehurst

British Library Cataloguing in Publication Data:
A catalogue record for this book is available
from the British Library

Copyright © David Rose 1996

ISBN 1–873376–76–6

First published in the UK in 1996 by
Spellmount Limited
The Old Rectory
Staplehurst
Kent TN12 0AZ

1 3 5 7 9 8 6 4 2

The right of David Rose to be identified
as the author of this work has been asserted by him
in accordance with the Copyright, Designs
and Patents Act 1988

Typeset by Palimpsest Book Production Ltd,
Polmont, Stirlingshire
Printed in Great Britain by
Mackays of Chatham PLC, Chatham, Kent

To the three women in my life –
my Mother, my Wife and my Daughter

The Final Road

O now that days of mental effort
quietly fade to misty past
and lofty thoughts of self-expression
seldom come and never last,
'tis now we see ourselves in letters
received and sent when we were young,
read, and re-read, thoughtful treasures,
delights for days still yet to come!
And when the mind no longer can,
assimilate, create the picture,
then must we, like all of man
accept the last and final stricture -
the end of all sweet Nature's plan -
and prepare to meet what lies ahead
when we've laid down our mortal head,
in faith, alone, at our last tryst,
to end mortality in Christ!

Andrew Duncan

PREFACE

General Sir Michael Rose
KCB, CBE, DSO, QGM, ADC Gen

David Rose has set out to write his reminiscences, in the expectation that readers of a very different era – whether or not they have been privileged to wear the 'Red Hackle' of the 'Forty-Twa' – will be interested in his distinguished regimental service, packed as it is with active duty.

Drawing on his letters to his wife, Lady Jean, and to and from others amongst his family and friends, he was written a narrative full of vigour and force. He and those who fought alongside him knew what they were about and accepted with courage and energy their tasks in battle. Straightforward in his views, David follows the progress of operations in Palestine before the Second World War, and during it the fighting in Somaliland (where he won his first DSO), North Africa and Burma where he led a Chindit Column of his own Black Watch Jocks. A very experienced battalion commander by then, he commanded with distinction the 1st Black Watch in Korea, during the famous battle of the 'Hook'. His skilful use of artillery cover on his own positions, well prepared with overhead protection, defeated the enemy's 'human wave' tactics, and reduced his battalion's casualties to a minimum. He was awarded a bar to his DSO.

Gaining a fine reputation was one thing, but following his story in *Off the Record* and reading between the lines, he was clearly a hard taskmaster on himself and his superiors. Nothing was too much for him in defending his Jocks from the inefficiency of others. But his huge sense of fun in viewing the unfolding situation is a lesson to all would-be leaders.

His anecdotes at times are hilarious and his letters are a pleasure to read for their candour and realism. He had three brothers, each with a fine war record with the HLI, Argylls and French Foreign Legion respectively. What a handful of young men they must have been to their parents. As a distant member of the Rose Clan, I can only wish I had met them all!

For all these reasons, and because above all *Off the Record* is a charming and very human book, I commended it to all who enjoy reading about regimental soldiering and a man who has led his life to the full.

Michael Rose

Contents

Foreword

My grandfather, George Rose, lived at Inverness at a house called 'Hillview', now a youth hostel. He had five sons. His wife, Florence Latham, died when the children were still quite young and they were brought up by the Housekeeper. They were all educated at Fort Augustus.

David, the eldest, left home at the age of 19 with his shepherd, a dog and £100. He founded a family in Texas, where they own a ranch to this day. My father, John Latham, was next. He inherited a small legacy and became a soldier, an officer in what was then a rather smart regiment, the HLI. Some of their officers were very wealthy men and my father was unable to stand the cost of champagne in the Mess. He transferred to the Indian Army and became a Gurkha.

The next two sons, George and Hugh, went to Canada and joined the Canadian Mounted Police, settling eventually in British Columbia. George was a founder member of the City of Kalona and for many years was the Editor of the *Kalona Courier*. Hugh grew wonderful apples but never made any money. The two brothers stuck together all their lives: they had no children.

Frederick died of enteric fever in the South African War.

Brigadier General John Rose, my father, brought up our family in Argyll, at Fanans, the Dower House of the Campbells of Inverawe and Dunstaffnage, my mother's home. We were very much in the shadow of the First World War. My mother and father used to get, every fortnight or so, books from the Times Book Club, which as far as I remember were nearly always histories of the war or biographies of the great men. Churchill, Allenby, Haig, Foch, Rawlinson and the names of all these people were frequently to be heard at our table when we had guests of my father's age to stay in the house.

My brothers, Rhoddy and Angus, both went to Wellington College and there was no doubt that they would follow in their father's footsteps. Neil and I were less certain because we went to Glenalmond, which was by no means a Military School, although it had a fine War Memorial to the many young men who had given their lives for their country. I was supposed to break new ground and go to Cambridge, but I didn't work hard enough and I failed the exam. After a short time at a crammer, I succeeded in getting a place at the Royal Military College, Sandhurst, like my brothers. Neil, my younger brother, had bad luck with illness but he joined the Cameronians, a very tough Lowland Scottish Regiment and was recommended for a Commission. Again he fell ill and, after a long convalescence at home, he ended up in the Foreign Legion.

Colonel Hugh Rose of Kilravock, our Chieftain, was commanding the 1st Battalion Black Watch in 1912, the year I was born. I was to have this great privilege 40 years later.

Before launching into my tale of years gone by – sometimes they seem as yesterday – there are some heartfelt thanks to express. Many friends have seen the book in various stages of writing and offered some suggestions, but mainly encouragement. Patrick Mileham, whose father John was with me at Staff College in Haifa during the war, and with his charming wife and daughters used to take our garden cottage at Trian each year, acted as my editor and sometimes referee! Linda MacDougal, Jean Gemmell and particularly Carolyn Laing did sterling work on the word processor, as did Pat Stevenson. Regimental Headquarters provided extra illustrations from the museum collection set up so many years ago by George Rusk, who lived in our lovely house and garden before we did. So the circle is complete.

Trian House   David Rose
Glenartney   1996
Perthshire

List of Illustrations

CHAPTER ONE
Early Days

Boyhood

My father returned from India in 1919. We settled in a house called Saxon Lodge at Seaford in Sussex, where we were at a school known as Kings Mead. The house was only about 200 yards from the sea. At the end of the garden, and it wasn't really a garden, there was a kind of cement structure called a gazebo, I suppose to give some shelter from the constant wind.

Our house was quite small. I think it was all painted white inside. There was rather a pretty white panelled parlour where my parents sat. We had a long low loft, where we could lay out our lines of lead soldiers on wet days. To get to the dining room, we went down several brick steps, which made the square room quite high. I think it must have been the kitchen in olden times as it had a huge open brick hearth with a large oak beam at the chimney breast. We burnt logs on the hearth and always left the ashes.

We didn't seem to do anything at Seaford, except walk along the path on Beachy Head. That was fun, but it was only along a path. It was dangerous to stray off the path because the chalk cliff often broke away and the sea was about 150 feet below. We were made to run down to the beach in our macintoshes for a dip before breakfast. It was supposed to make us manly. I hated it and often shirked the awful shock and then felt rather ashamed of myself. One day we went to a lovely place in the country called Alfriston. It was so beautiful after Seaford, it just made me gasp. It was wonderful, downland with lots of cows and sheep. I was seven.

My mother and father bought a new house. I think the object was to be nearer to the golf course. My mother wasn't at all happy at Seaford. One day I heard her say in a very cross voice, 'This is no place to bring up the boys.' The new house was put back on the market and sold almost immediately for a thousand pounds more than they had paid for it, so there were no more cross words about 'that horrible redbrick villa'. My father loved his golf, but I think the other members of the club were not the sort of people he was used to and he often just played with the professional.

The very next holiday we set off for Scotland in the third-hand, pale blue Maxwell. It had a cape hood and side screens. I think

1

most of our things were sent by rail. It took us two days to get from Seaford. We had seven or eight punctures on the way. My father ran every tyre to death, right onto the canvas. I can't remember where we stayed the night, but when we had another puncture in the morning, my mother and I walked back to York and bought a ham. The ham cost much more than several punctures and my father was rather angry. When we got to Fanans, Neil and I were very excited. Everything smelt quite different. We had got rid of Rhoddy and Angus, who were living in the big house. Neil and I were in a lovely little cottage at the end of the drive with Mum and Dad. It was rather nice not to have Rhoddy and Angus bossing us all the time.

In the morning we met Fergusson the ghillie. He lived at the gate of Fanans House in a little white cottage. His wife Mimi had only one tooth and looked like a witch. Duncan Fergusson smelt very strange. A funny kind of smell – a mixture of sweat, tobacco and something rather nice – it must have been whisky. His skin was like leather. We were told that he only had a bath on the 1st of May each year.

One afternoon, we all went up to Fanans House to see Aunt Jane. She was in bed and she looked like a witch too – but a very pretty witch. She had a lovely lace cap on her head and she spoke very kindly to us. She was obviously very tired and we didn't stay for long. We went back to Seaford after a lovely holiday.

The next year we went to Scotland properly. We went by steamer from Tilbury Docks with the Maxwell on board. The ship was the SS *Perth* which I was to meet again later in my life. It took two days. We had a wonderful breakfast at the Station Hotel at Perth. What a breakfast! Porridge and cream, followed by fish and poached eggs, followed by all kinds of scones and blackcurrant jelly and creamy milk. How one can recall such meals.

It took the whole day to get to Fanans from Perth in the Maxwell. We only went at 25 miles per hour. Dad said the potholes were really terrible. We hardly met one car on the journey.

This time we were all in the big house. I suppose Aunt Jane had died but no one told us. It was lovely to have our own home and there were rabbits everywhere. Neil got terribly over-excited and didn't know what he was doing, just ran about all over the place, shouting.

In the morning Mimi Fergusson brought up a large bucket of milk. We had a cow and she milked it. Next to the byre there was another shed with a notice on the door 'Tinker's Hotel'. When a tramp or a tinker was using it, there was always a can of milk and a small bucket of porridge put down at the door. We were told that it was an old clan custom that the family gave hospitality to all who should pass by.

We had the salmon fishing on the River Awe two days one week, four days the next. The Taynuilt Hotel shared it with us. It wasn't a very good beat, the left bank from the Bridge of Awe up to the Pass of Brander. The wealthy Huntingtons had the right bank, with the famous Pol Verie pool, and another mile below the bridge. However, my father and his guests sometimes got a salmon or a grilse, and in the gloaming we often had great sport with sea trout and finnock.

Neil and I still had to go to our prep school in England but we knew where our real home was and didn't sleep a wink when we came north in the railway sleeper. One day I made a bold approach to my father.

'Must I really go to Wellington? Rhoddy and Angus both hate it and Rhoddy says the food isn't fit for dogs.'

'Well I could send you to Glenalmond in Perthshire. That would save me all the expense of sleepers and a man to take you across London.'

So it came about that Neil and I went to Trinity College Glenalmond, and when I was 16, I was allowed to drive the car with my father's chauffeur beside me – Neil in the back seat would beg me to go faster, much faster.

I loved fishing. I didn't mind at all if I didn't catch anything, and I seldom did because Father and Rhoddy had covered the pools before I got a chance. But what I loved was being quite alone – just the river, the grey wagtails, the endless flow of the brown water. I spent so many completely useless hours on the river, changing my flies, covering every inch of the water, most of it quite unsuitable to hold a fish. No one taught me about where they would lie and I really didn't care. I would hum a lot when I was fishing, and when I was in a very noisy rapid, I would sing loudly against the water.

Sometimes I would think about what I wanted to do when I had finished with school. I had a great desire to be a crofter. I wanted to live on an island on the West Coast and to have sheep and cows and fish in the sea. It was a wonderful dream. There was nobody else in that dream, just a happy me.

We had lots of people to stay. They came for at least a week, sometimes more, and most of them were old. One morning each week one of us had to help Mother, immediately after breakfast, counting the laundry. It was Rhoddy's turn and I was keeping a sharp eye on him, because he always slipped away after going to the loo. I saw him come out of the loo and make for the front door. I could imitate my mother's rich contralto voice almost exactly.

'Rhoddy, don't forget that it's your day to help me with the laundry.'

'Alright, coming mother.'

When he got to the top of the stairs, he found only me – 'You young bastard!' 'You didn't get away with it this time,' I said. I had timed it perfectly.

My mother was coming up the stairs. 'Oh how kind of you Rhoddy and David too! We'll get through it in no time at all.'

The laundry was a terrible job. Dozens of double damask napkins, many pillow cases and then all the single and double sheets. My father had a chauffeur valet, an ex-naval man named Lyon, but he wouldn't do anything like the laundry. He took the big hampers to the station in the shopping car, where they were sent on to Oban. We also had a table maid and a kitchen maid, but they were busy making the beds I suppose.

My father had met two officers at Seaford who were in the Machine Gun Corps; they were both married, but neither had any children. They came to stay each summer for several years. They fairly stirred things up and we greatly looked forward to their visits.

Bill and Allan (as they were called) would take us out shooting to places father couldn't get to. Everything was properly organised. There were no more arguments, no talking, we were under discipline. Bill and Allan used to write lovely things in the visitors' book – 'I shot my first grouse; I landed my first salmon; marvellous grub. May I come again?' When they went south on the train from Taynuilt, we would stand on the railway embankment on the other side of the river and fire a salute with our various guns as the train went past.

We had other people to stay, but they were all much older and didn't come with us, but they gave us some nice tips, according to our age. We didn't get much pocket money and what we did get mostly went on bicycle repairs.

There were two other families in the neighbourhood who had children of our age. The Campbell Prestons lived on the other side of Loch Etive and you had to pay a toll to cross the bridge at Connel Ferry, so we didn't see much of them. They had two sons and three daughters – Bobby and Patrick, Faith, Hope and Charity.

At Bonawe Ferry there was a wealthy family named Huntington. They had a big property in the south. They rode to hounds in the winter and had race horses. Charles, Bill and Jim, Enid and another sister, whose name I have forgotten.

We didn't see much of each other because there weren't many cars in those days and we all had things to do on our own

4

doorsteps, such as fishing, rabbits, a few grouse and boats on the lochs.

The Oban Games was the great meeting place at the end of the season with two nights' dancing. Everyone went to the Games – the Duke of Argyll and all his Campbell cousins in their finery, all the other Lairds and the summer visitors who had rented various properties.

The winter in Argyll was really terrible. It just never stopped raining. My father simply didn't know what to do with himself. So we started going to St Andrews in Fife for the winter. We rented a very nice house in Abbotsford Crescent from a well-known liberal family, the Grimmonds.

So my father's needs had now been met to the full. He was within walking distance of the Royal and Ancient Golf Club, where there was abundant convivial company, and he could play golf and bridge to his heart's content. The green fees were free to rate-payers.

Rhoddy was now at Sandhurst and Angus was soon to follow him there. They had moved into the teenage lifestyle with jazz records and Rhoddy started playing the ukulele. He made a terrible noise, but thought himself quite the thing. He had some pretty fast friends in the RAF at Leuchars airfield.

We still went to Fanans at Easter and for the summer. Joyce and Rosemary Kirk came to stay for the Oban Balls. I fell in love with Joyce. She was gorgeous and very sophisticated and she was very kind to me. I had her picture above my bed at school. They all came back from the second night of the Oban Ball in broad daylight. Rhoddy thought they would get into their rooms unobserved by giving the girls a leg up through their bedroom window. Unfortunately my father was afoot earlier than usual. There was an explosion of what Rhoddy called 'generalism'. 'How dare you treat young ladies in such a cavalier manner.' Father did not know that on the way back from the Ball, they had decided to ride some horses in their kilts with the girls mounted behind them!

By the next year Rhoddy had his Commission in the HLI. He was in a very smart party given by Lady Masserine and Ferrard. She had been a famous beauty, like the Duchess of Argyll. Rhoddy was very good-looking indeed; he had a slim moustache like Ronald Coleman and all the girls were after him. So was one of the matrons! I overheard my mother say to Rhoddy at breakfast, 'Don't let that woman make a monkey of you.'

'What do you mean mother?'

'You know very well what I mean, Rhoddy.'

I remember one incident on the gravel outside the front door at Fanans as though it happened yesterday. Rhoddy was about to drive south in his car, a green two-seater, 'the Grasshopper'. His Regiment was in Aldershot and they were shortly to sail for India where they would be for many years. Rhoddy would not get any home leave for three years.

My father said, quite without any emotion, 'Well Rhoddy, I don't suppose we will meet again. You will enjoy India.' So the birds were leaving the nest. Now there was only Neil and me.

My parents decided to move to a more salubrious climate. My father chose the driest county of England, Suffolk, and they found a nice house at Woodbridge on the River Deban. It had an excellent golf course and lots of very nice people round about – landowners, retired admirals and generals and many sportsmen. It was still the fashion to leave calling cards on newcomers and I used to drive my mother round the country returning the calls. I was soon being asked to shoot at some very fine places. Suffolk was great fun and we made a great many friends there.

Royal Military College Sandhurst

I enjoyed my time at Sandhurst. I was given no alternative but I very soon realised that it was the right choice for me. It was very hard work. I particularly enjoyed the Riding School, compulsory then even for infantry officers.

I made my first real friends and we three went everywhere together. Pat Smylie was from a well-to-do family and had been fox hunting for several years. He was destined for the Cavalry. He was delightful company, 'bone idle' as we expressed it in our jargon, and remained a mere Gentleman Cadet. Peter Saunders' father, like mine, had been a Gurkha and that was where Peter was intending to do his service. Peter became Captain of the Cross Country Team and ran against Oxford University. He was a terrific enthusiast and had a twinkle in his eye and a keen sense of the ridiculous. He and I became Junior Under Officers.

I had only one remarkable experience at Sandhurst. A Cadet named Openheimer was put in the lake. He was in my Platoon. This was the way that Cadets showed their utter distaste for one of their kind. It was something you couldn't live down, so you had to pack it in. But it all went too far.

I had to visit him in hospital. Poor fellow, he was in a proper mess. His backside was like raw steak. He had been pulled across the square by his heels, before they threw him in.

I told the other Under Officers what I had discovered and we decided that we must do something about it pronto. The Senior UO was John Freeland and under him were four of us, Bob Moran,

Douglas Davies Scofield, Peter Saunders and me. Freeland said I was to read the riot act. So that was that. The whole company was assembled in the Big Hall. My great friend, Peter, gave me a dig in the ribs and said, 'You can do it. You know you can.' We all walked in together. There was a complete hush. I said, 'You fellows have made a real mess of Openheimer. I've seen him in hospital. You have also made a complete hash of our chances of being Champion Company.

'They are trying to teach us here how to be Officers and Gentlemen. No Gentleman would have done to anyone what you did to Openheimer. I have got to see the Adjutant after Church Parade and I can tell you, I am not looking forward to it. Fall out!'

As we left the Hall, Peter Saunders said, 'Well done. You got it just right.'

I walked up the stone stairs to the Adjutant's Quarters. His batman, smartly dressed in Blue Patrol jacket answered my ring. 'Captain Gwatkin is in his bath. I will tell him that you are here.' I heard him say, 'Under Office Rose says you sent for him.'

'Captain Gwatkin will see you now.' He opened the door and there was my Adjutant in a cloud of steam, with an enormous sponge providing necessary dignity.

'Rose, have you seen Openheimer?'

'Yes, Sir, he is in a bad way, but now fairly comfortable.'

'Why did it happen?'

'His name, Sir.'

'And what have you done about it?'

'Sir, with the other Under Officers, I read the riot act.'

'What was their response?'

'They were very ashamed of themselves.'

'Well done! James bring us some sherry.'

That was my first brush with authority; there were to be several more in the years to come.

Captain Norman Gwatkin was a magnificent figure on parade in his Brigade of Guards uniform and riding on his white charger. He was always polite, smartly dressed, smiling and radiated calm confidence. We all thought he was the very model of an Officer and a Gentleman, and so he was.

I was in my last term at Sandhurst when my father died. My eldest brother Rhoddy had been with the Highland Light Infantry in India for more than two years. My brother Angus was well settled with the Argyll & Sutherland Highlanders at Folkestone. My younger brother Neil had just left home for South Africa to be trained by the 1820 Memorial Settlers Association as a farmer.

My mother and I went to London to get me fitted out with everything that was required by an officer in those days. Savile Row of course; Maxwell for boots and shoes; Hilditch & Key for shirts and under clothes. The bill was staggering to me. 'Must I really have all this finery, mother?' I said. 'Yes, you must be a credit to your Regiment and if you look after your clothes carefully, they will last you for many years.' We ploughed on, tail coat, morning coat, top hat and bowler from Locks; tweed suit for race meetings, dark pin striped grey flannel suit; plus fours for golf and shooting, I had everything. They *did* last for many years, until my elder brothers raided my room when I was away in Burma! Only the useless tail coat and morning coat were left.

Colchester

I joined the Regiment in January 1932. My pay was £12 per month, my Mess bill was always a pound or two more. We had to pay 'extra messing' which was about eight shillings a day. This was for things like cold ham on the side board. The Mess staff wore livery.

My mother gave each of us an allowance of £250 a year. This kept us solvent, with sometimes recourse to a small overdraft. My mother also gave me the shopping car, an elderly Citroen, with a canvas hood. Bernard Fergusson and Pat Campbell Preston, who had joined six months before me, didn't have cars when they joined, but had just acquired jointly an old Bull Nosed Morris, for £23. It stood outside the Mess for several weeks, polished but unused, for they hadn't the cash to fill it with petrol. Petrol was one shilling and sixpence a gallon.

If you were posted to the battalion which was on a foreign tour, you could pay someone below you on the list to go in your place – probably for the price of a polo pony. I was warned for posting to the 1st Battalion at Meerut in Northern India. I didn't much want to go because of my mother's recent bereavement. Pat said he would go in my place. His father had also died, so he was going out anyway as he was escorting his sister who was to be married out there.

Any thought of promotion was years and years away. Our adjutant, Thomas Rennie, was still a subaltern with 15 years' service. He had passed through Staff College, but that made no difference. We had eight Officers in the Black Watch who had brothers in the Argylls. Our Roper-Calbeck was offered a captaincy in the Argylls over his younger brother, but he refused it. He had no wish to leave his regiment and all his friends – and he was having a wonderful time at Perth.

In those pre-war years, there was only one voice heard demanding reform of the armed forces. They were the years when Winston Churchill was in the wilderness. We had a Conservative government but financial stringency ruled everywhere. We were paying the debts of war. One Secretary of State, Hore Belisha, did eventually in 1939 introduce promotion to captain at nine years service, provided you had passed the promotion exam.

My first CO was Guy Rowan-Hamilton, rather an awesome figure with a very prominent chin and a breastful of medals and decorations. Our first battalion exercise was 'Defence of the line of the Roman River against an invasion from the Sea'. It was only a few miles' march from barracks. A bit of a joke really. We were to carry poles with yellow flags to represent anti-tank rifles. We were to dig trenches, but were to make sure they were properly filled in before we returned to barracks the next morning. In the evening I received a message 'Mr Rose and Mr Fergusson may withdraw to Bn HQ for supper'. There was quite a spread, a white table cloth and the waiters had come out in livery.

Glasgow

My second CO was Frankie Chalmer. He also had a breastful of medals and decorations. He was portly and benign and liked a quiet life and a good table.

Glasgow was quite frightful at that time. It was in the depths of the Depression. Quite apart from the gloom of rain and fog, the people were in despair. Meths drinking and 'red biddy' was obvious in the streets; the people were thin and pale and sour. The book of the day which told the sad story to the world was *No Mean City*.

Michael Young and I were in charge of the Cross Country Running Team; The Duke of Cornwall's Light Infantry were the army champions at that time. We decided we would win the title from them. There was quite a good local team, the Maryhill Harriers. We decided to train with them, and night after night we set forth in the dark and wet streets to build up our stamina. The local chaps were so ill-nourished that we used to take them first to the NAAFI for a 'char and wad'. After a few minutes, we would set off on our run. We didn't let them beat us, but on the other hand we didn't want to shame them. After the run they would have a shower and a NAAFI supper with our men. Mr Rose would pay the bill with a small grant from Regimental Institute funds but he often had to dip into his own pocket to make up the total.

Michael and I once tried to penetrate the Gorbals in disguise. It was not a success! They knew at once who we were and did not conceal the fact that we were to clear out. We were quite frightened.

My Company Commander was a wiry little man, also covered with decorations and medals. Adrian Hamilton had once commanded a battalion of Black Watch when only 20 years of age. Every other officer had been either killed or wounded. He simply could not endure the rain, the fog and the idleness at Maryhill.

One morning he said to me, 'Rose, go and find me a training area and then make out some draft training exercises.'

'Can I use my car?'

'Of course you can, but don't expect any petrol allowance.' I found the Great Park at Buchanan Castle, the seat of the Duke of Montrose.

The first exercise was to be billeting. We marched out of the gates of Maryhill Barracks but came to a sudden halt. Our mule-drawn limber was very smart but the spokes had not been wet for twelve years and were so brittle that they shattered. The limber and its heavy load lay inert on its belly. A voice from behind said, 'So what do you do now?'

'If it was war, Sir, I would commandeer one of those vehicles.'

'Right, get on with it.'

'But Sir!'

'Write the requisition order, before you choose the vehicle.' I complied.

'Now I'll go back to barracks and get a 15-cwt truck,' he said. This was getting interesting.

The billet was to be the village hall. I had obtained £3 from the training grant for the rent. Sentries were posted in case the enemy should surprise us. The cooking area was selected, water drawn, the men constantly being told to stop the chatter.

John Elphinstone was junior to me. 'John shall we sleep in the pub?'

'Good idea.'

'I'll go and book rooms.'

I returned a little later. 'Afraid there's only a double bed. Do you mind?'

'No, of course not.' We had no fear that we would be accused of being homo.

The next morning's exercise was 'Advance to Contact'. Hammy had his caravan in the Ducal Park and his small son with him to act as umpire.

'Mr Rose,' he said, 'Daddy says your dead.' It was John Elphinstone's turn to be tested.

Ceremonial

There are high spots in all our lives. I once had to carry the keys of Edinburgh Castle on a parade when our Regimental Colonel, General Cameron, was installed as Governor. My Company was the Castle Garrison, detached from Redford Barracks. We gave a cocktail party the night before the event and behaved no-how. The following morning, my escort and I assembled in front of the hospital block. Some of the staff came out to chat us up.

'Sweet Nurse,' I said with questing brow, 'would you have pity on a wicked man and give me a shot of something to get me through the parade?' She returned in no time at all with a prairie oyster – raw egg, Worcester sauce and a shot of sherry. I swallowed it in one gulp and off we went down the steep hill to the Castle gate.

'Sweet angel,' I called back, 'I will never forget you.'

Just before the portcullis we broke into slow time, but as we emerged through the arch the heavy keys with the large gilded labels shot off the plump velvet cushion. I took them at half volley and the press failed to get a scoop, which might have dogged me all my life.

High Life

When on the Balmoral Guard, I dined one night with the King. He had decided to leave London ahead of Queen Mary. He wasn't very well. It was a rush job for us to get to Ballater to do the Guard of Honour. My batman had only packed my civilian brogues, so there was much telephoning to the Officers' Mess to rectify this situation. Blow me down, we were commanded to dine the very first night!

We assembled in a small room. It was an all male party. Just the Comptroller, the Equerry, Michael Young and me. I stood with my feet concealed behind a small sofa. We made our bow as the King entered.

'When I became your Colonel in Chief, the Regiment very kindly gave me all the accoutrements, the sporran, skean dhu and gold buckles for my brogues, and they were gold – much too heavy. Come out from behind the sofa, Rose and let me have a look at you. What's this – what's this? Silver buckles?' he said in his gravelly old voice.

'I am sorry that I am improperly dressed, Sir, but we came up in rather a hurry and my batman only packed my civilian brogues.'

'Oh what rotten bad luck, but you have a proper sporran. Can't stand these small sporrans they all seem to wear nowadays.'

We went into dinner without further delay. Michael Young sat on his right with me on his left.

'This is a good champagne, Rose, I am sure you will like it. I'm not allowed to drink champagne, so I have this wine from my own vineyard in France. It's called Bernkastler Doctor – very delicious.'

His hand rested for a moment on the table between us. I was intrigued to see the exquisite manicure. He always shot in gloves. His cuff links were small Union Jacks! Dare I ask who had given them to him? No better not – rather cheeky.

'Now tuck into the grouse, Rose. I'm sure it's very well cooked. I'm not allowed grouse, but I have a very nice young partridge – out of season of course!' He spoke to me just like a father. I was entirely at ease with him. Only a year later I was to slow march behind his coffin with a fine body of NCOs and men at my back.

I once danced with Queen Mary at the Mar Lodge Ball. The first dance was called the Flirtation Waltz, a kind of Paul Jones. The band always stopped when the Queen was either opposite to me or Michael Young. At the end of the dance, she gave each of us a hand and led us across the floor to the dais. 'George these are my beaux,' she said and he replied in his deep gruff voice, 'Splendid, Mary, splendid.'

Michael and I were in need of a drink after that. We found the Dining Room and there we saw an opened bottle of champagne and two glasses. We had just finished the bottle, when in walked the Duke of York (our future King George VI) and his host. It was quite obvious for whom the champagne had been intended.

'There will be a penalty to pay for this misdemeanour,' said the Duke. 'You will have to dine with me.' We were then invited to shoot with him each Tuesday and Thursday.

One evening Queen Mary gave a big dinner party for twenty or more people. Lord Shaftesbury was Comptroller of the Household, and his beautiful daughter and very wild son, Paddy, were there too. Paddy had dined with us at the Ballater Mess, but that is a story which is definitely not for publication.

The table was wonderfully decorated with fruits and flowers and pressed leaves on the white cloth. The candelabra threw a magical light over the silver and crystal. We sat down to a full dinner, course after course.

After dinner we all moved to a very large drawing room. By the time I got there, Queen Mary was standing in front of the fire, one hand resting on the gilded fire screen. She was a perfect picture.

Each of the male guests was taken up in turn. I made my bow.

'Are you enjoying the Guard, Mr Rose?'

'Yes, Ma'am, it's wonderful. We're having so much fishing and shooting.'

'Have we ever met before this?'

'Well, Ma'am, not really, but once you visited my uncle and aunt, Admiral and Lady Henderson in Sussex.'

'Oh yes, I remember, she has a very nice collection of Bristol glass, which interests me, but I don't remember any children.'

'Well, Ma'am, we were considered too ragamuffin to come to tea, but we watched you through the keyhole.'

Queen Mary burst out laughing and so did I. The whole room was watching. I went bright pink. The Equerry was at my elbow. I made my bow and moved slowly away.

'What on earth did you say to the Queen?' he said. 'No one has made her laugh for ages.'

The Depot, Perth

The 2nd Battalion was now due for a period of foreign service. The 1st Battalion had left India and, on the way home, was stationed in the Sudan. There was a certain amount of cross-posting of those who still had time to serve abroad, but instead of returning to the 2nd Battalion, I was posted to the Depot as one of two training subalterns; the other was Neil Blair.

A posting to the Depot in any rank was much coveted. There could not be many jobs at home with greater opportunities for sport of all kinds and a wonderful social life.

The supervision of training was not very onerous; it was very much left to the NCOs. Our main job was with the Territorial Army. We very soon got to know all the officers of the Black Watch battalions and the Fife and Forfar Yeomanry. They were the local businessmen, solicitors, wine merchants and farmers. These were the men who were to lead our battalions with such distinction in the Second World War in north Africa, Italy and northern Europe. I can remember nearly every one of them.

Before the First World War, Scotland had been the playground of the very wealthy. Punitive taxation was, over a period of some 10 years, to bring great changes in the life-style of the great noble families. It was also to have a very adverse effect on agriculture and the landscape of the whole of Britain. The demand for more and ever more produce from each acre, the massive use of artificial fertilisers and pesticides, and the harvesting of silage on a vast scale was to devastate the habitat of the partridge and many other wild birds. However, between the wars there was still wonderful sport to be had everywhere. Small fields and many very old hedges produced the insect life and the necessary protection for nesting, and dung farming produced the worms and beetles so essential for all wildlife.

13

The old Duke of Atholl gave us wonderful winter shooting at Blair Atholl. The only penalty, he said, was that we were to have tea with him and the Duchess after each shoot, to tell them all about it.

Mungo Mansfield, Joe Airlie, Evelyn Forteviot, John Dalhousie and Timothy Bowes-Lyon who owned large tracts of Perthshire and Angus, were all very keen and very good shots and were kind enough to invite us on many occasions. Other estates like Errol and Burkhill had wonderful autumn days, with large bags of partridges and ducks. In those days the farmers were very pleased for us to shoot the large numbers of geese who raided their young corn in the spring. In addition to all this sport, there was also sailing and inexpensive golf and curling in the winter and spring.

Towards the end of our time at the Depot, Neil Blair got married and I was his best man. I also made an attempt at marriage, but the well brought up young lady thought I was too wild and I am sure she was quite right. So I went off to Palestine to rejoin the 2nd Battalion.

Palestine

At the end of the Great War, with the collapse of the Ottoman Empire, Palestine was handed over to the British as a 'mandate' territory. We had the unenviable task of not only controlling the Arabs, whose political ambitions had been raised enormously by the revolt, partly engineered by ourselves during the war, but the Jewish population as well. Zionism was in the ascendant during the period and the demands for a Jewish homeland to be established were reinforced by the steady flow of Jews returning to the Middle East after many generations of dispersal all over the western world.

Nevertheless Palestine was fun for young officers. We sometimes tangled with an Arab gang, or we lined out over the hills searching for gangs in hiding. My company was for some time based in a pleasant hotel at Ramalleh. One night, when we were having a cinema show in the garden, an Arab fired a blunderbuss at the screen over the wall – not a good mark for our security precautions!

The sentry on the roof of the hotel opened fire, and then there was a cry 'casualty on the roof'. The foolish fellow had fired into the parapet and the ricochet had hit his companion.

The next order was, 'Mr Rose, clear the perimeter.' Mr Rose duly charged off with a dozen men beside him and reported that the perimeter wall was all clear.

Another company was based at the Citadel in Hebron. This was, and still is, a very tricky Arab stronghold. One night the Citadel came under long-range rifle fire. The officer in charge, Richard Boyle was having his supper. Richard was a charming fellow, an Etonian and very 'laid back'. He suffered from quite a bad stutter.

He ordered the Corporal on the roof to 'f..fire a f..few shots' in the general direction of the incoming fire and returned to his supper. A few moments later there was a stream of automatic fire and he returned to the roof, rather angry.

'I said f..fire a f..few shots,' he yelled. Uncontrolled fire again streamed forth for several seconds.

'F..f..f.. what you f..f..f..ucking well like,' he ejaculated and returned to his supper. It was very, very funny; it was just Richard all over.

I was on detachment at Allenby Bridge on the Jordan when Britain declared war on Germany and the Second World War began. We had been the only battalion in Palestine at the start of the Arab Rebellion, with platoons and companies scattered literally from Dan to Beersheba. Now there was a steady build up of Yeomanry and several other regiments. There were red tabs to be seen in the King David Hotel and we heard that there were two Major Generals, one called Montgomery and one called O'Connor. We also started getting operational orders from a Brigadier instead of from our CO, which we didn't quite understand. The Brigadier told us that he was going to bring the rebellion to a speedy conclusion, which nobody else had been able to do.

The Hal-Hul/Muckmas Incident

One day the Brigadier gave orders to A and B Companies for the surrounding and internment of the inhabitants of two Arab villages not many miles from Jerusalem. We were to enforce a strict regime and work the able-bodied men very hard, with restricted rations of food and water. When they became cooperative and started handing in their weapons, the restrictions would be modified. It was a perfectly straightforward operation, and in due course, a wire compound had been built for the detainees – the old men, women and children had been confined to the school. My Company Commander then drove off to Jerusalem leaving me in charge.

I had a Jewish interpreter and an Arab cook. I was almost always on detachment in Jericho, at Allenby Bridge or at Enab on the road from Jerusalem to Jaffa. I didn't much care for 'all-in-stew', so I hired myself an Arab called Joseph, who made nice kebabs and rice and fresh vegetables. He also had his ear to the ground, but he didn't manage to teach me much

15

Arabic. I had a sunproof tent with a red lining. I liked being on detachment!

At about midnight I was aroused by the Guard Commander.

'Mr Rose, there is a terrible carry-on down at the cage, I think you had better come. I can't do anything with them.'

There certainly was a real shindy, groaning, shouting, men convulsed with malarial rigor. I ordered a distribution of water and a blanket for each man and things quietened down. In the morning I made my report to my Company Commander. He was furious and red in the face. In future I was to obey orders to the letter . The following day they continued to pull down walls in the appalling heat and dust. No rifles were produced. The night which followed was a repeat performance, but worse. I again rescinded the orders. Once more my Company Commander blew up, turning bright purple, but this time I stood up to him.

'When you are not here, I consider that I am in command. Please take me to see the Colonel.'

I was taken in to Colonel McMicking by the Adjutant, Malcolm Wolfe-Murray. I told him what had happened and said that I thought the orders were preposterous and would bring shame on the regiment. He said he would take my complaint to the Brigadier and come out to see me at Muckmas the next morning.   The following morning he gave me written orders in the Brigadier's own script and signed by him. I was horrified – they were entirely unchanged. I folded up the letter and put it in my pocket.

'I am to return the orders to the Brigadier,' Colonel Neil said.

'In that case,' I started and then shut up. I did not say the dread word 'refuse'. I said 'I will use my discretion.' The CO drove off without another word.

The following day was Day 4. A very large man in khaki drill, with no badges of rank, got out of a truck and told me to line up all my detainees for medical inspection.

'And who are you?' I said with some asperity.

'I am the Chief Medical Officer and I am here on orders from Downing Street. Haven't you heard what has happened? Five Arabs at Hal-Hul jumped down the well and drowned themselves. It's all over the world press. You are to withdraw as soon as I am finished.'

I was damned if I was going to clear off and look a bloody fool, so I assembled the whole village and with my Arab and Jewish interpreters beside me, gave them a short talk on the need for cooperation. Then I gave the women the unexpended portion of the day's ration of bread, margarine and potatoes. We left with clapping and handshaking and mended feelings.

I knew that there would be a barrage of questions when I got back to the Mess, but I was fairly certain that they would not know what had happened at Muckmas as no one but the Adjutant could know, so I decided to play it dumb. When I walked into the Mess, there was an unnatural hush. 'What goes on?' I said. 'A Major General is holding an enquiry in the Dining Room. For God's sake keep quiet.' I went off to have a bath. When I returned the chat went like this:

'David, how did you get away with it?'

'The Colonel was very considerate.'

'Not even a bollocking?'

'Not really.'

'So poor Douglas (Lord Douglas Gordon) takes the can!'

'Not a bit,' someone chipped in. 'He is to be flown home tomorrow so that the Arabs can't get him.'

'Lucky Douglas!'

'And what about Neville (OC BCoy Neville Blair)?'

'Oh, he is quite wild about something. Goes round spluttering, "Bloody fellow, perfectly bloody fellow, ought to be booted out".'

We were to have more trouble with that Brigadier.

Not so many years ago, I wrote to Neville Blair and asked him to tell me his recollections of the incident. He, like me, had remonstrated, but for some reason which I cannot understand, he did not receive the considerate treatment that I did from McMicking. He was told to obey orders or hand in his Commission. Neville, however, knew the rest of the story because he was present throughout the enquiry. The Brigadier did not accept any responsibility. He said Douglas Gordon had exceeded his orders. But there was no proof because the orders were not given in writing. The head of a subaltern was not sufficient. He considered that the Company Commander had not given sufficient supervision. Fortunately General O'Connor arrived at this point, and when he had been given a run-down of the evidence thus far, he said he was dissolving the court. He should have known what was going on in his district and he took full responsibility for everything. He would settle the matter with his superiors.

I had written to my mother by air mail, to warn her that she might hear that I was in trouble. Her reply by cable was, 'Don't let your heart rule your head'. But should the heart and head agree, what then? Go for bust?

The battalion's next head-on encounter with this Brigadier was over the defence of Heraklion in Crete. Colonel Hammy Hamilton fought him for ten days till he was at the point of a nervous breakdown. The Brigadier wanted us on the beaches; Hammy was

17

absolutely certain that the battle would be fought on the airfields and he was right. But once more his constitution let him down and he had to hand over command to Andy Pitcairn.

They fought what was probably the 2nd Battalion's most successful battle of the war, against the invading German paratroops, on whom they inflicted very heavy casualties.

Aussies and Pommies

My next task was to arrange a Platoon Commanders' Course for the Australians. I was a bit scared. I had been told that they didn't much take to Pommies. I had the pick of the NCOs as instructors.

One of the Aussies was a fellow called Phil Parbury. He was obviously English-educated and just like one of us. They all liked him, so why should they give me a hard time? In fact we got on splendidly from the very start. We worked extremely hard. They were tough and keen and used to the heat.

One morning I felt we were pushing it a bit too hard, so I said, 'Today we will take a holiday. I'll take you down to the Dead Sea and show you my Roman Fort. We call it Kilo 33. It's built like the Romans used to do it in the time of Christ. It has a fresh-water channel running down the hill beside it, which is why we built it there.'

I knew a nice place to bathe in the Dead Sea, close to the Khalia Hotel, where there was a fresh-water shower for afterwards. We jumped out of our trucks and I gave them a few words of warning about the water.

'Now I know that you chaps always dash in, like you would on Bondi Beach, but DON'T. This water is lethal; go in like an old woman'. I slipped off my shorts, but before two seconds had gone, there was a mad rush of naked figures dashing past me in Bondi fashion. They struck out, heads below the water, feet thrashing.

'Oh my eyes! Oh my balls! Oh golly, this is frightful.'

Salt! In the softest parts.

I called out, 'I will lead you to the fresh-water shower. Each man take the shoulder of another.' With one hand on their blinded eyes and some clutching their private parts, the humbled Aussie procession followed me to the fresh-water shower.

There was then a mad fight to get under the healing trickle. After a time it developed into a wild free for all and no holds barred! I wished I could have taken a photograph of them. The scene would have made a splendid fresco.

I had taught them a lesson. 'You *must* be prepared to take advice, even from a Pommy Bastard!'

Visit of Cigs

Before we left Jerusalem for the Canal Zone, we were visited by the Chief of the Imperial General Staff, Field Marshal Lord Gort, VC. He seemed to be a very pleasant old chap, but do you know, he had nothing to say to us. He didn't even ask any questions. I wonder if he knew that we had never seen a shell fired out of a gun; never worked with tanks or armoured cars; never laid a minefield or set a booby trap. We had never staged a raid or even carried out a fighting patrol. We were certainly not ready for war because we had been chasing Arabs for two years. We hadn't even got a machine gun company.

Evacuation of Families

My last job in Palestine was to evacuate families across the Suez Canal at El Kantara. There was no bridge, so we had to take them across in a ferry boat.

My Company Commander, as at Muckmas, was never present when there was an emergency. He was no doubt staying with his wife in Jerusalem. When he returned at midnight to find the camp almost deserted, he sent peremptory orders demanding my immediate return. I returned about two hours later, when the job was finished, to face the full blast of his temper. Once more I had to appeal to Caesar. This time it was Adrian Hamilton in Command. Neil McMicking had been promoted to Commander British Troops Egypt.

'Please may I be transferred to another company?' I said.

'No, certainly not. You are the only officer who has any control over him. Just stick it out. I will have a talk to him and I think you will have no more trouble.' The Jocks called him 'Peas in the Pod'. He had four barrels to his name – Lindsay-Orrock-Graham-Scott, but he was known by all as 'Major KG'.

KG was an extraordinarily insensitive man. He looked like a Prussian colonel and that is how he spoke to the men.

'Do it at once.'

'You must scrub the floor until it is as white as snow.'

I followed him around quelling each potential mutiny.

One of his peculiarities was his complete lack of finesse regarding how you should sit when wearing the kilt. He would sit behind the table in the company office with his knees wide apart, allowing a complete free circulation of cooling air.

Sometimes I would catch the eye of a young soldier on company orders looking aghast at this awesome spectacle. He knew that I knew what he was looking at with such rapt attention, and he would then cast his eyes to the ceiling in a vain attempt to stop his giggles. Each time he would look at me, I had only to raise an eyebrow and off he would go again in a paroxysm of uncontrollable laughter.

'What are you laughing at? This is no laughing matter, Private McPhee, as you will soon discover.'

'Sorry Sir, I reckon I am just very stupid.'

'March him out Sergeant Major and give him a good talking to.'

After a suitable interlude McPhee was brought in again. One glance was enough. The situation was quite unchanged. The CSM, now in the know, had a good look and of course got the giggle bug too. Everything was revealed – flesh and fur together. Should I but purse my lips, the unfortunate young man would burst out with renewed and uncontrollable mirth. The proceedings were quite beyond control. The CSM bawled out 'Right turn – Quick March.'

Half an hour later, with tears still streaming down my face I tried to tell KG that he must try to conceal the full extent of his manhood; it was just not fair on the defaulters. Even he had to laugh.

A lot of changes took place in quick succession. Major George Rusk, who was to become my greatest friend, got command of a battalion of the King's African Rifles and Major Bucknall, another lifelong friend, got command of the Worcestershire Regiment. The officers from the First World War had nearly all left us. A new and inexperienced generation was to take their place.

Tailpiece

For a short time we were stationed at Moascar on the Suez Canal. We were not yet at war with Italy and so their ships were constantly passing through the Canal. We were given orders not to provoke hostility and I expect they were too.

We spent much of our time sunbathing and swimming. One day I saw a gathering of Jocks on the bank apparently in deep discussion. A big Italian troop ship was approaching. The Jocks all 'fell in' in a single rank.

The Sergeant or Corporal in charge gave the order, 'About Turn – Bum-bags down – Touch your toes – Bum Bags up – About Turn – Fascist Salute – Fall Out.'

They were obviously delighted with their well thought-out insult and jumped into the water. There was no response from the ship.

CHAPTER TWO
Middle East and African Adventures
1940–1943

May 1940
The French armies were in the Maginot Line – the great linear fortress on which they had spent so much of their national wealth. The British Expeditionary Force was busy extending defences from the Maginot to the coast. Nothing much happened. This was known as the Phoney War. Then all hell broke loose as the Germans invaded first Belgium and then France. My brother Neil was in the thick of the fighting, serving in the French Foreign Legion in northern France.

Then came Rhoddy's turn for action as his battalion faced the German army racing across France. The only anti-tank weapon they had was the Boyes rifle – a veritable pea-shooter. He was awarded an immediate Military Cross. My mother was a very proud woman. His citation reads rather well:

'On May 29th, this officer set a splendid example of coolness and courage, when enemy tanks which had broken through another formation, suddenly attacked the battalion in a reserve area. He quickly organised all possible anti-tank resistance and himself fired over 40 rounds with an anti-tank rifle with great effect. The tanks were kept at a distance until nightfall, during which time one was completely put out of action, one badly damaged, and a third hit so badly that the crew were forced to vacate it. Under cover of darkness he helped his C.O. extricate the remainder of the battalion, and himself commanded the rearguard very successfully.'

Somaliland
On 10th June 1940 the Italians declared war against the British. They were already established in Libya – a threat to the Suez Canal which was under British protection. In 1936 they had annexed Ethiopia (Abyssinia) to add to neighbouring Italian Somaliland and Eritrea. They then invaded the small colony of British Somaliland, an act of aggression which proved that the whole of British East Africa was likely to become their battleground.

21

We were rushed down from Palestine to Aden on the cruiser HMS *Southampton*. After a week or two, we went over to Berbera in small transports, but this took several days to complete. A and B Companies were in the first flight and were attacked by three Italian bombers. There were a lot of dead fish floating round the harbour but no casualties. We went straight up country and deployed by companies in scrub-covered desert. Colonel Hammy was rushing all over the place, looking for possible defensive positions. We, of course, were digging slit trenches. We got attacked again by some bombers and put up a tremendous fusillade of rifle and Bren gun fire. It was reported that Colonel Hammy was rather angry about this. The birds were too high. In future we were to wait for the bugle to sound from Battalion HQ before we opened fire. However, shortly afterwards, a fighter plane came down the road and, without any bugle, we brought it down. We saw the smoke rising only a mile down the road. Of course, C Company also claimed it!

The following evening, my A Company got its first job. We were to escort a convoy of supplies to the front line. I think the drivers were Somalis supplied by a contractor, but they may have been from the King's African Rifles. As Company Second-in-Command I was at the tail of the column, with Major KG in the centre and two Bren carriers leading us. We had gone only a few miles, when we suddenly came under heavy fire. The convoy all bunched up. A lot of the drivers ran away and I had to find replacements from our own men. I worked my way up the column doing this till I came to Company HQ. Major KG was having his head bandaged. He had fallen out of the truck and was obviously badly concussed, so now I was in charge. Eventually I got to the leading truck. I opened the door of the first vehicle. The driver had been shot through the head and was jammed behind the wheel. I pulled him out onto the road. In front of the leading truck was a wrecked Bren carrier. In the moonlight I couldn't tell whether it had been blown up on a mine or had been hit by a shell. Somehow or other we toppled it over the bank into the gully. Then I got into the cab and drove off much too fast towards our destination.

Quite suddenly there were lots of chaps waving their arms and shouting, 'Stop, stop, you are in the minefield'. I reversed gingerly back without turning the steering wheel. I had never driven a heavy lorry before. That was a close shave!

There were friendly greetings from the chaps of the North Rhodesian Regiment. 'What is that terrible smell?' They had been charged a few days before by cavalry. The bodies of men and horses were lying out in front. They all seemed to be quite used to the horrible smell.

The return journey still lay ahead of us. I called an Orders Group. There was a Lt Colonel present from GHQ Middle East. I can't think what his job was, but he disagreed with everything I said.

Eventually I said, 'Right, Sir, you give the orders, I'll bring up the rear'. That fixed him!

Not very confident, I resumed my place in the leading vehicle. My orders were: 'Drive slowly. If any vehicle breaks down, run it off the road and climb into the next vehicle. If we get shot at again, just keep firing a few shots into the scrub till we get through. Try to find a spare driver for each vehicle. Good luck.'

It was bright moonlight, so we drove without any lights, and then a wonderful stroke of luck, a huge cloud veiled the moon. We got through the ambush with only some long-range fire from a machine gun, which did no damage. When we reached Brigade HQ I went to report.

'Who are you?' said the Brigadier.

'A Company,' I replied.

'Gosh,' said the Brigadier, 'Your black drivers are here and they said "Major killed, Captain wounded, all finish, no good!"'

We left the vehicles, as they now had their drivers again and marched off to our own company area, just as dawn was breaking. They gave us quite a cheer. That was my baptism of fire.

The next job for the battalion was to hold the Barkasan Gap, so as to give time for the withdrawal of the troops in front of us. It was a poor prospect. For the next two days we were very busy digging our fighting trenches and cutting thorn bushes to camouflage them. We had no air support, no tanks and only one Bofors gun with a dozen shells. All pre-war training had laid down that the defence of a position was to be built up on the fire-power of machine guns, the rest of the dispositions being designed to fill in the gaps. We had no machine guns and the position was two miles wide. The final dispositions were the best that could be made. My company was on some slightly rising ground just west of the road, covering the road block, which was manned by Sgt Major Sandy with the Pioneer Platoon and the Bofors gun. Four Bren carriers and a section of 3" mortars were under my command. On the other side of the road was D company commanded by Capt. Richard Flemming, and Capt. Richard Boyle's company was echeloned back on my right and to the rear, to deal with any turning movement. Captain Alistair Hamilton was in reserve with B Company, close to Battalion HQ and the remaining Bren carriers, for counter attack.

The first troops to arrive were not Italians but two platoons of

Punjabis, who had been cut off a day or two before. They were carrying their expended cartridge cases in sandbags, just as if they were coming home after a field firing exercise. The enemy were not far behind. Some enemy trucks came down the road led by some motor cyclists. What a wonderful target if we had our machine gun company! We could have mopped up a whole battalion.

We opened fire and they all ran into each other and the troops scattered for cover and more trucks came up behind. Now everyone was firing. Suddenly, to my horror men started 'falling back'. This was absolutely not allowed without express orders. I got very angry and jumped out of my trench, waving my pistol. I shouted to them to turn around and get back into their trenches, fix their bayonets and then come with me. One platoon was commanded by Richard Fairlie another by Platoon Sgt Major Grieve. They were milling around somewhere, and then we all started shouting and chasing the enemy. It was exciting.

Nothing ever seemed to happen to anyone I shot at, and reloading my revolver with shaking hands was an absolute nightmare. Never again would I rely on a pistol; I must have a rifle next time. We went on and on and we killed some of them, but not very many. Were the others all as bad shots as me? And then quite suddenly I was bowled over with a shot through my shoulder and went arse-over-tip just like a shot rabbit. The Italian Black Shirts were starting to pop up from the wadis where they had taken cover, and were regaining their courage. Someone helped me to my feet and we returned to our slit trenches in good order and took a breather, waiting for the next attack. I asked the CSM to look for my bottle of whisky. Someone had been there before me! And just as well! The temperature was 120°

After a bit of a rest, I went back to the Regimental Aid Post to get my wound attended to. I had a bit of a laugh with the MO Hoot Gibson. He told me that Major Alistair Gilroy was now in command, and Colonel Hammy was absolutely done in after so many days of hard work and no sleep. He then sent me on my way to the Casualty Clearing Station. On the way there, walking down the perfectly straight road, I was being shelled – I couldn't believe that anyone was actually aiming at me, so I just walked straight on. The CCS turned out to be nothing more than a 15-cwt truck! There were a few other men there already and someone took a photograph with my camera. When the truck was full we drove off to Berbera.

I eventually reached Berbera Harbour and was put onto the New Zealand cruiser *Hobart*. I had no shirt on and so no badges of rank, and I had a most enjoyable evening with some of the crew. By morning they had somehow discovered that I was a Captain and one of them, who had a wonderful curly beard, came to ask that I shouldn't give them away, nor all the stories they had told me. Later that morning the cruiser drew out of the harbour and stood off-shore to destroy the city and all the many vehicles which had been closely parked in the square. The bombardment continued for some time and then we sailed for Aden, leaving behind a great column of black smoke. On reaching Aden, I was transferred to a hospital ship, the SS *Perth*. So I didn't see any of my friends for many months, not until I rejoined the battalion at Tobruk.

Only a few years ago, I had the very great pleasure of reading in draft the autobiography of Angus Montrose, not long before he died. He told this story about Berbera. He went ashore with his Sub-Lieut. Milford Haven to get news of The Black Watch. His great friend Richard Fleming was one of the five Rhodesian officers who had joined us in Palestine. In the town he met a senior officer who told him that 'there was no hope for the Regiment, they were all cut up'.

Commander Angus Graham, as he was known in those days, said, 'Well is anyone doing anything about it?'

He and his young NO collected stokers from his corvette and drove some lorries up to the front. They met a small party of Black Watch, marching towards them, in good order.

To their enquiry for news of the battalion, the Sergeant replied 'Och, they're all coming along alright. Some silly bugger has blown the bridge and our transport is on the wrong side of it . . .' The naval drivers then ran a ferry service for the Regiment.

Commander Maurice Vernon, RN was in charge of the embarkation of troops, which he seems to have done almost single-handed. In his account of the evacuation there is this remarkable account of his interview with the GOC, General Godwin-Austen.

Vernon:	'We haven't got The Black Watch down yet. Three or four wounded came along and then no more.'
Godwin Austen:	'I'm afraid The Black Watch are a write-off. You won't see them again, Vernon. The last I heard of them they were doing a bayonet charge of one battalion against a Division of Italians. The odds are pretty high.'
Vernon:	'You can't write off a whole battalion just like that, General. The Black Watch can't be exterminated.'
Godwin Austen:	'No, but another tragedy is that the only bridge

at La Peron was blown up by mistake by the
Sappers. We did of course have it mined, but I
didn't send the signal. How they got it, I don't
know, but the bridge was blown, so they can't
get back.

What a General! No wonder Churchill was angry. I wonder if
that Lt Colonel who was with my convoy when we were ambushed
was the man who made a report to Churchill?

Reflecting on my battle in the comfort of my hospital-ship bed,
I came to the following conclusions. I was a bloody bad shot. I
wasn't very brave, but rather desperate. My desperation saved a
rotten situation. My mortars had fired all their bombs in about 15
minutes and after that they were just riflemen. I hadn't made any
use of my Bren carriers for mobile fire power, because I couldn't
speak to them. Must do better next time!

To India

I was put into the enormous Bombay Hospital. The 'Butcher's
Bill' as General Wavell put it to Churchill, had been light. I
was in an Officers' ward with 59 empty beds. I used to go
along the verandah in the afternoons to visit the other ranks
who had also been wounded in Somaliland. Corporal Clark, my
Company Clerk, was the most serious case. His right arm was
in an awful mess, as he had been hit several times. You had to
sit up-wind when you visited Corporal Clark! He had maggots
under his plaster and sometimes they came out! I was horrified
but the nurse reassured me that it was the best thing for cleaning
up his frightful wounds. He seemed to be remarkably cheerful. My
batman, Private Campbell, was killed while trying to pull Corporal
Clark back into the trench. I didn't know anything about this till I
got to Bombay.

We all had lots of kind visitors with fruit, books and periodicals
and I had several very nice invitations to go out to the beach at Juhu,
where rich people had wonderful parties under the palm trees.

My erstwhile Company Commander was also in the hospital,
still apparently suffering from concussion, but he never visited me
or the men. One day the hospital padre said to me, 'Well, I suppose
you will be best man at Major Graham Scott's wedding.'

'Padre, you must be joking. He has a very nice wife in Jerusalem.'
I sent a signal 'ADJUTANT – BLACK WATCH – M.E.F. URGENT.
SAVE MARRIAGE – SEND MURIEL SOONEST – ROSE.' They
lived happily ever after!

The nurse in charge of our wards was a very charming and bonny young Scots woman called Bremner. She was always teasing me because she claimed that we had met before. I had absolutely no recollection what-so-ever of any meeting and she stubbornly refused to give me a clue to work on.

One day she came down the long empty ward with the doctor, carrying a bottle of champagne.

'Captain Rose, we are very pleased to tell you that you have been awarded the DSO and we have come to celebrate with you. Now do you remember the last celebration when you had too much!'

'You are my Angel of the Prairie Oyster,' I replied. 'May I be forgiven.'

After a time I was put into the Taj Mahal Hotel graded 'sick in quarters'. It was real luxury – air-conditioned dining room and wonderful food. My arm was up in the air, supported by plaster-of-paris, forever giving the Hitler salute! I was also a bit of an 'object', because of the DSO. In my opinion I was over-decorated for a very junior officer, and I was rather shy about it.

General Bertie Tucker, the Director of Military Training in India, was told that I was lonely and rather bored and he sent for me to go to Delhi. He was sending officers with war experience round India on lecture tours and thought I should do something useful during my convalescence. At his office I met Colonel Ian Stewart of the Argyll and Sutherland Highlanders. My brother Angus had been his Second-in-Command in Malaya. The Colonel and the Adjutant and my brother had been told to escape to tell the dreadful story.

'David, I hope you will come to my lecture tonight,' said Colonel Ian. 'Don't be late.'

The Delhi Lecture
The spruce and athletic young Colonel Stewart sprang onto the platform.

'Orderly. It is 6 o'clock, please shut the doors and lock them.'

A hush fell over the large audience.

'Gentleman, I have come here tonight to tell you why we have suffered such a devastating defeat at the hands of the Japanese. I would draw your attention to the two front rows of this great hall. The seats are empty. Where are your senior officers? Are they too busy – or are they still on the polo field? Wake up India – there is a war on!'

The lecture which followed was brilliant. He pulled no punches. He described the inefficiency of Brigade and higher Headquarters, lack of confidence and decision; the unreadiness for war of units whose training had been on the tennis courts and at cocktail parties rather than in the jungle. The Argyll and Sutherland Highlanders were the only battalion who knew how to cope with the Japs.

The top brass in India would not accept his criticism and he was sent home straight away. I, as a humble Captain, had to do my lectures, but in a low key of course. It wasn't much fun.

Colonel Ian Stewart was a very good soldier. He seemed to have the ability to think a problem right through to its practical conclusion. It all came out of his own head. The jungle tactics which he had worked out for the Argylls became the basis of the teachings which my brother drew up for the Indian School of Jungle Warfare.

My brother Angus was also a very fine soldier and a great athlete. He had the heart of a lion. After the disastrous Malayan campaign and his escape to Java in a man-of-war, constantly under aerial bombardment for two days, Angus wrote an account of his recent experiences, while crossing the Indian Ocean in a Dhow. The book was published by Jonathan Cape under the title *Who Dies Fighting*. I have the slim volume marked 'Author's Copy'. In the fly-leaf at the end is written, in his neat small hand, the whole of Wordsworth's 'A Soldier's Creed'. I am quite sure that Angus saw himself as 'The Happy Warrior', and that is what he was to all his brother officers.

My Indian Lecture Tour

It wasn't much fun, but I saw a great deal of India from the railway carriage window. I enjoyed mulling over the well-known names – Rawalpindi, Peshawar, Simla, Gilgit, the garden city of Poona and all the Gurkha hill stations. I had to do one lecture every day and sometimes two; it really was a bit of a strain.

As I rumbled along my way, I had plenty of time to think of the past glories of the Indian Empire, of the great victories against stupendous odds directed by our greatest General, Lord Wellesley, later Duke of Wellington. A man of few words, but of brilliant despatches, the General rode many battlefields seemingly careless of his own life, but always thoughtful for the lives of his men, using reverse slope positions to gain surprise and to shield his troops from murderous artillery fire. My brother Rhoddy's regiment, the HLI, had greatly distinguished themselves at one of the Duke's greatest battles at Assaye and were granted a third colour, the Assaye colour, for their valour. Rhoddy had the distinction to be chosen to carry it when trooped in 1930. Very sadly for many Glasgow families, the HLI does not now exist. They were amalgamated, against much opposition, with the Royal Scots Fusiliers.

My father had two campaign medals for the NW Frontier, 'Tirah' and 'The Punjab Frontier'. He also had 'The Relief of Peking'. He was the Brigade Major of that very first International Force. He also had a Somaliland medal from an earlier war.

The name Punjab immediately brings to mind the name of the Governor General, The Marquis of Dalhousie, that far-seeing administrator who gave his health and his life to the Punjab and India.

The long hours in the train passed remarkably quickly as I fell into a kind of reverie.

Reverie

Ghulmarg – that was the name that brought back a family story about my mother. I think it must have been one of the many hill stations.

The Colonel Sahib was out fishing for trout. The Memsahib was to bring out the 'tiffin' at one o'clock. The Memsahib was in a long white summer dress and was wearing a broad-brimmed sun helmet and carrying a huge white parasol.

Juspahadur, the bearer, was walking tall, with freshly-ironed pugaree, a cane under his left arm, the 'tiffin' basket in his right hand. On the narrow hill path, with trees on either side, they met a large brown bear. Juspahadur threatened the beast with his cane, but instead of running away, it attacked him and with one swipe tore off most of his face, knocking him to the ground, and lay on him. The Memsahib launched a counter attack with the point of her parasol to the most vulnerable part of the animal's body. The bear rose and took a swipe at her head and got its claw stuck in her topee. The Memsahib started to thrash the bear about the head: it flung away the topee and, making one last swipe, hit the Memsahib in the centre of her back and fled down the hill. There would be no 'tiffin' and whiskey-pane for the Colonel Sahib that day!

My mother tore up her petticoat into bandages, put back poor Juspahadur's face, then took the almost blinded man home on her arm. White iodine and fresh bandages were produced by the other servants and a messenger was sent off for the doctor.

By the time my father returned from his fishing with a fine basket of trout, the house was in its normal state of tranquillity. My mother gave a brief account of the incident and my father went off to have his bath and the long delayed whiskey-pane.

The guests for the dinner party arrived in rickshaws and not much was said about the 'unfortunate incident', but towards the end of dinner the doctor arrived on a pony. He was taken to the servants' quarters to attend Juspahadur. Some time later he appeared at the dining room door and was invited in for a glass of port.

'But Jock,' he said to my father, 'I really should have a look at your Memsahib's back. I hear that she has quite a bad wound.'

'You never told me about that Connie,' said my father.

'It's really nothing,' said Mother, 'you go on with the port and your stories – I'll be back in a few minutes.' The party went on with discussion of who was to be 12th man for Ranji Singie's cricket team against Calcutta and who had shot the most sand grouse at Patiala for the fewest cartridges.

My mother returned to the party some time later and said everything was just fine. The dinner party was a great success.

When the guests had all departed my father said:

'Connie, you made rather a fool of me not telling me that you had been hurt.'

'Johnnie, I didn't mean to do that, but just not to spoil the party. It's been such a job to fix it all up. Must I always have that crashing bore Rory next to me? He can't talk about anything interesting.'

'Connie, he is a very useful partner on the tennis court.'

The battered sun helmet hung in the hall for many years. My father would not allow it to be thrown away. It was my mother's MID (Mention in Dispatches).

As a small boy, I well remember being allowed to touch the scar on my mother's back with my finger, and my children performed this ritual too.

Soliloquy

As hour followed hour, rumbling across the plains, I fell to thinking about my father.

When he left the HLI, because he couldn't stand the financial strain of all the champagne and claret drinking, he went to the Gurkhas. He was a great sportsman and he had a wonderful life playing good class cricket, golf and tennis and when he got a long leave he would go off on some expedition to the Pamirs, to shoot ibex and red deer. He was universally known in British India as Jock Rose. He was very popular and was always ready to make a jolly party. In those days everyone was expected to have a 'party piece' in the mess or when entertained in the houses of the Civilian Administration. My father's stand-by was 'The Laird of Cockpen' (Ramsay, of the Dalhousie family), which he would perform late on in the evening with gusto and many gestures, finger to nose, naughty wink, female falsetto voice, etc.

When we lived at Fanans in Argyll, we would sometimes get Dad to do his party piece. It was quite a job. The underlying object of the exercise was to get the stopper out of his port decanter. Perhaps it was the 14th of August. That was Angus's birthday and we would be celebrating anyway, but he had also shot his first grouse.

Rhoddy would say 'Come on Dad, let's have "The Laird of Cockpen".'

'Oh Rhoddy, you know I can never remember the words.'

'I'll help you Dad, I know them all.'

'Very well then, I'll try.'

In his deep throaty baritone voice he would sound off:

The Laird of Cockpen, he's proud an' he's great,
His mind is ta'en up wi' things o' the State;
He wanted a wife, his braw hoose to keep,
But favour wi' wooin' was fashious to seek.

'Now that's enough,' says Dad.

'No, no,' says Rhoddy, 'I'll sing it with you. Now, off we go Dad.' Both together:

Down by the dykeside a lady did dwell,
At his table head he thought she'd look well,
McClish's ae daughter o' Clavers-ha Lee,
A penniless lass wi' a lang pedigree.

'Now that's enough, boys.'

'No, no, Dad, the rest's easy. Can we have some port, Dad? That would help.'

'All right, just this once and only half a glass for Neil.'

'Oh Dad.' Both together:

His wig was weel pouther'd and as gude as new,
His waistcoat was white, his coat it was blue;
He put on a ring (gestures), a sword, and cock'd hat,
And wha could refuse the Laird wi' a' that (proud look)?

He took the grey mare, and rade cannily (gestures),
An' rapp'd (thumping table) at the yett o' Clavers-ha Lee,
'Gea tell Mistress Jean to come speedily ben, -
She's wanted to speak to the Laird o' Cockpen.'

'Now that's enough, boys.'

'No, no, Dad.' Off they go again:

An' when she cam' ben he bowed fu' low (deep bow).
An' what was his errand he soon let her know;

31

Amazed was the Laird when the lady said 'Na' (female voice),
And wi' a laigh curtsie she turned awa'.

Dumfounded was he, nae sigh did he gie,
He mounted his mare – he rade cannily;
An' aften he thought, as he gaed through the glen,
She's daft to refuse the Laird o' Cockpen.

Next time that the Laird and the lady were seen,
They were gaun arm-in-arm to the kirk on the green;
Now she sits in the ha' like a weel-tappit hen (contented look),
But as yet there's nae chickens appear'd at Cockpen.

Neil with innocent mien, 'Angus, what is a well tappit hen?'
'Shut up, Neil.'
Neil with glee, 'I know! I know! Ha, ha, ha.'
Rhoddy with some confidence, 'Pass the port.'
All together. 'Well done, Dad!'
Little did I know that the family of the Laird of Cockpen was to feature in my future life.

How am I to make my lecture about our little affair in Somaliland of any interest? Shall I tell them the one about Mungo Stirling being refused a drink at the Berbera Club, because he hadn't been made an Honorary Member? Only four days later he got his own back by handing out all their gin and whiskey free gratis to all comers. Or should I tell them about the Fuzzie-Wuzzie who offered me the corpse of the Italian Fighter Pilot as a trophy?

Here goes – only five more lectures to do – Secunderabad – Chin up – and smile!

Staff College, Haifa
I had bought a correspondence course in military subjects when I was serving at the depot before the war, but I dropped it when I went to Palestine. It really was deadly boring and I didn't think that I had the capacity for such sustained mental effort. So to get to the Staff College without doing all that work really was a bonus.

Just before the war started, I was sent to Egypt to attend a Desert Dispatch Riders' Course for Liaison Officers which was the greatest fun and I even learnt to jump. I was the proud possessor of Tartan Pantaloons (Scottish riding breeches) as all officers in the Medium Machine Gun Company were mounted. It was a very smart turn-out with Glengarry bonnet. This was my rig for motor bicycling.

I had always wanted to explore Palestine. Now was my chance. I bought a second-hand civvy bike and planned to explore the hill country, which had previously been impossible during the rebellion, and perhaps watch some of the war against the Vichy French up the coast road.

In the early mornings, I used to go down through the suburbs of Haifa to the beach in my bathing trunks. After a swim, I would do a dash down the completely empty sands. It was wonderful to be so free. I felt like a million dollars.

One weekend, I made friends at the front with an Australian Gunner FOO (Forward Observation Officer). He showed me how he did his job, and after some instruction, he would allow me to give the orders while he ate his lunch.

One day I was scanning the country at the front through my field glasses and I saw in the far distance an attack going on. I saw little bunches of men and I could faintly hear the sound of automatic fire and a few crumps of shellfire. What I was watching was in fact the battle of the Litani River. The Scottish Commando, commanded by Colonel Dick Pedder, had come in from the sea and turned the flank of the Vichy French. Dick was a great friend of my brother Rhoddy in the HLI. He was killed that day leading his men. A few days later an officer came to the Staff College and gave me his personal possessions to send to his wife.

On another occasion, I was watching the small town of Sidon through my glasses. I noticed that there were some civilians walking about and waving their arms in the air. I jumped onto my motor bike and went cautiously along the coast road. The people were all laughing and coming towards me. I had taken the surrender of that ancient city all by myself! I raced back to Battalion Command Post and told them to get cracking. The people were trying to find someone to surrender to. I then slipped quietly away before any questions were asked. Back at the school I had a really funny story to tell, but only to my few friends, who were sworn to secrecy.

One Saturday morning I was down at the Haifa Docks, looking at an Australian light cruiser named HMAS *Perth*. A naval officer told me they were just going up the coast to bombard Damour. Would I like to come? I put my motor bike into a secure shed and went on board. We hadn't gone far up the coast when the ship's alarm went off. There was a scramble for gun stations. All the AA guns opened fire, the very hell of a racket. The Captain took sharp avoiding action and I went hurtling across the deck. A stick of bombs exploded about 400 yards away, all down our right side. I was experiencing rather more than I had bargained for! We had been mistaken for a Vichy French ship by our own planes. Scare over, we proceeded to carry out the task against Damour, but then there was a change of orders. We were to proceed to Crete instead of returning to Haifa. That put me on the spot! I would be late for work on Monday morning. Would I be returned to my Regiment without completing the course?

When I arrived at the college on Monday morning, all the students were sitting on the steps and the stone wall. There was a bus strike on and one of the instructors had gone off to hire taxis. The truant was undetected!

GHQ Cairo

After Haifa, I got a junior appointment in General Wavell's headquarters in the Training Department. I more or less invented a job for myself. I would find young men and officers in the bars and hotels, who had just come back from the desert, and get their stories out of them. They had thrilling experiences of mobile warfare, ambushes and minefields, all kinds of things that other young officers, like myself, had not yet experienced, but were longing to hear about. I condensed these stories and tried to draw lessons from them which I then published in the Middle East Training Pamphlet. They were greatly appreciated.

A few words of explanation are necessary concerning the next part of my narrative.

During 1940, the British had occupied much of eastern Libya, pushing back the Italians. During 1941, the Germans reinforced the Italians in north Africa and advanced eastwards in great strength. Tobruk garrison had been reinforced by the 2nd Black Watch in October. The ensuing attack on the garrison by the Germans and the fight of The Black Watch has been described in the Linklaters' regimental history.

A summary by an artillery officer of the battle went like this. 'I class the attack of The Black Watch as one of the most outstanding examples of gallantry, combined with high class training, I have ever seen. Not one of us who was there will ever forget such supreme gallantry.' Some said that the CO, George Rusk, should have been awarded the VC for his personal leadership.

The Battle of Tobruk

One afternoon when I was doing this debriefing job, a young officer said 'I suppose you know about the awful battle The Black Watch had yesterday?' I had heard nothing, so rang up Bernard Fergusson. No, they didn't know about it at GHQ.

This extract from Bernard Fergusson's memoirs 'The Trumpet in the Hall' gives a graphic description of this dreadful episode in the regiment's history, and our experiences of the week that followed, when we went as reinforcements to Tobruk.

34

I was working late in my office. The others, including the weary John Ormiston, had gone home. My telephone rang and at the other end was David Rose.

'Are you coming back to your flat soon?'

'Well I could come back now. Where are you speaking from?'

'Your flat. Have you seen the casualty list?'

'What casualty list?'

'The Battalion's. It's bad.'

'I'll be back at once.'

I found David in the flat having a drink, with a slip of paper in his hand. It contained the names of all the officer casualties sustained during the break out and it included almost everybody we knew. Nine officers had been killed and sixteen wounded; the figures for the other ranks ran into hundreds. David and I between us could think of only three officers not on the list, though there would be others lately joined whom we wouldn't know of. But twenty-five officer casualties meant that at best they would be down to half a dozen.

Next morning at 8 am I waylaid Arthur Smith as he arrived at GHQ and told him the form. He said 'Come up to my office.' I showed him David's list. With a grim face he wrote at his desk and handed what he had written to me. He said, 'Come back and see me before you go and I am sure the Chief will want to say goodbye to you'.

1. Major B. E. Fergusson, The Black Watch, to be relieved of all duties with effect from this morning.

2. Major Fergusson is authorised to collect all officers and men of The Black Watch, whatever their duties, who are fit for active service, and to take them up with him to rejoin 2 BW in Tobruk.

3. Major Fergusson and his party will be given top priority to get them to Tobruk as soon as possible.

A. F. Smith
Major–General.

I rang up David Rose and we got together at once collecting people. It took a lot of time, but within three days we were on our way to Alexandria, six officers and sixty-four men, ex-staff, ex-leave, ex-hospital, including of course Peter Dorans [Fergusson's batman]. We were stuck for two nights in the transit camp, however much I might brandish General Smith's magic piece of paper, there wasn't a ship ready to take us up at that moment. On the third day, at crack of dawn, we boarded the *Chakdina*, a British India ship.

Beleaguered Tobruk was sustained by two types of convoy. It

was winter and the nights were comparatively long. The first type consisted of swift in-and-out trips by destroyers during the hours of darkness; the second of convoys which had to risk much of the passage by daylight; but still arrived, discharged and departed in the dark. *Chakdina* had not done the run before, but our convoy was to be in theory one of the second category. As the various ships assembled off Alexandria, a destroyer steamed close by us and addressed us through her loud-hailer.

'What speed can you make?'

'Seven knots,' came our answer.

'Christ!' said the destroyer: and paused before adding: 'well, in that case, good luck!'

We then saw the rest of the convoy creaming off with all speed to the westward, while we churned along breathlessly astern, with the gap between us widening every minute. Long before the afternoon was over, all the other ships were out of sight, though we passed a few lighters on their way back from Tobruk. Loaded though the ship was, we were able to prowl around a bit and I found one or two old friends. We were ordered to remain fully clothed, with our greatcoats on in case of trouble. It came just about dawn. We had passed all the other ships in our convoy hastening back to Alexandria. Our slow speed had condemned us to entering and discharging by day. The alarm suddenly went and we all stood by our boats, while a German aircraft, seeming to hover just above us, launched an aerial torpedo – and missed. In the growing light we saw the white houses of Tobruk beyond the harbour.

The entrance had been partly closed by a boom; so that it was only a cable wide. As we drew near, enemy guns opened up and the gap looked like a mass of water-spouts. We had been warned before sailing to bring only what we could carry with us; now the ship's loud-hailer told us to disembark with all speed as soon as we came alongside. Between the water spouts we could see the masts and funnels of sunken ships sticking out of the sea all over the harbour.

It seemed incredible that we should get through unscathed: but we did and berthed by a ship which had been sunk alongside the jetty. Aboard her, a bearded naval officer, despite the racket of the shelling, was calling out orders calmly through his megaphone. Gangways were immediately lowered and we filed quickly across the sunken ship and ashore.

Over innumerable cups of tea we heard details of that single bloody morning hour in which the Battalion had been reduced to a quarter of its strength – out of thirty-two officers and 600 men, eight officers and 160 men were all that was left an hour later. Two of the companies had no officers at all: one had fewer than ten men and was being commanded by its CSM.

After dark we climbed into trucks and were driven by Gordon Nicholson the Transport Officer and his men as far forward as was safe. We were then led stumbling through the night to the position. [The end of Bernard's account.]

Tobruk Reinforcements

When we got to the Colonel's dug-out, we were greeted by a brusque command, 'Don't bring the whole desert down with you.' The Colonel was drinking a mug of tea made with the brackish water from the very bottom of a well near the harbour. 'Well, Bernard,' he said, 'very pleased to see you all. You will take command of HQ Company and start building a cage right away for all these Italian POWs. You David, become Adjutant. Sit down over there and get stuck into it.' The gilded Staff Officers had been given proper jobs of work to do. It was wonderful to be back!

The next morning Rusky (George Rusk) decided to visit the forward companies and I was to go with him. We climbed out of the big square dug-out and proceeded to walk across the perfectly flat desert. As we went Rusky's conversation was something like this.

'Are you used to this sort of thing? Ever been under fire? I've had quite a bit of it in my time.'

I replied that I had been under very light artillery fire in Somaliland for one day. (Rusky, I knew, had been at Mons, Le Cateau, Ypres, the Somme, and never a scratch.)

'Well, walk behind me,' he said 'and do what I do.'

We hadn't gone very far when there was the loud crack of an 88mm German AA gun. Rusky dived for a hole in the ground. It was all so sudden that I was left standing, fortunately, for my poor Colonel had chosen an Italian shit trench for cover. I pulled him out and did my best to scrape off the horrors to very little effect, so we had to go on to Major Jim Ewan's dug-out in a sorry state. Jim, newly promoted during the battle, was of course on the look out for his CO. I told Jim what had happened and asked him to find some water and a stiff brush. It was no use; it just spread the muck around and made it worse. Rusky took it all very philosophically and decided to return to his own HQ in woollen vest and long johns, just as though nothing had happened .

Once or twice, I tried to talk to my Colonel about the recent battle, without much success. He was very taciturn. I knew he was grieving. He had lost his Adjutant, the debonair Sir Keith Dick Cunningham of Prestonfield, and he had lost the young officer whom he loved like the son he never had, the charming and cheeky Mungo Stirling of Glorat.

In my view the battle had been a balls-up and, except for George Rusk's personal bravery, might have been a complete disaster. The planning was faulty. Where had the Brigade Major been trained? Did he know about markers, guides and tapes for night attacks? What about the tank Squadron Commander? Had he ever been taught how to use a compass? His troop was not only very late on the start line, but went out on the wrong bearing. He was rather a 'Tally-ho a hunting we shall go' sort of fellow.

Colonel Rusk had two Bren carriers shot away from under him. He then got hold of a 15-cwt truck and chased the errant tanks and brought them back onto their objective. I was not there, but from what I heard, this action of his saved the attack from becoming a disaster. I thought there should be some form of enquiry so that it didn't happen again. No, the book was to be closed; no post mortem.

At the end of December, we got orders to move back to Egypt. 'Come on David, we'll leave the battalion with George Green and have a bit of luxury in Alex.' We drove hard, passed all the debris of former battles and arrived in good time to have an hour in the bath before dinner. What luxury – champagne with a very fine dinner and then a wonderful night between cool clean sheets.

Ranchi

The Division was moved to India in the SS *Mauritania*. We were stationed in camp at Ranchi. One evening I received a signal: 'VIP visiting you 0900 tomorrow. Provide Guard of Honour.'

My hero, General Archie Wavell, wasn't wasting any time to pay a visit to the regiment in which he had been born and bred. General Archie could thrash the enemy even when he was their inferior in numbers. My friend Bernard Fergusson was on his personal staff and had told me a thing or two. In the First World War, he was no gilded Staff Officer in polished boots. As a young Brigade Major he was constantly in the front line trenches, getting to know the officers and their men and doing everything he could to help them in the most appalling conditions.

Nearly every officer and man was out on training. I scraped the barrel to find the guard and gave them a few minutes' practice. The plane landed and there was a gathering of Red Tabs with map boards. The General waved them away and walked with me straight to the guard. As we walked I gave him a briefing and then introduced Cpl Savage.

'What is your job, Cpl Savage?'

38

'I do the MT (Motor Transport), Sir.'

'And how is the MT, up to standard?'

'Sir, you canna have a good MT on half a gallon of petrol per carburettor per week.'

'Thank you, Savage.'

Next man, a very small little fellow, just a boy. 'Your name?'

'Pte Weak, Sorr.'

'You don't look very happy.'

'I'm not, Sorr. I have no freens yet and we are confined to camp for the first ten days. It's terrible.' And so on and on, every man was encouraged to talk to the General, and received a kindly word.

Before his plane had touched down at Delhi, signals started to flow. 'On no account will the fighting elements of the Division be restricted to the present level of fuel consumption. Every effort must be made to produce entertainment and games for troops restricted to camp.' The Desert Army loved him and so did we.

I was very proud of my Colonel. He was like a rock. He was 50, I was 30. He wasn't clever but he knew how everything should be done – Audits, Summaries of Evidence, Courts of Enquiry – his precise minutes on every document left no one in doubt. He was very tired, but very regular in everything he did. He wouldn't spend more than a few minutes in the office. He seemed to know when there was something waiting there for him. I worked early mornings till late at night. I had nothing else to do but work. He left everything to me. The trouble about Ranchi was the utter boredom. It wasn't like pre-war India with young wives giving dinner parties and girls out from home, the 'Fishing Fleet'. There was absolutely no escape from the mess.

I had lost a very great friend in Keith Dick Cunningham. He loved music and he had taken some voice training. I often used to get him worked up in the evening to sing snatches of opera. 'Now let's have that castrato one,' I would say, 'or should I call it "counter tenor"', and off he would go, until we were both convulsed with laughter and started off again with something more robust. Mungo Stirling was always good for a laugh and he had gone too. Then there were all the others, who had been wounded and were no longer with us – Neville Blair and John Benson, and others.

Shillong Assam

Quite suddenly everything was changed. I was required to go as Brigade Major to 113 Indian Infantry Brigade. I expostulated: to start with, I couldn't speak Urdu.

The Brigade was in Assam recovering from the long retreat from Burma. The Brigadier was a bachelor, a podgy fellow appropriately named Fatty Bourke. He said, 'I suppose you have been sent here to make us or break us.'

I replied, 'No not quite that, but to report on the fitness of battalions for future employment.'

Each morning at 6 o'clock, the Brigadier and I would go riding. It was glorious – the lovely clean air; the scents of tea and herbs; the red earth tracks along which we cantered almost silently; the little native fellows with their bows and arrows and their horse-hair snares which they so deftly set in the bushes. It was all such a joy after the many months of dust and deserts and the heat of the plains.

My charger was a dream of comfort, a veritable armchair. We gently cantered for miles it seemed and then broke into a quiet trot. Back for a dip in a large galvanised bath, then breakfast and to work.

One evening when I was sitting with Fatty Bourke and having a convivial chat over a rather good whiskey called Black Dog, I asked him how he had managed the long march from Burma. 'Oh, I had three Sepoys who got me here,' he said. 'One carried a wet towel to mop my brow, one carried a thunder box on which I sat when we had a halt, and one carried the Black Dog.'

Nothing more was forthcoming. We got on with the whiskey.

It is always difficult to talk to someone about a campaign if the other party is completely ignorant of the general background. I knew absolutely nothing about Burma, the Japs, the Jungle or the Burmese and Indian Troops. No wonder my Brigadier found it impossible to find a starting point.

I know now about Brigadier Bourke's experiences during that very arduous campaign from that wonderful book, *The Hell of a Licking* by James Lunt, but that was only published in 1986. What a wonderful tale, and Fatty Bourke comes out of it very well indeed.

After a week or two the Brigadier informed me that he was going to Kashmir on leave. I was on my own. He hadn't been gone more than a few hours when I had an angry Colonel from the Punjabi Rifles in my office, lecturing me about the customs of the Indian Army. He had heard that his men in my HQ were being subjected to certain things which were simply not done in the Indian Army. Hindus and Mohammedans did not feed from one kitchen. They each had a corner of their own. And he had heard that the British troops in my HQ were all bathing naked with his men and ragging about in a most undignified manner. Would I kindly put a stop to it at once.

I was trying to build up the esprit and the fitness of the regiments with regular route marches. The Sikh battalion was good. The Punjabis were a bit wet, the British battalion was beyond belief, perfectly frightful. They fell out in droves. On the third day's march, I issued orders that no man would be permitted to fall out, without a chit signed by the MO or the BM (Brigade Major).

I eventually made my report. The Sikhs were fit for active service. The Punjabis needed a new CO and a stiffening of officers. The British battalion was only fit for guard duties on the L of C (Lines of Communication) but there were a few officers who should be posted to other regiments. I was then allowed to return to the haven of my own regiment, where all duties were carried out by young men whose only desire was to please their Colonel.

New Delhi

The C-in-C General Archie Wavell was now Viceroy. He and his wife, who was affectionately known as 'Queenie', found a good use for the huge palace and the hundreds of very smart servants, who had nothing much to do in the stringent times of war. They turned it into a leave camp for British troops. (They had done the same thing on a lesser scale when he was C-in-C.)Ten officers and 100 NCOs and men were invited to stay each week. On every man's pillow were three stamped picture postcards to send home. The Viceroy's staff had done a splendid job. Every minute of the day was filled with some activity, football and hockey matches, horse-riding and so on.

In the evening the Viceroy would lay aside the burdens of his office for an hour to mingle with the officers before dinner and then return to work. What a wonderful couple they were. Always thinking of us, who were far from home and often lonely in a foreign environment.

Salerno

I was next sent as India's representative to observe the landing at Salerno, just south of Naples. When the amphibious equipment was finished with in Italy, we were to use it for a landing in the Arakan coast of Burma.

I reported to Headquarters in Tunis and was taken in to see General Bertie Tucker, who had sent me on that lecture tour in India.

'David, you must get lost,' he said. 'General Montgomery has just incarcerated one hundred observers from the War Office in Malta. My staff will do what they can to help you, but I must not know anything about you.'

His staff fixed me up with an Austin 7 and a driver, and booked me a place on one of the Landing Craft on Day 2. I went off to explore the town.

A young man in uniform came up to me, saw my Red Hackle and said, 'I have just come down from the hospital. There is a very senior chap in your regiment up there who is desperately ill. I don't know his name or his rank but I think someone should visit him.' I thanked him for the information and took the tram up the hill. I walked through many wards asking for anyone in The Black Watch and had almost given up the search when a door into a private room was opened and there was my best friend of pre-war days at the depot, Neil Blair. The nurse said I mustn't go in. He was very seriously ill. I pleaded my special case – I had been best man at his wedding. I was leaving for Italy the next day. Could I just have a quiet word?

We had a very brief chat. It was a sniper's bullet, when the battle was over. 'Yes, I will write to Betty and tell her I have seen you.' He took his hand out of the bed to say goodbye. It was covered with blood.

'Nurse, nurse come quickly,' I cried out.

'Press your thumb firmly here; press hard. I will be back in a moment,' she commanded. A team of young doctors sprang into action and I was pushed out.

'I think you saved his life. He would have been gone in a moment or two,' said the nurse.

Neil would have gone a very long way had he not received that dreadful wound. His father and his grandfather had both been distinguished soldiers. Both had become General Officers. Neil won the Sword of Honour at Sandhurst and was obviously destined to follow in his father's footsteps. He was astute, methodical and tidy-minded. He had beautiful handwriting. What fun we had together at the depot, shooting, golf and fishing. He was one of the first members of the Regiment to go to Staff College at Camberley and I think he was an instructor there during the first years of the war. After the war, he transferred to the Foreign Office, where he was employed in writing *The Secret History of the War* and was awarded a CMG. He retired to Perthshire and we had many happy years together.

Salerno Bay was crammed with landing craft and transports of all kinds. Sometimes the sirens would sound off and a few bombs would be dropped. The men-of-war put up a barrage of AA fire. For a day or two there was considerable confusion, organised confusion, but gradually the organisation of the beach groups got going. The Germans put in a strong Panzer attack, and for a whole day and night it seemed that everything was in the balance. They were trying to drive a wedge between X Corps and the Americans. One day I noticed a lot of heavily-laden Americans coming back to the beach sitting disconsolately on their huge packs, as though waiting for re-embarkation. I was glad that they had nothing to do with me. The flap died down, the full swing of the landing got going, and X Corps was well into the hills.

One day I thought I should go forward and try to make contact with some of the Junior Staff Officers, to get their reactions to the whole operation. I worked my way up the Lines of Communication in my small car, but everything came to a sudden halt when an ammunition dump started to explode. I was standing beside my car trying to figure out what to do, when I saw the stalwart figure of General 'Noisy' Graham coming towards me, cross country. I offered him my car and he lent me his Humber, which was the other side of the fireworks display. He told me to get in touch with him later in the day when the obstruction had been cleared and drove off.

I spent the morning trying not to be a bore to the rather harassed staff officers, but to get from them their 'off the cuff' opinions about the organisation, something on which I could build the course which I was to run in India.

Contact had been made with the 8th Army which was moving up from the heel of Italy. The road to the south was open so I drove off to Brindisi. I thought of the 100 War Office Observers having a compulsory wartime holiday in Malta. I wished I could go off to some lovely resort, but I had no friend with me. I don't think anyone would have noticed my absence on a bit of French leave, but I took the next plane to India. I landed at Gwalior where I was intercepted by a Staff Officer from General Wingate's headquarters.

Interlude
Before plunging into the jungle of Burma, I feel some words about my brothers' war service are appropriate.

Rhoddy had started the war with the 71st or 1st Bn HLI in the BEF. He was adjutant at the time of the withdrawal towards Dunkirk, as rearguard of 127 Brigade. Nearing the port, the battalion held a position at Rexpoede against tanks and motorised infantry. Rhoddy, acting as a one man anti-tank platoon, destroyed two German tanks with a Boyes rifle, confirming his marksmanship as well as his courage. He was awarded the MC. The battalion managed to escape via Dunkirk in due course.

Rhoddy was in action again in 1944, commanding the 4th HLI during the seaborne invasion of the Walcheren Islands of Holland. These low-lying islands with canals, embankments and tidal mud flats were particularly difficult terrain to conduct any sort of operations. The 5th HLI captured the key areas of Molenberg and Fort Rammekeins. The whole expedition had been a success.

In early 1945, the 5th HLI were heavily involved in the advance to the border with Germany. Rhoddy's battalion captured Havert on the border on 19th January. Within weeks the allies were firm on the banks of the Rhine. Rhoddy was awarded the DSO for his exploits.

Having commanded the 1st Battalion for two years until 1947 in Palestine and Egypt, Rhoddy was again called to command from 1950–53. It cannot be given to many officers to command three times. In later chapters in this book, some of his letters to me are published. It is not hard to realise why he was such a successful commander. His reputation in the HLI was immense.

My brother would taunt me with this ditty.

> 'Here comes the 42nd
> Here comes the Forty Twa.
>
> 'Here come the Bair-Airsed Bastards
> Marching to the Burma War
> Some o' them hae Heilan' Bonnets
> Some o' them hae nane at a'
> Some hae boots and others hav'nae
> Here come the Forty Twa.'

His regiment were 'Gentlemen', they wore Trews. I, however, had the last laugh. After the war, the HLI, by popular demand, were allowed to adopt the kilt, to Rhoddy's fury.

Angus was also a man of strong character. 'In anticipation of a European war,' he wrote in his book *Who Dies Fighting*, 'I was enjoying long leave at home during the summer of 1939. Glorious days spent on English cricket fields and paddocks were freely mixed with the glittering nights of the last pre-war London Season ... I concluded my leave to the accompaniment of the Russo-German Pact, the embodiment of the Territorial Army, the invasion of Poland and the uncorking of all the Krug '28 that I could lay my hands on.'

The 93rd, or 2nd Battalion Argyll and Sutherland Highlanders, were despatched to Singapore. Spending his time there and in India, Angus did not see active service until early 1942. During the first part of the withdrawal through the Malayan Peninsula, Angus witnessed fighting while on the staff. Later he was instrumental in a daring seaborne raid, a hastily drawn together commando, whose purpose was to hit the enemy lines of communication.

During the latter part of the withdrawal to Singapore Island, Angus commanded another *ad hoc* force 'Roseforce', comprising a squadron of Indian Cavalry in armoured cars, the Malayan Independent Company, some Garharwahalis Dogras and some British Marines. He rejoined the 93rd for the last days of the battle for Singapore Island and was one of a handful of officers ordered to leave before the surrender – to take back the lesson learnt from the disastrous campaign. He commanded the 7th Argylls for a time and later the 2nd King's Own Scottish Borderers in 1945 in Burma.

Angus was an all-round sportsman of distinction. He won his army athletics colours in 1931, being second string to the Olympic runner Rampling. He represented Scotland against Ireland in athletics a year later, and played wing threequarters in the army rugby team, having a trial for the Scotland team as well. He was a single figure golfer in his prime, and later as a batsman in the Free Foresters and I Zingari, he played the No. 3 position. He was also the 'possessor of a laser beam throw from cover point'. He could draw well and was a competent handyman and mechanic. After the war he served in Greece and Kenya, retiring in 1950.

Neil, the youngest of the four brothers, was rather a problem. He was always in trouble at school – a rebel if ever there was one. My mother realised that he would never conform to the required standards of middle-class life and found him a place in South Africa with the 1820 Memorial Settlers Association.

He soon broke away from that training school and went off on his own looking for emeralds in the Belgian Congo. There he got into serious trouble and was deported as an undesirable alien. Taking a job as a stoker on a ship in Dar-Es-Salaam, he reached Suez. There he wired to me in Jerusalem to send him some money. The £25 I later learnt had been spent in Cairo having a fine party with some young officers in the Scots Guards.

He then stowed away in a ship leaving Alexandria, which took him to Toulon. There he enlisted in the French Foreign Legion. He had found his true home, the romance of soldiering, comradeship and discipline. My brother Neil was one of the best of men, and was to become a very fine and much respected soldier. But he did it in his own way.

One day there were the following headline in the *Daily Mirror*.
'GIANT SCOTSMAN IN FRENCH FOREIGN LEGION SLAYS NAZIS, Brothers in three famous Highland Regiments.'
The article announced he had been awarded a week of privilege

leave for his exploits in the Maginot Line. We were to hear no more of him till after the war.

Long after the war was over and his death, I managed to get from the French authorities his Médaille Militaire and his Croix de Guerre and Palme.

CHAPTER THREE
Chindits (1944)

Chindits

General Orde Wingate had organised the first Chindit operations crossing the Chindwin river into Burma in early 1943. The purpose of his highly-trained jungle fighting columns was to cause maximum disruption to the Japanese lines of communication deep inside Burma. The more lasting effect was to undermine the enemy's morale, and make the regaining of Burma by the allies easier. The Chindit columns marched between 1000 and 1500 miles during the four month period of the operation. Air supply, chiefly by the USAF, was an integral and vital aspect of sustaining the operation. Success of the first Chindit operation encouraged Wingate and the high command to plan a second operation.

Wingate told me that I could forget about my mission to Italy as I was now to command one of two columns of Black Watch in the Chindit Force, 'No 42'. The other was 'No 73', the number of our 2nd Battalion. I told him that I had no jungle experience. He said that I would be attached for fourteen days to a fully trained Chindit column on their final exercise. I would soon learn their techniques for silent movement and concealment and the various drills for supply dropping and river crossing. I would then have time to train my own men and would do a fourteen-day exercise to try out all these techniques.

I was not best pleased with this sudden change of role. I knew a bit about the Chindits from Bernard Fergusson, now a Brigadier. However, there was nothing to be done about it and I was still with the Regiment.

After the first week with the 'Experienced Chindit Column', I was convinced that they would be no match for the Japanese. Their lack of discipline was something I had never experienced in any Regular or Territorial battalion. They wore no badges of rank; unpleasant duties or patrols were undertaken by volunteers; officers and men were unshaven and scruffy. The Column Commander was often 'out on recce' when requested to speak on radio to his Brigade Commander.

I asked the Chief Umpire on the radio to send an experienced Chindit officer to take my place, but my request was not accepted.

My report at the end of the exercise was forthright. I was not questioned about it by the G1 or by Wingate.

At the end of the exercise, all the officers of the Chindit Force were assembled in a large cinema to hear General Wingate's exposition of his strategy for bringing the Japanese attack on India to a standstill. You could have heard a pin drop throughout his masterly discourse. He described how we would construct a chain of fortresses astride the enemy's L of C. Each fortress was at first to be supplied by air-drops, but very quickly landing strips would be made for re-supply and evacuation of casualties. To invest and attack these forts would require far more men than their defence and as each attack was mounted, the Japanese would be ambushed and harried by mobile columns of Chindits. He even described how we would eventually plant vegetables to supplement our rations! This was too much for me. I looked round at the young faces who were trying to absorb this graphic description of their future. Certainly none of them was laughing! 'In conclusion,' said General Wingate, 'I have one very unpleasant thing to say. The officers and men of the . . . Regiment should be thoroughly ashamed of themselves. Their conduct on this exercise has been disgraceful. They will return to the jungle for Christmas and the New Year and if they make the grade, they will be permitted to re-join the rest of the Force, when we go into Burma.'

I was sitting in the midst of them!

General Wingate's strategic dream was masterly. His grand design was just the concept that would appeal to Churchill. Our Prime Minister's advocacy won the ear of the American President and he had the power to provide the necessary air support. Roosevelt was appalled when he heard that many casualties in the first Wingate operation had to be abandoned to the enemy or to the jungle, and to overcome this problem he provided the light aircraft for the evacuation of casualties.

There was some very strong opposition amongst the top brass in India to Wingate's plan, mainly because it would absorb troops and resources, which were so badly needed on the main battle front; also because he had out-flanked them, by going straight to Churchill.

Neither the President nor the Prime Minister knew anything about jungle warfare and the General Staff in India were still very ignorant. I knew from Bernard what we were to be up against.

First in importance was to combat malaria. A man with high fever and no rest from marching was doomed. We were to take a suppressive pill every day. If you failed to take it, you were certain to become a casualty. The problem was how to make sure that every officer and man, without fail, would take his daily dose. A rumour went round that the pill made you impotent! Some men would rather become casualties, especially if there was a light plane available to get them out!

The second enormous problem was just living in the monsoon, marching with wet feet, sleeping wet and rising wet. Now add to that fighting wet, caring for the wounded wet-through and marching away from the battle soaked-through, and the full enormity of the situation becomes apparent. And what about the men who were so badly wounded that they could not be brought away?

I was convinced that we could overcome the malaria problem with our high standard of discipline. To become a fever case was tantamount to a self-inflicted wound. So we had an evening drill. 'Don't forget your pill, take it now.'

The only thing we could do about the monsoon was also based on good discipline – the routine care of feet and socks, attention to sores from leeches and abrasions. The other dreadful problem, what to do with a casualty who could not be moved, gave me much cause for thought. We were to carry with us a brick of opium, with which we could bribe the natives for intelligence purposes. This might come in useful to get shelter for very badly-wounded men.

I had a wonderful Adjutant named Graham Bishop. He was tireless, good humoured and a great worker. When the day's marching was over, he and I and the wireless operators had to get down to work with India – demands for the next supply drop, plans, codes and all the administration. I had a Major from the Burma Rifles named Michael Condon, brother-in-law to General Roy Urquhart HLI and Commander of 1st Airborne Division at Arnhem. Condon and Bishop were both about my own age. My Company Commander Hew Dalrymple was also my age or more. Hew Dalrymple and Graham Bishop were very great friends. We were a close-knit team. I think we quite enjoyed the training, crossing wide rivers without boats or rafts, teaching the mules and ponies to swim in the right direction, doing it all against time. Then there was the close-support bombing. This was something absolutely new and we were determined to make full use of it. Just imagine having your own bombers at call!

General Wingate's strategic plan seemed to be just the thing, but had he studied the men he had been given to carry out this most imaginative form of warfare? We were certainly not supermen, inured to a hard life and frugal living. We were not volunteers who had passed any stringent physical tests. We were the ordinary product of urban life. We were not used to

49

killing the food we ate, nor even digging up the vegetables. Who was going to cut the throat of the bullock? Who was going to cut the carcass up into platoon sized joints and share out the liver and tongue – and then roast it over a fire and share it out before marching on? We had no pots or pans. How long would all this take? It was quite beyond my comprehension. I would rather have had a bag of muesli and dried biltong.

We were in fact to live on the American K Ration. The American dieticians had devised the perfect ration for civilised man – three neat waxed packets a day. The waxed wrapping was good for starting a fire to heat the water in each man's mug. It even had three Camel cigarettes and three sheets of loo paper in the breakfast package!

Life in the Jungle Column was very basic – not democratic, because no one had a vote, but absolutely no privileges. We all ate the same food, we all carried the same loads and we all slept on Mother Earth, with just one lightweight green blanket. When we took a supply drop, anyone who received any 'goodies' from home had to hand them in for sharing out. I well remember watching Hew Dalrymple's 100 Balkan Sobranie cigarettes being shared out, two by two, first to him and then round the circle. One Jock said, 'Oh, I have the Camel Dung!' Hew had to barter his sweets or whatever, to get some of them back.

Of course, there was no alcohol, so that ironed out a lot of troubles. But there were really no punishments for keeping any difficult chap in order. So discipline had to be based on the principle 'all for one and one for all'. We were absolutely dependent on each other. If you became a casualty by neglect of your feet or because you had failed to take your anti-malaria pill, you were not to be pitied, you had let the side down.

We had one chap who was constantly giving cheek to his Corporal and failing in his duties as a sentry. He thought he could get away with anything – but he couldn't! After every effort had been made with him, he had to punish himself. There was a little ceremony at the perimeter. He was given a map and a compass and his friends filled his pack with their rations and wished him good luck and goodbye. He was then told that he was free to go off to India. We didn't want to guard him any more. He sulked for an hour or two some way from the laager, but eventually asked to be allowed to return if he behaved himself.

Out of the blue

My fourteen-day exercise was half way through when I received a signal from Chindit HQ 'VIP will visit you midday tomorrow at Map Ref —.' We were in a teak forest.

The next morning just before 12 o'clock, we moved into the laager, our hedgehog formation when at rest. We heard the vehicle approaching and I stepped out of the forest onto the track. General Wingate was standing there, his famous Wolsey Topée on his head, his hands clasped around a long forked stick.

He came straight to the point. 'I want a column of volunteers to carry out experimental forest landings in the American gliders which have just arrived. We must also learn how to load animals and some heavy machinery for the construction of landing strips.'

'I'll discuss it with my officers. Shall I come to see you at the end of the exercise?'

'No, I want the answer now.'

'Can you give me ten minutes?'

'Yes, certainly.'

I walked back into the forest and blew a long blast on my whistle. This was not the usual means of communication in the Chindit book. Our rule was silence. Then I called out, 'All officers and men, close on Command Post. Repeat the order.' I heard the steady crackle of dried leaves as they moved towards me and sat down.

It was seldom that I saw them all together. The training was hard; marching every day with weapons and packs. Sometimes we carried as much as five days' rations. They were bronzed and lean and looked clean. I have never seen Jocks so fit before or since. I wished the General was standing beside me, but apparently he did not want to see them or be seen by them – a strange Commander.

'General Wingate is here,' I said. 'He has asked me if you will volunteer to be his experimental glider troops. No man need feel ashamed if he doesn't wish to volunteer. We shall all end up in Burma on our feet or by glider. Discuss it for a few minutes.'

They sounded like a huge swarm of bees. One young soldier, in a high pitched voice called out, 'Please Sir, I don't think I would be much use jumping out of a glider, I have terrible weak ankles.' There was a rumble of subdued laughter. I returned to the General and told him that he had his volunteers and added, 'I presume that the exercise is now ended. May I march back to Camp?'

We moved off down the track like normal British troops. We were in high spirits. For a time 'jungle bashing' was at an end and new problems and a great challenge lay ahead.

The American Commander of our Air Task Force was Group

Captain Cochrane. He had won a reputation in the Battle of Britain, as a fighter pilot of the first order, and had won several decorations. His circus included medium bombers, fighters, dakotas, the gliders and L5's (light planes for the evacuation of casualties). This was the man with whom I was to carry out these experiments. His nickname was 'Railroad'. As a fighter pilot over France, he was often a bit vague as to his location and would dive down to the nearest railway station to read the name of the town or village and then return to his map!

His 'circus' was not an easy command. I was told that some of the L5 pilots were minor stars or extras from Hollywood. When they got a bit browned off with the rigours and boredom of jungle living, they would take a 'hard landing', which would ground their machine for a day or two, so that they could go off to Calcutta for a spree.

We learnt to load our mules and how to restrain them with bamboo stays. We also had twelve ponies with each column to carry our wounded. The last of the animals were the bullocks. We were to carry meat on the hoof. You can perhaps imagine the Jocks' ribaldry when the flimsy gliders had holes kicked in their sides and when the inevitable explosions of excrement had to be cleaned up. We learnt as we went along.

The first day landing was a success. Trees down the chosen landing strip were cut off close to the ground with a collar of gun cotton. The bulldozers could be broken down into manageable loads.

The night landing went very well but for two gliders. Mine was one of them. My pilot missed the precise moment to 'pull his plug' and had to do a forced landing. He called out, 'Lift your feet' and flew his machine deftly between two trees. The wings took most of the impact and we came to a rather bumpy halt on the floor of the jungle. None of us was injured and we proceeded to the RV, which was only a few hundred yards away. By the time we got there, all the other gliders had been checked in. The RSM came to me and reported that only one glider crew were missing, Captain Dalrymple and his HQ.

I reported to Lord Mountbatten for whom the exercise had been put on, to prove that such a thing as a night landing in forest was a possibility. He said in a very grand manner, 'Well, Rose what are you going to do about that?'

'I understand that our Dakota pilots are able to snatch a glider off the ground. I think I better go back on the same route as we came and see whether Captain Dalrymple has crash-landed and lit a fire,' I replied.

Bloody foolish kind of answer, just like on a TEWT (Tactical

Exercise Without Troops). Come to think of it, a silly question too!

'Good idea,' says Supremo, 'Do that.'

I gathered, I know not why, the RSM, the Doctor and several chaps who were standing round and we all climbed into a glider over which was erected a kind of rugby goal post, with a cable stretched between. We heard the thunder of the plane above us, but nothing happened. It passed over a second time with no result. I asked the pilot if this often happened.

He replied, 'We have only done it with dummies till now!' The next time over, we were suddenly jerked into the air with a shuddering and juddering as the enormous fishing reel released its nylon cord through the nose of the glider. Quite suddenly we were in normal flight.

Nothing could be seen below but black forest. I began to think of the awful letters I would have to write to Hew Dalrymple's father, Lord Stair, and all the other parents of these young men killed on a training exercise. I heard the order from the Dakota, to cut and land. We circled once and made a perfect landing, close to the Air Control hut. Rather despondent, I walked over to the hut, opened the door and there was Hew Dalrymple sitting at the table playing cards! When Hew's glider took off, his cord had got crossed with the twin and the pilot immediately 'pulled the plug' to avoid an accident. The Dakota, with only one glider, had continued to the Landing Zone. So all was well. We had quite a celebration!

When it came to doing the real landing in Burma, it was not my column that was used, despite all the training we had done. It was the column who had blotted their copy book on that exercise some time before. Their landing was unopposed, but through lack of air-recce or air photographs, the gliders crashed into huge tree trunks which were scattered over the chosen landing ground concealed in the long grass. The column suffered very heavy casualties and the mechanised equipment which was to make the landing strip was also rendered useless.

The reason why there was no air recce is well told in *Out of the Blue* by Terence O'Brian, Chapter 4, page 53. The blame was entirely due to General Wingate's refusal to listen to the advice of his RAF staff. He had an obsession about secrecy.

The Ambush

Not long after my column had landed in Burma, I got wounded in a minor incident. This is how it happened.

We were moving through open jungle in our usual formation. Suddenly we were under fire. I was under fire. A shot hit the magazine of my carbine. I jumped behind a tree. A shot went through the haversack on my left hip. I looked all round. Why could no one see them? Then suddenly – 'Look up, Look up,' I cried.

There was a fusillade of shots. I was shot in my right biceps and ribs. The Japs didn't fall out of the trees, they were tied to them. They had sprung a fast one on us. They were well-trained and brave soldiers.

We 'harboured up' and the doctor did his stuff. We had supper and then got down to work with India as usual, but this time also to order L5s for the evacuation of our casualties, but not me. I was going to be OK.

It was a lovely night when I woke up. I felt fine. I would just take a turn around to see that the sentries were alert. I was barefooted and just wearing my pants. I spoke to one or two men who were also awake and asked after my wound. I told them that I was just fine, nothing to worry about. 'The Column Commander is drunk you know,' I overheard one man mutter to his pal. After weeks with no drop of alcohol, the doctor's administration of morphine or whatever had put me on a high. No wonder I felt so well!

We prepared the landing strip not very far from our laager. The half dozen casualties were all ready to move as soon as we were in contact with the plane. When we got to the landing strip, there were some men there already from another column. I will not name the Regiment, but I soon discovered that they were malarial cases. I was furious. I had met this Regiment before in Tripoli and had little respect for them. They had driven into a riot in their 15-cwt trucks and thoroughly deserved to be lynched. Now they were getting out of Burma with SIW's (self inflicted wounds), but not before my battle casualties!

In my opinion indiscipline and slackness should be exposed, not hushed up. So often we fail to face the truth that indiscipline is the cause of many casualties, sometimes a whole battalion. What was to be the fate of this Regiment with so many fever cases in the very first weeks of the campaign? In a week or so there would be no more L5s to fly them out because of the monsoon. There would be many a broken heart when wives and parents received the news 'died on active service'. They would blame the jungle, but the power of the jungle to kill could be held at bay by good discipline.

I was wounded in this early skirmish, but was able to remain in command of my column for some weeks, but eventually I had to hand over to Michael Condon. The sticking plaster which was necessary to hold the dressings on my wounds induced acute prickly heat which spread all over my body. I suddenly realised that I was becoming short-tempered and unfit to act responsibly. I was terribly disappointed to leave my column after all the work we had done together, but I knew they were absolutely first class and would meet every challenge.

Bernard Fergusson wrote a very good account of the deeds performed by 73 and 42 Columns in his history, *The Black Watch and The King's Enemies*. As Bernard's book is now out of print, I have obtained permission from his son Geordie to reprint those parts which are relevant to this story. I do this out of admiration for the officers and men who went through it all and were the backbone of the brigade till the bitter end of that feat of the utmost endurance.

Extract from *'The Black Watch and the King's Enemies'*
General Wingate's penetration campaign was going well. Brigadier Calvert had established a block across the enemy's main line of communication to the north and was holding it against all comers. But viewed as a whole the Burma theatre was in a bad way. The Japanese had crossed the Chindwin in force, and were advancing irresistibly into the mountains of Manipur. Exposed Indian formations were fighting their way back to the plateau about Imphal. Some were saying that the High Command of the army would try to divert to its own uses those formations of Special Force which had not yet been committed; others were expressing the same views in less respectful language, saying: 'If we aren't careful, the rats will get at us.' General Wingate was quite prepared to let Imphal stew in its own juice, provided that there was no interruption to his own campaign; and he resolved to add 14 Brigade to his force in Burma before he could be ordered otherwise.

Green received his first orders from General Wingate's Chief of Staff at about 8 p.m. on the 22nd of March, and the first half of his column flew in on the following afternoon. The flight was extremely bumpy, and the ground below looked most inhospitable. There was still light enough to see the Chindwin as they crossed it; and by the time it was wholly dark the first lift was completed. They found themselves on 'Aberdeen,' a Dakota strip set up initially by another Brigade on its way past; its location was in the Meza Valley, near Manhton, two days' march from the considerable garrison of Indaw, which a Chindit Brigade was at that moment attacking.

First impressions of Aberdeen, where the second half of the column joined the first half next day, were distinctly pleasant. It lay in a deep green valley with jungle on the hills, and open paddy-fields on either side of the slow and shallow river. Beside the airfield was a village, Naunghmi, with its houses standing, Burmese fashion, eight feet above the ground on tall rounded logs. Villagers were moving about in their picturesque dress, and both the people and their dwellings were kinder to the eye and to the nose than their equivalents in India. There were also American ground-staff and British troops; some of these last had only been 'in' a few days; others were bearded, haggard and not over-clean members of 16 Brigade, who had been 'in' for two months and had marched 500 miles; this formation had come on foot, starting at the end of January.

42 Column was flown in on the 25th; and on that day, too, General Wingate paid his last visit to the Battalion. He told Green to congratulate the men on being the first Scottish troops to land at a Scottish airport in Burma, his final words before taking off. That night his aircraft flew into the ground not far from Imphal, and he was killed.

Wingate's death was also the death of the campaign as he had conceived it. That and other factors combined to result in many changes of plan, and still more changes in orders. It was sad that much of the energy and physical fitness with which the Battalion had entered Burma was expended in marching and counter-marching. Each man carried a load of seventy pounds on his back; the weather, already hot, was getting hotter; and the monsoon, an ordeal which British troops had never before deliberately defied, was little more than a month ahead.

Rumours and scares were the daily bread of Long Range Penetration, and each new unit arriving fresh to the game took a little time to become initiated, and able to distinguish between fact and fancy. After 73 Column had moved out, and while 42 Column was still receiving its last few details and girding up its loins to march, a major scare developed among the Americans, that an attack on Aberdeen was imminent; and the light aircraft, for the first and only time, took wing and disappeared. Patrols, partly from the Column and partly from some veteran Chindits who happened to be in Aberdeen, established that the story belonged to the 'fancy' category. The only Japs who appeared were airmen, who bombed and strafed the airfield, killing nine men, two of whom belonged to 42 Column.

73 Column, heading south on its way to the Banmauk-Indaw road, had its first skirmish near a village called Sittaw. The first intimation that there were Japs about came from the refusal of the Burmese guide to enter the village – a symptom analogous to the pointing of a gundog. A few shots were exchanged, and one Jock wounded. Already the congestion of British troops in this area was

proving to be an embarrassment: 73 Column played hide-and-seek for two days with a Gurkha column; but a lost and wandering English private from the Queen's Regiment in 16 Brigade was brought in by a friendly native, and he, at least, had cause to be grateful for congestion. Nevertheless, the number of formations in the area caused confusion in those early days, particularly in the matter of supply-drops: aircraft seeing troops on the ground were apt to mistake them for their consignees, particularly as a hard day's marching across country was to them but a three-minute flight. By various means, including stricter discipline and a more elaborate signal procedure, the supply system became less happy-go-lucky.

On the 4th of April, contact was made between the two columns by Major Rose arriving on a horse to meet Colonel Green. The commanders co-ordinated a plan to lay an ambush on the Banmauk-Indaw road, a pool which was always good for a fish. The ambush took up its position on the night of the 5th, platoons taking turns to man it. At 9 p.m. the Japs arrived, in three truck-loads; the waiting men could hear them singing as they drove along the road. The first truck was attacked with a Piat and with hand-grenades, and most of its men killed before they could dismount; those in the second had time to jump out and assume fire positions; the third turned and got away. The platoon had two men killed and two wounded; the Japanese dead included two officers. One of the trucks was taken over, and used for several days by 73 Column on the Banmauk-Indaw road and subsidiary tracks.

Both columns by this time had an accumulation of sick and wounded, and for various reasons – one of which was the heavier fighting going on in other columns – there was some delay in the arrival of light aircraft to evacuate them. This laid a sore burden on the medical officers. Captain Chesney, the Canadian MO with 73 Column, had already performed a remarkable operation on the man wounded at Settaw, whose wound was a dangerous one in the stomach. Chesney did an immediate operation in the fringe of the trees, under the protection of the Column's Vickers machine-guns; it took him half an hour to complete it, the man was taken away on a horse, he visibly regained strength during the next few days and finally completely recovered. Captain Langwell, with 42 Column, who had been MO with the Battalion ever since Tobruk, had a case of acute appendicitis. It was dark; there was a heavy downpour of rain; and he had to improvise his theatre in the space under a house in a village. Such torches as still had batteries were pressed into service, life-jackets were inflated to make a bed for the man. Captain Dalrymple's sponge was borrowed for a swab, and clips to hold back the edges of the incision were improvised from the bent handles of mess-tins. The Animal Transport Officer was anaesthetist. The operation was successful, the man was carried on by pony, and evacuated by Aberdeen to India next day. The stock of both MOs soared to the skies.

It must be recorded that the columns were equally lucky in their Padres. The 8th of April was Easter Sunday, and both columns had a church service. Holy Communion Services were held whenever possible, and family prayers almost every night.

On the 10th of April, 42 Column carried out its first attack with the new technique of direct air support. This up-to-date form of warfare consisted of directing the fighters or bombers to their targets by means of a wireless set on the ground with the forward troops, a system which had hitherto been turned down as often as it had been advocated. The American pilots needed no convincing about its feasibility; and Wingate's Force achieved by these means and by mutual trust, springing from close friendship between air and ground forces, a degree of air integration never approached on any other front. The wireless sets on the ground were operated by RAF signallers under the direction of an RAF officer marching with every column; and these officers were themselves drawn from air-crews with long operational experience.

The objective on this occasion was a Japanese dump in the small village of Singgan. Its approaches had been reconnoitred late on the afternoon of the 9th of April by Major Rose and two of his officers.

At first light on the 10th, the column, reinforced by two platoons and the support platoon from 73 Column, moved out towards the dump. While they were halted for a few moments, an enemy patrol of ten men walked into them, then made off, pursued by a few shots, to warn the guards upon the dump. The time for the operation was therefore advanced, and confirmation came through by wireless from India that the American Mustang fighters and Mitchell bombers would be over the target at 10 a.m. precisely. Plumb on time the Mitchells appeared to drop their bombs well and truly on the target; next came the Mustangs, who spent half an hour joyously shooting up the defenders; then the infantry went in. The dump was blazing merrily; and the Japanese had withdrawn to a safe distance from the exploding ammunition, into the jungle, where they had to be hunted. It was the column's first-battle and, for many of the men, their baptism of fire. The destruction of the dump was most satisfactory, with quantities of arms and ammunition, medical stores, food, petrol, electrical equipment and three 75-mm guns. Fifteen Japanese were found dead, and the column's losses were three killed and two wounded. Of the two, one was, unfortunately, Major Rose himself, who was shot through the shoulder in almost the same hole as had been made in Somaliland nearly four years before. The bullet was extracted that afternoon and he refused to be evacuated; he spent the next week on his horse, but on the 18th was marching again. The other wounded man was flown out the following day.

For the next few days the two columns marched and counter-marched in the lower Meza Valley. The weather was getting steadily hotter, and three hours' halt in the middle of the day was essential. This was the one treat to which the men could look forward: when boots came off, socks came off, shorts came off, and it was possible to sunbathe and to have a leisurely meal. It had been a Chindit principle to encourage the growing of beards; but Colonel Green was conservative in this and ordained that whatever other Chindits might do, The Black Watch would shave. But, pleasant though the mid-day halts were, there was a growing feeling that the campaign lacked direction, since the route followed by the column doubled and redoubled depressingly often; and, when crossing for the third time a track junction near Mankat, Colonel Green was heard to say: 'This ought to confuse the Jap: we don't even know where we're going ourselves.' To add to the discomfort, the rain was becoming more frequent; and, far from lessening the heat, each shower made the jungle more like a hot house. By the 2nd of May, 73 Column estimated that it had marched 150 miles since leaving 'Aberdeen,' and 42 Column only slightly less; neither had much to show for it.

Routine, that sure secret of such comfort as may be had in a Chindit column, had now established itself in both columns. An officer who commanded one of the rifle platoons in 75 Column until he was wounded early in May wrote some staccato notes after the war on memories prompted by a perusal of the War Diary, which conjure up some typical scenes in a few words:

'Apr 1st. Litter and north-country newspapers indicate a column here before us. What a bivouac! My platoon again has something dead in its area – a mule this time. Jocks shocked at litter and refuse, after our own strict litter discipline.

Apr 2nd. Hot morning march. Placid elephant lonely and content excites comments from Jocks. Jocks excite no comment from elephant.

Apr 5/6th. Supply drop on far side of *chaung*. S.H. [diarist] loses his party in jungle, passes same yellow bush four times, fourth time finds last member of party sitting there confidently awaiting him, Harris in Hampton Court Maze (*Three Men in a Boat*).

Apr 10th. Overheard on Walkie-Talkie:
John Fraser [Major and Rifle Company Commander 42 Column]:
"Where are you now, Jamie?!"
Jamie Richmond [Platoon Commander]: "At Milestone 27."
John Fraser: "You can't be, the Japs are there."
Jamie Richmond: "Well, to be perfectly honest, I'm sitting on the Milestone!"
Apr 18th Patrol to Tondaw etc. Company Commander had ordered no fires; to our great delight we find red-hot logs and brew up on them (spontaneous combustion?).

Apr 22nd. Jocks ordered to collect bamboo leaves for mules to eat: great indignation to find how many one mule can account for.

May 7th. [in an account of an ambush]. S.H.'s War dance with Jap mortarman amuses every one except S.H., who is trying to make up his mind which is correct way to kill with bare hands; in struggle, Jap drops after being disarmed, and runs, to be shot by almost every weapon in the platoon.'

The beginning of May brought the battalion's first considerable engagement in Burma. The main Japanese artery to the north was the railway running through Indaw to Myitkyina, 200 miles away, and one of the considerations which had weighed most in General Wingate's choice of this area for his operations had been the importance of isolating Myitkyina from the rest of Burma. Brigadier Calvert's object, from the moment of his fly-in, had been to put himself astride the railway and the road which ran beside it; and this he had successfully done. He had found and occupied a position known as the 'White City', consisting of three or four lone hills on the very edge of the railway. Immediately east of them, the main range of the Kachin Hills climbed to a height of some 3,000 feet; west of them was a broad stretch of paddy. Calvert had seized the White City on the night of the 11th of March, and since then Japanese formation after Japanese formation has splintered itself into fragments in a vain attempt to dislodge him. Now, at last, a policy for the Chindit campaign had taken shape. It was to drop all thought of taking Indaw (which 16 Brigade had finally failed to carry) and to draw north 150 miles, with a view to linking up with General Stilwell's Chinese. This entailed hauling down the tattered Union Jack which flew over White City and evacuating Calvert's tired but triumphant men from the position. 14 Brigade was to march there, and help him to break through a ring of baffled Japanese which had built up around him.

The White City was 40 miles north of where the two columns of the Regiment were operating; and it was not thought impossible for them to march straight on it, since this would have meant moving close to the railway, which was alive with Japanese. The choice of routes was limited: water was essential, and although the rains had begun, most streams were still dry. Since the railway valley was closed to them, there remained any one of three river lines as a means of approach. They chose the Nami Chaung, a broad and shallow stream, not more than two feet deep, with an ample flow of water for men and mules. On the 25th of April they were only six miles south of Indaw; from there they moved due south, then north-west by north; and the 3rd of May found both columns looking across open fields at the White City. They knew that they were in for some stiff fighting, and arrangements were made for the more vulnerable portions (the soft 'skins') of both columns to be united under the command of Major Watson-Gandy, and held back out of harm's way, in so far as that was possible. Early on the 4th of May, a patrol from the White City made contact with the two columns in order to lead them across the open valley; and this movement was carried out without interruption.

By 10 a.m. they were safely on the far side and scrambling up the Kachin Hills, whose gradients were proverbially steep. Heavy firing was to be heard, as usual, from the White City, which swelled to a crescendo during an air-raid. The columns passed through a battered piece of jungle, splintered trees and abandoned Japanese equipment, showing the site of one of Calvert's battles. A little before noon, they chose a bivouac deep in the jungle, moving into it in the fashion taught by Wingate, which left no traces and which ensured immunity from being trailed.

Various officers from the White City garrison had visited the columns as they moved, and their information, supplemented by the columns' own patrols, gave a fair picture of the enemy's habits in this neighbourhood. The enemy was known to use by night a certain track which, leading up into the hills and finally rejoining the railway farther north, enabled them to by-pass the White City block. This track it was resolved to ambush; and at 2 p.m. on the 5th of May, three platoons of 73 Column, with a three-inch mortar, moved down to lie in wait beside it. The remaining rifle platoon was left at the village of Napin, which had been burnt some days previously by the Japanese.These three platoons were under the command of Major John Fanshawe of the Argyll and Sutherland Highlanders, who had volunteered, while serving in the Middle East, to throw in his lot with the Chindits. The journey took longer than they expected and they did not reach the site of the ambush north of Nathkokyin until 5.30 p.m., half an hour before dark. This delay in arriving made all the difference between a perfect ambush and an ambush which was not quite perfect, since they had intended, in the best Chindit tradition, to mine the jungle on that side of the track into which they had hoped to stampede the enemy when he came. For this there was no time before nightfall; there was barely time to choose fire-positions and to occupy them.

They had to wait some hours before anything happened, but at 11 p.m. the sentries shook them awake. There was the sound of movement along the track. The first arrivals proved to be some bullocks, but they were closely followed by a long line of Japanese soldiers, heavily weighed down with full equipment and large packs, and led by an officer on a white charger. As the officer reached the end of the ambush, so that as many of his men as possible were under the guns of the hidden Jocks, Private McLuskie shot him down, everyone else opened fire, and numerous Japanese fell dead upon the track. Recovering themselves, the survivors fled into that part of the jungle which should have been mined; but more casualties were inflicted on the tail of their column which, although outside the ambush when fire was opened, had pressed on along the track towards the shooting.

The firing and general confusion caused some loss of control; and there were moments of internecine fighting between groups of Jocks; but casualties were light. The Japanese left the Black Watch platoons in possession of the field, a large number of bodies, and two suitcases of informative documents. Three Jocks were killed and fourteen wounded, among these being Serjeant Ballantine, who was shot in the face while speaking into his walkie-talkie. The wounded were evacuated by light aircraft on the following day.

A similar but larger ambush was laid on the night of the 7th of May, which developed into the biggest single action of the campaign so far as the Battalion was concerned. Its purpose was to cover Calvert's move from the White City, by creating a diversion; and the spot selected was a point on the same track as Fanshawe had attacked, but south of Nathkokyin village. The safe harbour party was to move forward to a convenient point, and to move back to its old lair after the action. The ambush force was to consist of six platoons, making roughly two hundred men; and Green himself took command of them, leaving Rose in charge of the safe harbour.

The ambush settled in without incident, but the night wore on with never a sign of the enemy. At 4.50 a.m. the little force fell in on the track, and set off in a premature spirit of anti-climax for the safe harbour. In less than half an hour a runner came back with urgent gestures, and reported that a party of Japs had been seen fifty yards ahead of the leading scouts, completely unaware that there was anything afoot: the scouts were keeping them under observation.

Green gave his orders out quickly. McGuigan's platoon was to lead the attack; two platoons were to go in on the left of the track, two on the right of the track. The first blow was struck at 5.25 a.m. and a sharp fight developed. It was not long before Green realised that he had tackled an enemy very much stronger than himself, and this was confirmed by subsequent intelligence; the Japs numbered between eleven and twelve hundred. The impetus of the initial rush had given the Jocks certain advantages of ground, which enabled them to stem a series of bitter counter-attacks; but platoons became isolated, the number of wounded steadily mounted, and Green became more and more worried about how he was eventually to extricate them, particularly those who could not walk.

Some time after ten o'clock, when the fight had been going on for five hours, and the enemy pressure showed no sign of slackening, Green decided to break off the action, and gave out his orders to those of his subordinate commanders with whom he was still in touch. During this process, he is recorded as interrupting himself by saying: 'Excuse me, gentlemen', and picking off a Jap sniper. He then had the rally sounded on the bugle, and that was the last of him and his main body for twenty-nine hours.

Back at the safe harbour Major Rose and his men had been listening to the battle. They had heard it begin just before half-past five in the morning, with two loud bangs; and ever since the sound of mortars and light machine-guns had been continuous, sometimes spasmodic, sometimes swelling fiercely. It was impossible to estimate how the fight was going, and at 10 a.m. he resolved to send out some patrols. The first to leave was a platoon under Lieutenant Archie Wallace, the second, by a different route, another under Lieutenant James Ross: one of Wallace's sections returned after fifteen minutes having bumped into the Japanese and suffered three casualties, but the rest of the platoon had apparently given them the slip and gone on.

Soon after Ross had left, the first detachment from the ambush force arrived – Lieutenant 'Gory' Anderson and most of his platoon, plus three wounded, among whom were his namesake Captain W.A. Anderson. The Andersons' news was scanty: the platoon had been early separated from the main body, had fought a lone action completely surrounded by Japs, and had finally broken out with the bayonet.

A few minutes later Major Fraser arrived back with a much larger party and later information. He had no recent news of

Green, but had come back to safe harbour with such men as were
with him.

At 11.30 a.m. a fresh outburst of small arms fire was heard from
what had been the battle area, and Fraser set out with fresher troops
than those he had brought in, to try his luck at making contact with
the colonel and at picking up wounded men or stragglers. Bearing
in mind Green's intention of moving the safe harbour back to its
old abode, and hoping that Green and his men would appear in
the course of the afternoon, Rose warned Fraser that he would
remain at the present location only until 4 p.m., and that if Fraser
were not back by then, he should make for the old site. Meanwhile
Rose would send out some Burma Riflemen to learn what they
could from local villagers about the latest Japanese strengths and
dispositions.

Of the four parties – Fraser's, Wallace's, Ross's and the Burma
Riflemen – which Rose had now dispatched in search of news,
the Riflemen were the first to return. They arrived at 1 p.m. with
reports of a hundred Japs in Nyaungbintha village; and runners
were despatched to the White City asking that its 25 pdr. guns
should be brought to bear. Nyaungbintha was duly shelled during
the afternoon.

By 4 p.m., the hour at which Rose had resolved to move, both
Ross and Walker were back, the latter only just in time. Ross had
found one wounded and wandering man from the ambush, but
had nothing else to report; Wallace had no news, but he also had
found two wounded men, both unable to walk: they were being
carried in by his platoon. Of Green there was no sign; and at 4
p.m. punctually, Rose moved off, the wounded being carried on
stretchers made from bamboo; and the old harbour was eventually
reached.

There Fraser joined them an hour before midnight. He had
penetrated to the site of the battle, having brushed the Japs several
times without loss; but he had seen nothing of Green, nor of any
other men. The Japs, he said, were busy burying their dead.

It was an anxious night. The colonel and a hundred and fifty men
were missing; and it was in a distracted mood that the harbour
party set to work next morning to build a light plane strip from
which to evacuate the wounded. It was ready shortly after noon,
and at 2 p.m. four light planes flew in and loaded up with
casualties. And then, at 2.45, a joyful message came from a post
on the perimeter, to say that the colonel was arriving with a large
party, including eight wounded; and a few minutes later he walked
in. The relief was tremendous, and even the War Diary sheds its
customary detachment, and records: 'A happy reunion indeed'.

Green, after ordering the bugle to be sounded and extracting himself and those within reach of his orders from contact with the enemy, had found himself with a total of a hundred and five men, of whom eleven were wounded. He had three officers, Captain Swannell and Lieutenants Scott-Hyde and Richmond, of whom both the subalterns were wounded; Scott-Hyde had a bayonet thrust in the thigh, Richmond had been shot through both ankles while standing to attention addressing the colonel. Green had waited a little in case any of the other parties should manage to join him, lying up in view of the track; but as the Japs were interposed between them and the harbour, they had had to travel with caution. While lying there, they realised for the first time, not only how many Japs had been opposed to them, but also the extent of their success. For four hours they had watched, moving down the track, an endless procession of Japanese carrying dead and wounded; and it was obvious that there had been a great killing. They had left the area at 4 p.m. and made straight for the old harbour, that to which Rose had gone, cutting their way across country and sadly handicapped by the wounded. Two had died on the way; one had to be left behind with a broken femur, and was never heard of again; Richmond could only hobble with the greatest difficulty; and Private McGregor had been blinded in both eyes, though happily he was afterwards to recover the use of one.

All parties compared notes to find who was still unaccounted for. It was established that the losses were twenty-six killed, thirty-five wounded and a few missing. Among the killed were Lieutenants McGuigan and Douglas Nicoll; Nicoll had been first wounded in the head and bandaged, and then killed by a sniper at fifteen yards' range while speaking to Green and Swannell. Padre Mair held a memorial service that evening, near the Regimental Aid Post so that the wounded could join in; and every man not actually on duty as a sentry made shift to appear.

The action had been abundantly justified. Apart from the casualties inflicted, the White City had been evacuated under its cover, even the guns, which had fired their last few rounds at the Japs in Nyaungbintha having been flown out without interference (all except one, which got stuck in the mud and had to be put out of action and left). From Special Force HQ came a signal in clear: the familiar cry with many and old association: 'Up the Watch.'

There were still wounded to be evacuated; and when 73 Column moved off on the 10th of May to join the main body of the Brigade on the west side of the railway, 42 remained behind to see the last of them safely flown out. The final flight was made at 10.30 a.m., completing a total of thirty-two men flown out in the last twenty-four hours, all of whom, on the first expedition, would have had to be abandoned to the joint mercies of jungle and Jap. By evening, 42 Column had safely followed 73 across the railway valley, and found it once more reunited with Watson-Gandy's Party, from which the two columns has been separated for seven eventful days.

The whole force (except for one Brigade, which had been evacuated by air to India) was now moving steadily north through the hills on either side of the railway; Aberdeen had been abandoned. Wingate had expressed his belief that no column should have to operate in these arduous conditions for more than two, or at the outside three, months. 14 Brigade had now been in for half of the maximum period and for three-quarters of the minimum; and it was actually given out officially that once arrived at Warazup (far away to the north, on General Stilwell's road) the Brigade would be motored out to Assam. For the next few days, until this order was cancelled, failing hearts were cheered by a doggerel couplet:

> *Chindit, Chindit, don't give up*
> *There's transport waiting at Warazup.*

The rains had now begun to fall in earnest, and a hard day's work from dawn to dusk was pitiful when reckoned in miles. From now on, conditions became as bad as man could endure: one or two unhappy men, indeed, were to find them beyond endurance. Until the end of the campaign they were to forgo even the luxury of occasional dry clothing. They lived in a dripping world, where every fire successfully lit represented a heavy outlay of patience and ingenuity. Day after day of torrential rain and thunderstorms represented not merely discomfort but the threat of starvation; either might prevent the supply planes from flying, and thunder prevented the use of wireless to summon and direct them. During the march out to India, seventy men died of typhus, but both columns continued to fight several more small actions. Nearly every officer and man suffered the effect of the wet and lack of adequate food.

Thus ends Bernard Fergusson's account

Two further views of the campaign can be followed in the letters I received from Graham Bishop, the Intelligence Officer, and Pte W. S. Anderson, my batman.

From: Graham Bishop,
I.O. 42 Col. and later Adjt.,

2nd Bn. The Black Watch
(R.H.R.)
August 29th.   *India Command.*

Dear David,
   At last, I am able to write to you. I'm out! safe and fairly sound. I still can't really believe the perishing campaign is over, but the Colonel keeps assuring me that it is, and we have another whisky! He and I flew down here from the forward area in advance of the Battalion, ostensibly to get things straightened up here, but I quietly think the C.O. wanted a couple of nights in Calcutta, and did we have them! They have promoted me Adjutant, I can't think why, but I am frightfully proud of it. I only wish you over here to help me, you always did all my work for me anyway, still one thing is certain, the younger subalterns will get hell if not the Majors. I've got more liverish than ever. This trembling hand I am writing in is not drink, I am undergoing Blanket Treatment and feel pretty bloody.
   Well David there is so much for me to tell you, I hardly know where to start, or what the censor will say, but here goes. Before I start you must know that the Jocks and Officers of your Col behaved splendidly throughout the rest of the campaign, no praise is high enough for them, and except for the one or two you are bound to get, the reputation of the Battalion has never been higher. Well to the never forgotten day when we left you in your hammock, waiting to be evacuated. I can't tell you how much it affected us all, and how browned off you were to have to leave us. I should have felt 100% better if only we had been able to see you off in a plane. It seemed that we were deserting you, but Pat Hughes put my mind at rest about a week later.
   We arrived at our next port of call, where Geoffrey Lockett was holding the Pass to find that 73 and 59 had left to find another route over the hills, and we had to wait two days here, during that time got another change of orders came through and the CO's lot were ordered up the Pass, we followed the next day. We all expected to be up there about four days at the most, in actual fact your Col stayed a month. It was fairly bloody, and we were mortared and shelled for the first few days, which was unpleasant, as we only had about six spades between us, had quite a few casualties, and Michael and I were extremely lucky with an Air Burst in a tree under which our small trench was constructed. Our role up here was to hold the Pass and take offensive action against the Jap. We had most of our casualties during patrol down in the valley, which was perfectly bloody country, paddling 3 ft under water, and elephant grass made it almost impossible to deploy troops. Poor little Archie was killed on our fourth day up. The Japs put in a surprise attack on his new forward position,

which they were just occupying when the attack came in. Sgt Bain and three others of his patrol were wounded. Soon afterwards old Hew got hit in the hand during a patrol in the valley. Michael had previously decided that John needed a Second in Command, and as Bob Riddell was doing nothing, he took over admin and did it damn well. I feel very sorry about old Hew's patrol, but he made mistakes and was also let down by another unit. It was a minor patrol and the other unit's task was to ambush the road, stay there for a prescribed time, and cover Hew's return. Not only did they leave half an hour before they should have done, but they let 2 patrols of Japs through saying they weren't strong enough to cope. Hew ran into them when practically home and of course expected the track to be clear. I haven't seen him since he went out and I understand he is going home, and also that he is in mood 10 and very embittered. I wish I could cheer him up, but you will probably see him before I do. Sgt McClusky led a first class patrol and against heavy odds inflicted a lot of casualties on the enemy. He himself was wounded twice, but brought his patrol back, such Jocks as L/Cp McLelland, Pte Grant, and Madden put up an exceptionally fine show, carrying a wounded and leading a blinded man for about four hours, most of the time under fire, as it was one of the few times the Japs followed up. We were attacked many times at night, which was unpleasant, but the Jap always got the worst of it. They got through once though, God knows how, and sat over our water point for two days until Douglas Ross with great nerve and dash, leading 2 West African patrols cleared them off, and we drank again. And so a month passed by, raining like hell, and rather wearing on the nerves. The CO was in command of the Pass and of course did wonderfully well. He will tell you more about our Wilfred. Do you remember 'It's just not on Old Boy' when he comes home. Michael also wrote two amusing pieces of poetry which are going in the scrap pile, but which will have to be taken out on guest nights!!

And so we plodded on to our next port of call. It wasn't far and it was North and we all thought it was drawing to a close, but that was just wishful thinking. The weather was foul and at times the mud was knee high. You remember the brand which you hated, the smell of rotting vegetation. Quite a flap on the way 42 was in the lead when a report came in from a village about half a mile away that there were 200 Japs and four elephants there – pushed off with a few Barifs and found that the birds had flown and crossed the hills the night before. Arrived at our destination without further incident, but very tired and had 24 hours rest whilst REs went ahead as the villagers told us that our route was impassable to men let alone mules. 'Tom' [Brigade Commander] of course said absolute nonsense, and went up himself and came back exhausted and said, cannot move until strips are made, it was a climb of over 2,000 feet. All the REs got cracking and most of the patrols with matchets and were working for two days. 'Tom' exceedingly impatient by the time, sent 42 up on the third day, starting at 0500 we reached the top at 1930 hours. What a day, and was I tired. Total loss four mules, and my most precious wireless set, the one that did us as well on training. It fell over 150 feet down a ravine and was no more. Cpl Webb I think felt he had lost a great friend.

At the top a most curious situation occurred which took about five days to discover, the routes forward towards the valley, really was impassable to mules. There were three of them and we left them all. L/Sgt Todd did a first class patrol from here, his patrol being fired on from prepared positions outside a village, his leading scout was killed, but he outflanked the enemy, made his recce of the village, shot the Japs up from the rear and returned to bivouac. The CO made him a full Sergeant on the spot. After much deliberation it was decided to split, all the mules and Admin. to go back down the hill again and the battle groups to go forward with just their weapons, as it was at least a few days journey under such conditions. I was all against leaving the wireless behind, and we were the only Column who attempted it. We had to carry them up the most dreadful hills and through the most appalling mud I have ever seen, but we got communications which was the main thing, and it gave us comfort. Towards the end of this journey we had to wade down a river knee deep for six miles. It was pouring with rain when we started, and after an hour, believe it or not, the water rose 2 feet and the current was about 9 knots. We could not proceed, or turn back, or get out of the bloody thing as it had sheer sides. The only thing to do was to clamber on to huge rocks and hope for the best. We got the loads off the mules and put them on to the rocks and just held the mules' heads. We spent an afternoon and all night in this extremely uncomfortable 'bivouac' and it was the coldest and most miserable experience I ever had. But two days later we arrived at our destination, having taken 8 days to do about 12 miles.

Are you getting bored yet? because I have got a long way to go. Just light a cigar and have another glass of port and relax, it can't go on for ever. The MOs at this stage put their foot down and said the Battalion cannot move for at least 48 hours owing to acute foot rot. 80% of us had raw feet, it was the sand and the mud, and not being able to dry our feet for so long. 'Tom' kept on saying of course 'You must get on you know', but it was no can do, so the Chesney syndicate won. But two days were not really enough. You should have seen some of their feet. The guts shown by all the men was something terrific. And then we moved North East, getting nearer the village where we were to operate from. A party had gone forward to prepare a DZ so that we could get our heavy weapons dropped. When we arrived there it was to find that the DZ was overlooked by a hill occupied by the enemy, who had a heavy M.G. rather uncomfortable, but we got all our stuff dropped OK and then 73 promptly went up the hill and with mortar support, drove the Jap from whence he came, captured the MG, killed 6 Japs for certain, with no casualties. Ours was the next roll, in fact the Battalion took on all other next rolls, turn and turn about. Everyone was bloody tired by this time, but our Battalion was of course in far the best condition. 'Up the Watch' we reminded ourselves. A village five miles further on was our objective, and the next patrol went ahead. Ian Alexander did damn well with this patrol, woke up tremendously! It was a hell of a march again, and at dusk we met a guide from the Col who explained the route up the hill, returned about 14.00 hours with the report that it was just climbable. Bill Swannie took up two patrols to hold the top until first light when 73 would go through and attack, with a front attack by us, with mortar support up the main track. This worked so well that 73 took the village unopposed. We pushed on a couple of miles further on and took what the BBC described as a strategical junction, with no opposition. There at last was over R, of C. and six days later our soft skins were very depleted, 42 having no admin or RE Officer left. Even Bob succumbed and has been on the dangerously ill list ever since. We really thought well this is the end, but no, the old road and rail had to be patrolled offensively, so we upstretched and pushed on. The Yorks and Lancashires occupied a hill overlooking our next objective, and after two days fighting, we cleared the Japs out of the last village. It was a Battalion attack and a glorious finish to the Campaign. The pipes played during the assault and we had the pleasure of seeing 20 Japs running for their lives. Douglas Ross was magnificent, and how we made the effort at all, after all the handgrips we had I don't know. Next day we met up with our own Forces in the valley, and so after five months we found ourselves behind our own lines, it was a great moment.

Well David, there it is, just a peep at the real picture. George will give you details, by the score, many of which are hard to believe, in fact they are indescribable. CSM Stephen asked to be remembered to you when next I write. He did damn well, although he had shrapnel in his leg, he stuck it out to the end. Anderson my batman and Mac remained with me throughout and are fit and well.

And now how are you after all this time? I was very sorry to hear that you were so ill when you got out, although I felt it was bound to happen, you stuck it far too long. We all hoped to find you here when we got out, but you certainly did the wisest thing in going home, it is the only way of getting fit. The thing that worries us more than anything at the moment is who is going to command when the CO goes home. I think you had better come out you know. The CO says he will be home in time for Susan's birthday, if you don't know when that is, write and ask her, you will then know approximately when he arrives. I hope to get away on leave with that bad type Dod in about two weeks' time, which should be very pleasant. Are you married yet! or is this too previous? I bet you are having a whale of a time anyway. All the officers in 42 send their best wishes. Did you know that Guy Anderson got the MC also Wally Anderson (73), damn good show. If you don't come out here and command the Battalion, you had better get a Bde at home pretty soon, and when I come home next year I'll be your BM! Well look after yourself David, let me know your news some time. All the best.

(Signed) Graham.

Batman to Col.Comdr.   W.S. Anderson, 2759685,
                              H.Q. Company,
                              2nd Batt. The Black Watch, RHR
                              India Command,
                              31st August, 1944.

Dear Sir,

I arrived back at our depot yesterday, Colonel Green is also here, arriving a day in front of me, but the Battalion won't arrive for some time yet. I think they are undergoing their blanket treatment before they come here. The reason I am here is, Major —— Sgt Proctor, Cpl Webb, and I, were sent ahead to —— and when we arrived there, Major —— was given a direct order from the Force Commander to get on the first plane for making our stay in —— brief, lasting altogether twenty minutes. The organisation there was marvellous.

I was only a day in India when a small party of us were sent on to Depot Coy.

I was very pleased you were flown out when you did Sir, cause as time went on the light plane situation became more acute. I believe that on the last LP strip I say, as you will know most of it was done by seaplane after that, but as rains got worse, the conditions all round got worse. But we always got there and never once did we fail to achieve our objective. Thanks to Colonel Green, a great man and a grand leader, the men have nothing but admiration for him. After you left us Sir, forty two didn't seem the same. Major —— is a good man and was always very keen, but I think he just didn't have enough experience in LRPG and wasn't too sure about making decisions. Major —— I believe has gone to the Burma Rifles at ——.

We had two or three battles after you left us Sir, but the last one was the most spectacular of all. Major Ross and his Company took the last objective in real Black Watch style, bayonets fixed, pipes playing, and in they went. It would have done your heart the world of good to have seen and heard the pipes and the squeaks, that is the time Sir when you know you have Scottish blood in you cause it boils.

I had quite an important part in it all, I was at base plate, with the

71

Colonel, Brigadier and Major —— I was the sole means of communication between base plate and Reserve Coy, HQ, and if we couldn't get advance Coy on the other —— and I went. I think I covered more ground on that day than I did on any march.

I got your letter and the money from the PRI Corporal as soon as I arrived here. Thanks very much Sir, it was very good of you to remember me. I am seriously thinking of going to Simla for my leave. I am told it is very quiet and very reserved, so I better be on my best behaviour if I go there, but as for the Scotch Nurses, that is out of the question. I might meet one who knows my wife and then I'd have to behave myself.

I don't think it will be very long now Sir before I am due out. So I hope by the time I get home Sir you are Commanding a Battalion of the Black Watch, but if you are Sir you can be sure I'll come to it in on one of the drafts.

Well I really must close Sir and get off to the MI room for an injection for the plague that is here. So all the best Sir and I hope the climate in the UK restores your health back to normal.

Sincerely yours,
(Signed) Pte. W.S.Anderson.
P.S. Would you believe it Sir, I put on two pounds in Burma, pretty good I think.

Reorganisation

Not long afterwards, with reinforcements, they once more became the 2nd Bn. The Black Watch under John Benson – a fully qualified Paratroop Battalion, but sporting the Red Hackle instead of the Red Beret. They would have been the spearhead of the re-conquest of Burma had they not been spared that honour by the release of the atomic bomb on Hiroshima.

In Hospital

I was in a thorough mess with septic prickly heat. My wounds were healed but the root of every hair on my body was a tiny pimple of irritation. I was moved to Calcutta. Soon after my arrival, almost screaming with the irritation, I was visited by the Matron. It was my Prairie Oyster Angel, the charming Nurse Bremner, now the Matron of this vast hospital.

After a cursory examination she said, 'I know what to do with you Major Rose. Take a long bath in permanganate and when you are dry – no towel – cover your whole body with Ponds cold cream. I will go and get the cream.'

She returned a few minutes later with a huge 2-pound pot of her own precious ointment. After this treatment I had the first proper night's sleep for many weeks. We never met again. She was a very busy woman. I was allowed to walk the verandas in my sarong at night. Eventually I got to a ship in Bombay and sailed for home. I was permitted to remain in my cabin under a fan by day and was again allowed to walk the decks by night. The very day we got into the Mediterranean, a miracle occurred; my skin was healed!

CHAPTER FOUR
Taking Stock

A Soldier's Return

I was sound in wind and limb and I could look forward to some leave. My mother was well and had kept things going, despite many difficulties. She had cooked for her three grandchildren and their governess all through the war. For more than five years she had written to me, often not knowing for weeks at a time where I was or what I was doing. It wasn't a very cheerful homecoming. There was nothing to be cheerful about, except our reunion. She thanked me for my parcels of sugar and fats from the Army and Navy stores in Bombay, and told me how they often arrived only half-full as our own Post Office would stick a knife into the sugar and run it out, but they couldn't do that to the raisins and they had been a great help with feeding the grandchildren.

'And David,' she said 'the butter on your plate is a whole week's ration!'

The great armada of planes and gliders on their way to Arnhem flew out over our Suffolk house, a truly awesome sight; hour after hour the whole sky in every direction was filled with planes and gliders and we were drenched in the noise. Standing there on the lawn with my indomitable mother, we thought of Rhoddy somewhere at the other end with his Battalion of HLI bashing their way through the Low Countries and crossing the Rhine to the very heart of Germany. Angus was in Greece. We did not know whether Neil was dead or alive. I thought to myself about my ridiculous little experiments with gliders for Wingate and my pride in my ability with my close support bombers. This monstrous show above our heads put things into perspective.

My 'one and only' was still unattached and working with Scottish Ambulance from her home at Brechin. So off I went to persuade her to take some leave with me in London. She lived at Claridges, I at the Royal Automobile Club. It was the time of the V2 rockets which added excitement to my courtship. We would ring each other up about each big explosion and enquire how close it had been. Life was quite wonderful. Each evening we went to the theatre. It didn't matter what the play was. Sometimes we saw the same one twice, sometimes we arrived in time for the second act. There was no refusal this time.

When I returned to the mess, everyone seemed to be in remarkably good form. Then I noticed that they were making funny signs to each other and I was the object of their merriment. I could not stop laughing and neither could they. I was obviously bonkers! I wanted to sing all the time – I did sing – sometimes I wanted to shout – I did shout. The boredom and repression of years melted away like summer snow. I was free from bondage and on an endless high, without any liquid stimulant, something I had never experienced before. I was in love.

I had a letter of congratulations from Simon Fergusson, Bernard's brother in the Argylls. He said, 'I simply can't tell you what a difference there is in my life now that I am married. I couldn't ever have imagined what a change it would make. It's just wonderful.'

We were married in the spring at Brechin Castle and Bernard Fergusson was my best man. We went to the Shooting Lodge for our honeymoon and for the first few days we were in the snow.

I didn't get much leave, and had to go back to the Infantry School at Warminster, but this time as a married man, with a motor bicycle, given to me by my brother-in-law. We lived in a farmhouse.

That job didn't last very long. I was promoted to T/Lt Colonel as GSO 1 to the 61st Division, dubbed by all the 'Sixty Worst'! They were to be trained to fight the Japanese and I was to teach them the rudiments of jungle warfare. Can you imagine anything more impossible than teaching a collection of bolshie stockbrokers how to fight in the jungle in a very dense spruce wood in Kent? Thanks to the atomic bomb, my first job as a Lt Colonel came speedily to an end. So happily we went off to Suffolk on long leave.

In my own opinion I was due quite six months leave and I lived the life of domestic bliss, until some Staff Officer at the War Office (bless his inefficiency) woke up to the fact that I should have been downgraded to the Major's list long since. The job I was offered was once more overseas, the British Military Mission in Cairo and once more as a T/Lt Colonel. This was tempting for a newly married couple, as England was very drab with rationing and coupons and every kind of restriction.

To Egypt

My passage to Egypt was via Marseilles, so I was able to visit my brother Neil. Rhoddy had gone to the South of France for an end of war bash and had told various barmen that he was looking for a brother who had been with the Foreign Legion. He didn't have to look for Neil. Neil soon found *him*. So I knew what to expect at Bourmes les Mimosa. I took a taxi and there he was, a lank peasant figure, leaning on his hoe in the middle of a vegetable plot. I waved and waved again. Neil slowly put up a hand, then recognition.

'Mon Dieu! – David, David my brother David . . .' We ran to each other and for the first time in our lives, we embraced.

It was thirteen years since his farewell party at the Hungaria Restaurant in Jermyn Street.

Peasant Life

Neil had become an honorary member of a very remarkable French peasant family. When the Germans cleared the hospitals for their own men, Neil had gone south with all the other refugees to Free France. He had taken work in the Toulon docks, but wasn't up to the heavy task. One day he had been found lying on the ground, utterly exhausted, by La Mère Valentine. She took him into her home and nursed him back to health. After a time he joined the Maquis, but eventually became a regular soldier once more.

The extended family very soon heard that another brother had arrived and a great party developed. It was all alfresco – endless bottles of very rough Midi plonk, lots of food, non-stop talking, shouting, teasing.

In the morning with sore heads, Neil and I were to go to the Military Hospital in Toulon for his pension assessment. He was dressed in his best suit and sported the badge of Honour in his lapel. We were to go by train; he wouldn't hear of me hiring a car. The train was more than crowded, it was bulging.

'Really, Neil, we can't do this.'

'You just see.' He opened a carriage door and said 'Bonjour, mon frère et moi, we wish to be seated.'

Everyone got up. 'Certainement, l'honour, très heureuse.'

We ended up in two window seats with everyone clasping our hands and shouting friendly greeting.

'Vive l'Angleterre!' Their friendliness and the garlic was almost overwhelming. One man said he would give Neil a hive of bees for his small farm.

Neil had fought very gallantly for France, first in the Maginot Line, then next in the Maquis and finally in the Régiment Maritime on the Italian front. He received the very finest medical and surgical treatment for his many wounds. He had a silver plate on his forehead.

His Regiment was very proud of him and he of his Regiment. He was a local hero. He rose to the rank of Sergeant on the Italian front, but had to revert to the ranks 'for striking a deserter'. His loyalty was total. Neil had won the Médaille Militaire, the Croix de Guerre and Palm – as a Legionnaire!

The next day, we went for a long slow walk along the sea shore. The water was clear as crystal, a perfect spring day. He had considerable difficulty with his English to start with, but it soon came back. In retrospect, I am always utterly astonished that I can remember almost nothing that he told me. Was my amnesia due to the Midi plonk? I should have written it all down when I boarded the ship later that evening, but the cabin was full of other Lt Colonels and I had no moment to write an aide memoire. What a story he had. I am very sorry that I failed to record it.

AFTER THE WAR

Cairo
Our son was born in Cairo. The Mission to Egypt was a hopeless job. They simply would not do any work, but they would line the streets for some Pasha's funeral. After a little more than a year – and a most enjoyable year – with many friends in the Mission, I resigned. It wasn't a very popular move, but the Mission closed down very soon after.

Tripoli
I reverted to the rank of Major and became GSO 2 at Tripolitania HQ. Our daughter was born in Tripoli. One of my jobs was to arrange entertainment for visiting army and naval VIPs. The sand grouse shooting was very good and there were marvellous Roman cities to visit all along the coast, such as Leptis Magna, Sabrata and Homs.

Duisberg in Germany
After a year in Tripoli I was able to rejoin the Regiment in Germany. Bernard Fergusson was in Command and his 2I/C was our mutual friend, Pat Campbell-Preston. He had been a POW since the fall of France and the disaster which befell the 51st Highland Division at St Valery. It was wonderful to be with my old friends once more, and our three wives were almost as close as we were. Bernard was enjoying himself and so were we. He called me 3I/C and showed me every kindness. We had many convivial evenings together in our own homes and with all the other officers at the Club. The 1st Battalion was in good heart and everything was just like old times.

Our married quarters were substantial German suburban houses, with three floors above and one floor below ground. We were in a large square, just off the main road to the East and Russia. At night, when we were snug in bed, we would hear the thump, thump, thump of marching feet. If I stood at my bedroom window, I could see groups of men in ragged grey overcoats passing below the street lamps.

Sometimes in the very early morning, I would hear the distant sound of marching songs. Nearer and nearer they would come, swelling into well known German army tunes. I just had to get out of bed to see them.

Standing there in my warm flannel pyjamas, I would try to visualise what these young men had endured. These were the survivors of perhaps a million young men, some only boys, who had been launched against Russia and who had died there in cold and misery. We had not suffered carnage on anything like this scale. We had room in Africa to move and room to fall back from Burma to India.

Now they were nearly home. They had probably received no news from their families for many months. They must look their best – heads held high – 'Deutschland, Deutschland Über Alles' – it was very moving. I felt sure that if the tables had been turned, we would have played the same part – but we might have been shot down on orders from the tyrant had we dared to sing 'Scotland the Brave' or 'Rule Britannia'.

We had won the war, but what had we won? Nothing really, but we had kept our freedom. They had been defeated, but they had won their freedom from tyranny. Actually we had won it for them, but they wouldn't think of it that way. The Duke of Wellington knew the answer to this conundrum: 'There is only one thing worse than a battle won – a battle lost!'

We had a lot of fun shooting hares. The Germans were disarmed. You could buy a set of tyres for a hare or two, but they were even more valuable for dinner parties when there was such a shortage of everything, particularly when cooked as only Germans know how.

I don't remember how we met them, but my wife and I were asked to shoot by a noble family named Von Garlen. They had a very fine Schloss and there was a great gathering of the family for a big pheasant shoot. The family were well-known all over Europe as one of the few families who had been anti-Nazi from the very beginning. One member of the family had become world-famous, Cardinal Neimuller, who had been martyred for speaking out against Hitler.

Auntie Julie came to stand with me. Some very low birds came our way. Aunt Julie said 'Shoot, Major, Shoot.'

'No I can't shoot them when they are so low, I would blow them to bits.' More and more birds came, everything came to me.

'You must shoot, Major.'

'Why does everything come to me?'

'Oh, I feed them,' she said.

I shot a few going away behind, but I fear my score did not in any measure come up to expectations.

We went into the baronial hall for lunch. Outside the dining room door, on a large black velvet cushion, was the death mask of the noble Cardinal.

The Countess Von Garlen was a very beautiful woman, not painted or in any way made up, but in country tweeds, she was absolutely stunning. She told us a wonderful 'end of war story'. One morning their castle was surrounded by troops. She and her husband went immediately to the front hall to meet whatever might transpire. They had a plan. Just before unbolting the door they kicked a round brown paper parcel under the huge oak cabinet that stood there. The whole house was searched from cellar to attic, but not that one spot in the front hall. This package contained her priceless Von Garlen emeralds.

The Countess Sophie told us that they were still very uncertain about the future. They thought that the Russians might very well make another move further into Germany. Should they do so, they were going to make a quick getaway in their car with the children. Should they arrive one day at our home in Duisberg, would we take their children and get them safely to England? We will give you the brown paper parcel to pay for their education. It's always wise to plan ahead, but this bold plan did not have to be put into execution.

CHAPTER FIVE

Korea: To War Once More (1952)

My diary: Extracts from letters to my wife.
Some letters to and from the Colonel of the Regiment, General Neil
McMicking and my brother Rhoddy, who was commanding 1st Bn
HLI. Those letters are shown in Italics.

To war once more

It was a lovely summer day at Queen's Barracks, Perth. We were
all in the ante-room having our pre-luncheon drinks and planning
what to do in the afternoon, when round the door popped the
grisly head of General Keith Arbuthnott, the Highland District
Commander, who was acting as Regimental Colonel, as General
Neil Ritchie had settled in Canada with his Canadian wife.

In quite a loud voice he said, 'David, I have something very
unpleasant to say to you. Come outside!' We stood in the porch,
face to face. He wasn't one to beat about the bush.

'Pat Campbell-Preston has had a serious heart attack; you are to
take Command of the 1st Battalion immediately and you will fly
almost at once by BOAC to Japan. You'd better go straight home
and tell Jean.' He got into his car and drove away. I put on my
Glengarry and set off for the walk from the Barracks to the South
Inch where we were living in a Married Quarter at St Leonard's
Bank. I wondered how Jean would take it.

As I went along the well-known road, my previous years of
active service flitted through my mind – those dreadful transit
camps, the searing hot winds, the dust that got into one's back
teeth – but above all, the utter boredom when one was not actually
working.

This wasn't a normal army separation of a few months. It would
be for at least a year and probably for 18 months, with no hope
of any leave. So it was back to the celibate life with dreadful food
and no solace of music, literature or social life. Anyway, there was
no choice. It was wartime again.

But wartime with a difference. It wasn't our nation at war, it was
America at war, with a token of goodwill called the Commonwealth
Division. The rest of Europe had no real interest in it and just
carried on with life as usual.

The Queen Mother came to stay near Crail to say 'Farewell' to her much loved Regiment. She was in mourning for her husband, King George VI. She dined with the Officers at Balcares Castle and she addressed the Battalion on parade. I replied:

'We do not know what lies ahead, but I can assure Your Majesty that we shall do everything to uphold the great traditions of Your Majesty's Regiment.'

After a hectic few days of farewell parties, we drove down to our cottage in Suffolk and, for five wonderful days, lived a perfectly normal life with our adorable children.

My brother Rhoddy and I had always kept up a correspondence when we were at opposite ends of the world. I had enjoyed his letters from the N.W. Frontier in India before the war and his exploits on the Polo Field and Pig Sticking. We exchanged letters frequently while I was in Korea and I hope they will be of interest.

Malta

My dear David,

First of all, congratulations on being selected to Command your 1st Battalion. It is a mark of distinction, especially as it is to take them on active service. As CO's go these days, you are very young. In my Regiment even my contemporaries have not yet got command, and people like Dick Kindersby and Michael Bell will have several years to wait; so you see, at any moment now you may become a boy Brigadier and never have to answer bells in a staff job again. The disadvantages as I see them are not so much that there is a war on in Korea, but that it has such a bloody climate. That combined with the inconvenience to your family life is pretty bloody, but since we cannot afford to retire, you would have had to face a bloody period sooner or later and better now than when the children are at school.

There is no need to worry about lack of experience – you have bags of it, and, as you know, commanding on active service is simple compared to the peace time job. The only trouble is that the high-ups have got the army into such a mess that officers have to do NCO jobs and the soldiers can't shoot. After manoeuvres the Generals all think they have wonderful formations because they don't realise that the units consist of groups of a hundred men doing 'follow my leader' behind two officers. I got a terrific write-up for an assault crossing of the Thames by night, but it was all done by the officers, and as far as the men were concerned, they might as well have been climbing in and out of lorries or aircraft, as boats.

From my experience in the field, I would say the most important thing is visiting rounds. The British soldier will always go to sleep unless he is almost certain that an officer will come round during his turn of sentry. It is a great strain on the Company officers and has to be carefully worked out and divided up, so that there are at least three rounds per night. 'It may be forgivable to be defeated but not to be surprised.' After that I put good feeding, 'bunderbast' by the Company Colour Sergeants, and an example of calmness by all officers. A couple of nevers are, 'never believe any unit has been wiped out'. The chap who tells you so has always run away. 'Never do complicated manoeuvres as every attack will be a frontal one in the end, no matter how many circles you run.' Also try and give your orders on the ground as very few people can read maps anyhow, and most people aren't even issued with them. In Korea there will be special tips about which I know nothing.

No, Athens is neither leave nor operations but the closing down of our Mission, the unveiling of the Greek war memorial and something in the British Cemetery. The C in C with his whole fleet is going, together with Naval, Army and RAF Guard of Honour and our Pipe Band. My contingent is three officers and 100 men. The Admiral is entertaining the King and Q of G to Dinner and my pipers and dancers are the cabaret. There has been a tremendous amount of chi-chi over the whole thing and even the War Office have had a word or two to say over my band being in full dress and the officers carrying swords, etc. However, it has worked out all right and they are wearing just what I said they would.

The Navy are very polite and make a great distinction between Commanding Officers and other Lt Cols. For instance, the C in C writes personally to me to ask for the band and all the Admirals return my calls in person when I write in their books. It is really rather funny but a good thing for the Army to see, in these decayed times.
Yours ever
    Rhoddy

The Parting

Our leave was drawing to its end, so we went to London to say goodbye to my very dear mother. On our last evening we took tickets for 'South Pacific' and cast all care aside. It really was a memorable occasion. The romance, the laughing wife, the music and the joy of being alone together. The memory of this happy evening stayed with me throughout my time of separation.

The next morning after breakfast I walked round to Harrods to have a last proper hair cut. As the barber was finishing, I saw a very smartly dressed young man looking intently at me in the mirror.

'Last time I saw you,' he said, 'you were lying in a hammock beside a very rough landing strip in the forest. Come and have a talk.'

I told him I had no recollection of our former meeting, but I couldn't accept his kind invitation as I was just about to catch the Flying Boat to Korea.

'Good grief. Are you still at it!'

Standing there in the barber's shop he told me that he had gone straight back to his Brigadier and said that they couldn't possibly leave a Column Commander lying unguarded in the jungle, to wait for a light plane, which probably would never arrive. He would go and round up some of the Burma Forestry elephants, which he had noticed earlier in the morning. When he returned with the elephants I had gone. The West African casualties who were still lying beside the airstrip were put on the elephants and ten days later reached the Indawgee Lake, whence they were up-lifted by a flying boat and eventually ended in the same hospital as me in Shillong.

I told him that when the L5 arrived to pick me up, they also loaded a West African with a broken leg. They couldn't take off with the two of us, so the poor fellow was unloaded. With me alone, we became airborne. The West Africans were in a bad way when they reached Shillong, maggots and all, but the wonderful medical team there soon had them on the mend.

That was 1944: now to return to 1952.

We decided to make the break at the Station and I went on to the Flying Boat terminal alone. I don't remember much about the journey, except that I was deeply depressed. I got into my comfortable seat on the Flying Boat and soon the engines roared and we were climbing over France.

Quite suddenly and silently the dam burst: my tropical suit was a sorry sight! After a little time, the small voice of reason returned. It won't be so bad this time round. At least you will have your soul-mate to share everything and two adorable children at instant recall. No more Mr Solo. And so it was that I started there and then a correspondence which continued till we were reunited, more than a year later.

This following account of my months in Korea is not a 'history'. It was written over forty years ago at the time and I have had no access to war diaries, other than my own. I have left practically nothing out. Every incident was recorded on the day it happened, or one or two days later when more news had been collected. Although the official history of the Korean War has been written recently, I am told that individual accounts of war by professional soldiers are often of interest and should be taken to be complementary to the 'best sort of history', written by academics.

Journey to Japan

BOAC D1

My Darling,

So the partings are over and now we must rely for a time on future hopes and past memories. It has been a wonderful seven years for me and we have been very lucky to spend nearly all of it together – and there are so many sweet memories. As I write this letter we are passing over Dijon. Wasn't that a happy day and such a beautiful trip through France? It was such a lovely rest at Finn and so happy working, cooking, eating and sleeping, hearing those little voices and feet all over the place. My ticket is worth £240! So the Colonel is worth something to his country. I hope he can pay it back.

The land is in darkness now but we are still in the sun. F M Alexander is sitting in the seat directly behind me. Beside me is a nice young man, a Mercantile Marine Engineer whose firm has a ship damaged in Pusan – so we shall be all the way together. There was a great gathering of the press for the FM as you will no doubt see in tomorrow's paper. (We are now turning for Zurich.) I do hope you caught the train and got safely back to the dear wee cottage where we have been so happy together. I can't see the mountains yet but there is one big white cloud, much higher than we are, and it's the only pink one left.

I have just had a very good dinner. Clear soup, salmon, strawberries and cream and a glass of white wine. Couldn't eat the cheese!

Tell Isa (our Nanny) how grateful I am that she is sticking by us in these trying days and how much I admire the way she handles the children and how much I have enjoyed having her living with us. I can't think of any nicer or more sympathetic person – the product of kindly and charming parents – may our children be the same.

We are very high now and one feels it. Pat Campbell Preston would be *very* short of breath. I can just see forests and some rivers and it looks in shape like the Lake of Annecy of happy memories. It's nice writing to you as I go along my way.

BOAC D2

I couldn't write yesterday. It was too bloody hot. Karachi was like a furnace and Delhi was worse. They were just waiting for the monsoon to break. When we got to Rangoon it had happened. The fields were all wet and green and the air was lovely. Mick Baker met me and took me off to his bungalow for dinner. It was grand to have a bath and change and I slept well. Now I am in Bangkok. They turned out a band for the FM and a curious Guard of Honour.

Perhaps tonight I may see Charlie Anderson if he is not on the frontier.

Mick Baker was having much the same trouble with his Mission that Keith Arbuthnott had with his in Egypt. They aren't allowed more than a few miles out of Rangoon. All they really want is the weapons and if they don't get them soon, they will close it all up.

We passed the Gold Pagoda in Rangoon and at night it was all lit up – quite a sight. My companions are not very amusing and they couldn't be even if they tried, with the noise of the machine and the heat.

BOAC D3

11th June 1952

I told you, I think, that I dined with Mick Baker in Rangoon. He was sharing a very charming bungalow with the RAF Officer. Lovely lake in front of it and we sat there and talked and had a whisky & soda or two. Early to bed and an early start in the morning. Tried to get in touch with Charlie Anderson but he was on an exercise that evening.

We landed at Okinawa this morning. They had 10' of rain there the day before. It was crammed full of war stuff. There I met Malcolm Wallace for a few minutes, also on his way to Japan, but in a RAF plane. I shall meet him in a day or two when we fly over to Korea. He told me that our Air Advance Party had been very much delayed on their journey and was only a day or two ahead of us. Wasn't it a good thing that I got that leave?

I had a few minutes conversation with the FM but didn't get much out of it. He will visit our Division, a Korean Division and an American Division and the prison camp and return by Washington. I do hope he can do something, but I see no reason why he should be successful where others, who have tried so hard, have had no luck. We land in Japan in a few minutes.

Kure

12th June 1952

A great Guard of Honour of all nations met the FM at Tokyo and a large band and masses of photographers of course. I was met by that captain who was on the Movement Control Staff in Tripoli but can't remember his name. He was very good to me, fixed me up with lunch and some money and then bundled me straight into a sleeper for this place, Kure.

The train was very clean and comfortable – much better than British Railways – plenty of hot water, very nice clean sheets and the lavatories and passages were always being cleaned and swept.

It was a long and hot journey but gave me a very good look at the country. It's quite extraordinary. Every single piece of ground is cultivated right up to the walls of the houses. Some fields are only two yards wide and most of them no bigger than our vegetable plot at Finningham. Every stalk of corn is cut by hand and tied up in little bundles. As I went through the country they were cutting the corn and flooding bare fields for the second crop which is rice.

They have been very good to me here. I am living in a little Japanese house with the GSO1 and another colonel. Last night two Canadian colonels came in and joined us for drinks and I was very popular giving over half a bottle of whisky – the remains of mother's present. (They have no whisky here since the Treaty with Japan, as they would now have to pay duty.) After dinner we went to the Canadian's house and he played his latest rude American songs. Some of them were quite funny. I asked him if he had South Pacific – and he HAD, so we had the whole of that to my great enjoyment and then a few tunes from Oklahoma and so to bed. And did I sleep! This morning we had dressing-gown breakfast and I am now writing to you while my clothes are being washed by the two Japanese girls who cook and do batman duties.

Later on I am to go to see a draft of 40 men who are joining us and who have been doing some hard training here. Then they are taking me to HMS *Ocean* to meet Rhoddy's friend, Evans. Isn't that a bit of luck? I never thought I would have a chance of meeting him. Tomorrow I visit the Battle School and in the evening, drive off to another aerodrome where I sleep and fly to Korea early the next morning.

We are getting six days' training before we take over from the Leicesters. Things are pretty quiet up there just now and no-one here expects any fireworks in the immediate future.

There were lots of American families in the train from Tokyo. They had obviously just landed and were all being met by their husbands. Some of the children were very blonde and attractive. One couple, without children, who were sitting opposite me, started their reunion with the very dickens of a row about their sewing machine! He said why the hell hadn't she sold it for $300. She said she wanted to keep it for always and was tired of selling everything every time they had to move – and they went on and on about it. Little did they realise how lucky they were to be together.

Korea

A word or two is in order at this point to explain 'the war so far'. In June 1950 the communist North Koreans invaded the South. The US

86

rushed troops to the aid of the South. Owing to the absence of the Russians in the Security Council (they had earlier stormed out in a contrived political huff), the United Nations Organisation was the cover for the Americans and some other anti-communist countries to wage war ostensibly in the defence of the Free World.

The Koreans made great gains at first, but during the latter half of 1950 and through 1951 the war was conducted north of the border agreed some years earlier. By the end of 1951 the front line was mainly consolidated north of the 38th Parallel. The war of manoeuvre was over but the war of defence continued with huge numbers of Chinese 'volunteer' units as the enemy. The feature known as 'the Hook' was part of the front line defence in the Commonwealth Division's area of responsibility. It was to be our home and battleground over the months.

It should be remembered that much of the British Army at the time, including my battalion, was made up of conscript soldiers. Scottish soldiers, with a more fatalistic view of life, probably took to conscription in a better spirit than English soldiers in general, although we found that The Black Watch absorbed all comers as 'jocks', an expression synonymous with true fighters. Such was the Regimental spirit of the old-fashioned Regimental system.

15th June 1952

I have arrived at my destination. I went up to the Battle School from Kure in Japan and I inspected the draft of 120 men who are coming to us and who have been training there. They looked absolutely first-class and very fit. Actually they are all Englishmen, but I don't mind, as they looked such very good chaps. In the evening, my host, Morris Bryant, took me to the officers club to play Bingo – you know the game, when they call out numbers. I won two bottles of Champagne and we drank them the next evening before my departure.

From Kure I flew to Pusan and then to Seoul and at Seoul they met me with a light aeroplane and brought me right up here. Everyone has been quite charming and friendly. The Brigadier showed me to my tent and gave me the freedom of his own 'thunder-box'. It was the day of FM's visit to the Division and I was among a number of COs who had to meet him at an Observation Post. With him was our General of course, who greeted me in most friendly manner. I spent the afternoon going round other Observation Posts with Colonel Hutchins. There wasn't much activity and everyone was enjoying themselves, bathing and sitting in the sun and rushing about in Jeeps – making an awful dust. One of the companies got shelled a bit during the afternoon.

The food is *marvellous* – fresh turkeys and goodness knows what. In fact there is an abundance of everything and I gather that regiments vie with each other when they give a party and produce the most wonderful spread. Today I am to visit the Leicesters for their weekly curry-lunch and in the afternoon the KOSBs for the playing of Retreat. We were doing quite a lot of shelling last night, but I had a grand night's sleep.

I saw most of my Advance Party yesterday – all very busy rushing round Company positions – very pleased with themselves and already looking brown and fit. Denniston looked as though he had lost at least a stone and Peter Buchanan had fined down. None of them have had a Mail yet, but Nobby Clark has taken steps to find out where it is being held up.

I am to stay here at Brigade Headquarters for a few days. When the Battalion arrives, we go into a Concentration area for some training. After that we take over our section of the line, which will be temporarily held by an Australian battalion. I am told I have a very first-class Gunner, Reg Pont, and I have already met my tank Squadron Commander in the Dragoon Guards – a very charming fellow and keen sportsman. Oh, what a number of people I have met – I am in rather a whirl but no-one really expects you to remember all of them at once.

At this point I got the summons and disappeared for hours with the Brigadier. We walked up hot hills, talked and walked again. He was very nice – *very* slow, but full of good common sense, I thought. I liked him and felt the whole time that he was doing everything that he could do to make me at ease and tell me things without giving me a lecture. Eventually I went off to the Leicesters for their Sunday curry luncheon. Very hot, lots of gin, lots of curry, but I got away by 3pm and drove on with Malcolm and Raas McRae to the KOSBs. We were expected there for Retreat at 4pm, but were too late which didn't matter. Stayed for talk and drinks. Another hour with the Brigadier tonight and other chaps. Very sore with sweat and sun-burn. I also have a large jug of lime juice. Last night I had nothing to drink and was in agony by 7am.

Our guns have started firing. It's such a lovely night. Tomorrow I have a very hard day on a big mountain – our reserve position. The others are all going with me to look at our positions there, which have been dug for us by others.

The Brigadier treats me very much as his guest and couldn't take more interest in my comfort and my daily programme. I see everything that is happening from the best points of vantage and I am doing my best to absorb everything, while I am still free from daily duties. My Brigadier was also a Chindit – unknown to me. He told me all about it last night. We have had several long talks. His wife's brother was a great friend of mine, Terrence Close. Poor fellow, he died in his prime after the war of infantile paralysis.

I got up very early this morning and watched a tank raid from a Grand Stand OP. We put down a very heavy concentration of fire – results not in yet.

I have now met many of the other COs and they are all very helpful. I like Raas MacRae and think he will do me well. I can't go down to meet the ship, so I am sending Malcolm.

This is a very comfortable war compared to my previous experience; such good food and no shortage of anything. Of course the climate is wonderful at the moment, but soon the rain will come which will cut up the dirt roads and make things less pleasant. There are lovely flowers and birds. The swallows nest in tent and dug-out roofs and remain unmolested. I shall see Pat Douglas in two days' time. We all had a glorious swim in the Imjin this evening and lay on the sand sun-bathing.

I must tell you my funny story from the aeroplane. The Minister, Selwyn Lloyd, went along to the lavatory very early in the morning. One of the other passengers, his eyes full of sleep, rose from his chair almost at the same moment and not thinking that anyone else was awake, kept rattling the door handle and pushing hard on the door.

The pretty air hostess said to him, 'You can't go in there, the Minister is in.'

'Well, that's the nearest I shall ever be to a seat in the Cabinet.'

'It's rather awful, there's no paper in there. He just beat me to it,' she said.

'Oh,' said the passenger, 'that must be the first time a Cabinet Minister has ever been short of bumph!'

The Battalion Reunited for Training
23rd June 1952

They arrived yesterday at Rail Head in very good form and with three letters from you and one from Hughie. It was grand. I had such a day – left Brigade Headquarters at 4am and motored down in the lovely cool dawn with no dust from other vehicles. They had a wonderful trip and were magnificently entertained all the way. I think Pat made a great success of it and left new friends for the Regiment wherever they went. I brought Pat away with me from the Staging Camp, as the Leicesters were having their farewell party and it was a grand opportunity for him to meet everyone. Our General was there and the American Corps Commander and I had several talks with both. All the Brigadiers and their COs were there of course and they were charming to me. Brig MacDonald in particular, whose opening remark was:

'I hear from a friend of mine that the BW is first-class, but that you consider yourself the only weak link. Have you seen the paper today?' and laughed.

Afterwards someone gave me the paper. I can't tell you what a write-up I had!

After the party, we went to swim in the river in our '8th Army bathing suits' as they say. It was glorious and we returned to the hot dusty camp in the evening when it was beginning to get cooler. Ted Hutchins, the Leicester CO, insisted that we should stay to dinner and it developed into a really old fashioned party – cock fighting, through the tent ventilators and all the rest of it. This morning I am rather stiff and sore, but it was worth it, as we made great friends with our hosts and other people who were there.

25th June 1952

I am so sorry to hear that my letters haven't been arriving. Tomorrow we start work in a big way. It's very hot indeed, so we are trying to start very early in the mornings. The worst of it is that there is nowhere to get shade in the afternoons. My small caravan is like an oven. You can only just go quickly in and out again. However the nights are lovely and cool.

I may be very busy for the next few days so I am going to write again tonight in case I should miss a few days. I am to lunch at Divisional Headquarters tomorrow and dine there on 28th. Tomorrow is a farewell party for 'Iron Mike', the Corps Commander. The morning and afternoon are both packed with work so I shall be rushing about the country with no moment to spare. Tonight is the anniversary of China's entry into the war, so our guns are having a birthday party and there will be little sleep for any of us. Thank God it is our guns anyway. It's really very hot but one doesn't have much time to think about it. One just pours with sweat and I take plenty of salt tablets which make all the difference. We are getting the Mess going, but as yet I haven't succeeded in getting any water coolers or any squash. There is lots of beer for the evenings but cold lime juice is the thing in the day-time. We'll have it in a day or two.

Sandy Barnett, Peter's brother, sent me three packages of second-hand books from Hatchetts – for the Mess of course, not for myself. Wasn't that kind? Today we were all over the country – up hill, down dale, deciding where to do all our exercises. We ended up in the river which was quite perfect.

Pat went down to the rail head with the Pipes and Drums to play off Ted Hutchins and his boys. By his account they were having a *very* jolly party on the train. We would be doing the same no doubt if we were in their shoes.

28th June

I have just returned from dining with General Cassels. It was a good dinner. It is now coming down 'cats and dogs' and the roads are pure glue. My poor driver, Pte Dillon, whom you may remember, had his Jeep stolen in the Divisional Car Park. Can you beat it! And so I was driven home, with Dillon, in the greatest comfort in a huge Humber. I sat on the General's left at dinner and he was very nice to me. We talked a bit about his wife, Joyce, which no-one else can do because she never follows the drum, but I knew her well when she was a girl. We also talked a lot about Perth – his future job. Wasn't it awful having my jeep pinched? The General had gone as the new Corps Commander had sent for him on the telephone, but someone had to stay with me till all was arranged – only 10pm!! Now I am hoping that the rain will be so heavy that tomorrow's exercise will have to be cancelled.

29th June 1952

My first exercise is over and it appeared to go very well. The Brigadier was in good form and I hear that his staff was much impressed by his reactions on his return. Pat, in his cups, told me that I had won over the men of the Battalion by some aside I made at Crail. So despite the fact that I feel they don't know me, I am more confident.

Yesterday we got washed out. Many of them must be soaking tonight. Of course I am doing all I can to help them, but I am afraid it isn't much. Before the rain came it was very hot. In the morning I had been up to the top of our highest hill, conducting a reconnaissance party. I simply couldn't stop sweating so I went to the stream where all the men go for a dip, and I saw the most astounding thing – a complete rainbow round the sun in full colour. Men asked me what it was. Was it an eclipse, what else could it be? It was quite extraordinary, like our 'Blue Sun' at Invermark!

1st July 1952

Everything seems to be going well. I seem to be getting nearer to officers and men and all are very happy and natural. The floods have subsided and it is astonishing how quickly all the wet blankets have dried. Every day is full of activity – jeeping here, there and everywhere. Seeing this and that, issuing instructions and moving on again. Pat seems to agree whole heartedly with everything I do and say, which is a very happy position for us both. We had a nice swim in the Imjin this evening. There is so much to teach everyone, including myself, in such a short time. We have had very good officers to tell us the form, Gunners, Sappers, Doctors, they all have their bits to tell us which are of such immense value, if we can make use of their experience.

General Jim Cassels comes to visit us the day after tomorrow. When I dined with him he didn't seem to look forward very much to Perth. He said he hadn't a bob above his pay.

Did you notice that Brig Tom Brodie, whom I have often told you about in Chindit days and who lectured to us in Perth about Korea, has got Command of 1st Division.

I expect you have heard in Perth that Didee's half-brother lost his leg here a few days ago. I think I told you about the 'tank raid'. He got out of his tank and with some other men, walked into a booby trap. The Helicopter had him in hospital in no time, but the leg was beyond repair. I am told he took it wonderfully.

2nd July 1952

I came back from a demonstration a few minutes ago to find three lovely long letters from you. The mud is now dust again but it is a good deal cooler with a certain amount of cloud. We'll get more rain in a day or two, but next time everyone will have learned by experience how to cope with it.

Everyone in very good heart and working hard and me getting more confident in myself and my chief supporters. May everything continue well. We shall be giving a Retreat Party before we go further forward. Our Korean porters are busy making a small flat space as a parade ground. Coming back from dining with the King's Shropshire Light Infantry the other night, Pat and I picked up two men who were walking back to their camp, I discovered one drove a Bulldozer and asked him if he would work for us for an hour or two for a bottle of whisky. All went well but the rain undid most of the good work and formed quite a deep river through the middle of it. RSM Scott is now driving a Jeep round and round it with some iron bars like a harrow behind, to smooth the surface.

3rd July 1952

This is the night that Hugh was born, so despite the fact that it is now midnight, I must write to you. What a night that was for you – but what a success was the result. I do hope he has a lovely party tomorrow. All the guns are firing in his honour tonight – Independence Day. Tonight I was invited to take Nic (my Adjutant) and Pat and all my company commanders to Brigade Headquarters for dinner. I had been there also for lunch to meet the new Corps Commander – with the other COs of course. He was almost indistinguishable from the last Corps Commander, 'Iron Mike'. This one has a bigger tummy! It was a very nice, but quiet dinner. On Sunday, the Brigade Staff and many other people, are coming to us for Retreat. Every day is crammed full of activity. I start at 6.30am and usually finish at 11pm. Today was field firing exercises all over the place. Pat goes to those I can't fit in.

David Campbell's test this morning, with tanks assisting, was *very* bad and I had to be rather rough-spoken. The others have been well done. *My* big test comes on Saturday and General Jim will be there. There is a rumour – and this is only for you – that he will not now go to Perth but may become a Corps Commander – a result of the FM's visit no doubt.

6th July 1952

Yesterday we were hard at it from the middle of the night till evening – exercise 'Swift'. Everything went well and some things very well. I had the hell of a day. Went round all my positions as soon as we were established and then straight round them again with the Brigadier, who naturally wanted to see how well the men had dug their trenches and so on. We had over 200 Korean porters to supply our hilltop positions and Pat organised all that part of it very well. I had an unpleasant day, the previous day. I had to remove David Campbell from command of his company, replacing him by Malcolm Wallace – all goes well there now. In a few minutes time we have a Drum Head service, followed by Communion and this evening Retreat and a good number of guests. I do hope it doesn't rain again as it did last week, but there are some heavy clouds about.

I have chosen very well in Raas MacRae as my Battle Adjutant. He is methodical and accurate and unhurried and good on paper. They still go on talking vaguely about an armistice but it doesn't seem to get anywhere. Reuters' Correspondent out here said that he did not think that America really wanted one, now that her supplies and organisation were so well geared up.

In the Line for the First Time
9th July 1952

We have been forward for a bit and everyone is getting quickly used to their new surroundings. Tell Hughie we do a lot of shelling and firing with mortar bombs – and sometimes they post some back to us, but not very often. We had some heavy ones this morning but nothing worse than two rather frightened Sergeant Majors – one of them RSM Scott!!

It's a curious life up here and a healthy one. I climb hills most of the day and pour with sweat – inspecting trenches and fortifications and planning improvements. Then I try to sleep for a bit in the afternoon and get up feeling rather fuddled at 5.30pm when Nic comes up with papers to sign. After dinner real work starts and may go on all night but usually I can go to bed at midnight or soon after. Raas McRae, Peter Buchanan, Pat Douglas or John Moncrieff taking it in turns to sit at the telephones and wirelesses till 5.00 a.m. – one whole night each and most of the next day off. I have got such a nice and very expert Gunner. Early tomorrow morning I go up with the Brigadier to visit Malcolm Wallace. He has the nastiest bit of our front, but it isn't really very bad. It needs a great deal of work done on it, which Malcolm is doing all he can.

David Campbell is doing very well in his new job. He is too old for an active Company and lacks the knowledge and experience. I am so glad I spotted it in time.

13th July 1952

I am afraid we have had the inevitable first casualties – very sad – but it has made them realise that *all* the noises aren't our own. I have got them digging really hard and yesterday we received a good bombardment, without a scratch. They really are working well and cheerfully and have done more in a week than the other regiment who has been here has done in four months.

Today we had all the big-wigs to visit us. General Mark Clark, General Collins (chief of Staff American Army), General Van Fleet, Corps and Divisional Commanders. We had a small guard in the kilt and two pipers played while they were drinking tea. They were tickled to death! They didn't go up the hill to see the enemy. I suppose it was considered inadvisable after yesterday's shelling. I wonder if you will see any pictures in the papers? It is getting very sticky now, so the rains can't be far off. Very trying in the afternoons. I do wish they would arrive, despite the discomfort they will bring. Tonight we had one officer from each Company into the command Post for supper. We are lucky, in that we can cook fresh rations. Most of them have to eat from tins except for one fresh meal a day, which is cooked behind and sent up to them. They were all in very good form and delighted to have a change. We get five men per company out of the line each day, back to A Echelon where they have a bath, a good feed, a cinema, a swim and clean clothing. David Campbell and Peter Lindsay run it very well.

Nobby Clark (QM) is in fine fettle – very active and fit and very proud of his B Echelon. He is the senior QM in the Division, so naturally he has to set the standard – and what a standard!

16th July 1952

I don't know how I am going to reply to all the people whom you say are going to write to me, but things may quieten down in a day or two. Yes things have been a bit hectic, but I am getting into a routine. Late to bed, a few hours in the afternoon and a cat nap now and again. Feeling very well despite the heat and the irregular hours. The food is good, enough to drink and good company. They all keep in good humour and the staff and the Brigadier and the Generals are all nice to me. We all go very 'nunga-punga' when we are out of the line. Last evening I had a swim in the Brigade HQ swimming bath – a stream with sand-bags around it and a cement bottom. It was lovely and cool after a long hot conference.

Tomorrow I shall be out of the line for an hour or two. Princess Patricia's Canadian Light Infantry have asked 3 of us to a buffet luncheon. It will be a nice change. We had a Public Relations Sergeant yesterday among many other visitors. He spent the day with some of my Companies and returned here in the evening. He wanted to photograph me, but I insisted on having my Staff with me. While he was doing it, there were a few shells landing which made it difficult for him to do his job. Much laughter from us. So you may see us all soon in the 'gutter press', as my mother would say.

19th July 1952

All continues to go well but we are going through an unpleasant time – a few casualties every day. Malcolm's Company are getting the worst of it: really very unpleasant. I ordered Malcolm out of the line for a day's rest today. He came back here with me for a 6.30am breakfast - sausage, egg, bacon and fried bread, coffee and fresh rolls. Our cook makes such good rolls. He had a good rest and a bath and dined with me tonight on his way back there. He's such a good chap. And Keith Denniston has carried on very well in his absence. They have started to get one or two cases of nerves and shell-shock – the weaker links of course. However, I shall have them in a quiet area the day after tomorrow when Angus Rowan Hamilton takes his place. It isn't really bad but in this country we are forced to be very concentrated on the hill tops which makes shelling most unpleasant. In the day time there is really no threat of attack so I make Malcolm's men 'thin out'. In other words, I remove about 30 of them to the back areas for rest and washing. No-one seems to have thought of this before. And we have a good cinema there for those who want it. I must tell you another nice story.

We had a funny American here the other day. He said in his drawly way 'There are just two things I simply loathe about Korea – wet lavatory paper and Second *Lu*-tenants.' I like it.

Tomorrow is Sunday. I read the lesson at 11.30 and then I go with Pat to lunch with Colonel John Orlebar of the Norfolks. He had lunch with me today on his way back from a reconnaissance. A very charming fellow.

22nd July 1952

It has been pouring with rain all day, with heavy thunderstorms. It's very warm, so one just splashes about in the wet and everyone is busy trying to keep the ditches open and the water from flooding their dug-outs. The roofs are all leaking, my papers are all wet, everything in a thorough mess. We may get a break of fine weather before the big rains set in and we shall have to make good use of every moment, if we are to be ready for them. It's all very difficult. However, we had Turkey for dinner! And Pat and I enjoyed our Curry Luncheon with John Orlebar – quite a party finishing up with liqueur brandy. Next week I am invited to the KOSBs and to the Princess Pat's Canadian LI – and to take two others with me on each occasion. We can't do anything in return till we are out of the line, but we have many visitors every day who come our way on duty.

I am reading Ponsonby's 'Three Reigns' and like it. His name reminds me of a silly story. When Ponsonby's son and heir was born he went straight to the nursing home and insisted that he should be circumcised at once. The doctor told him that this was usually done after a week or so, but agreed to do it then if he insisted. The next day he brought a flask of brandy with him and insisted on the child being given some to drink. Then he took the boy to his mother and put him to her breast and stood there looking more than delighted. The Nurse asked him why he was so pleased.

'There you see a true Ponsonby,' he said. 'Sore cock, stomach full of drink and mouth full of tit.'

23rd July 1952

I am very happy because there is a bit of a let up in the shelling and everything is going well. Golly, it's hot and humid! Today I had the CO of the Royal Fusiliers, whose battalion arrives shortly. He wanted to spend all day and a night with us. I have farmed him out to Angus Irwin for the night, so that he can see what goes on in the line. Angus has Larry Trotter as second in command and they run a very good show together. Angus and Malcolm are without doubt my best Company Commanders – Angus a little quicker on the up-take. I shall see the colonel back here for breakfast at 6.30 or 7. Isn't it a good thing that I am a natural early riser?

The sun set off a small ammunition dump of ours this afternoon. It was the smoke bombs which started it. That's Pat's department.

David Arbuthnott becomes a Captain tonight and Peter Carthew a fully fledged subaltern. We all drank their health. The big bridge over the River Imjin is opened tomorrow and they have asked for my pipers for the occasion. It means a relief of troops in the line, but the Americans adore the Pipers so much I couldn't refuse them. I wish I could tell you more about what is going on, but I know that would be wrong. After pounding up and down the hills with the visiting colonel, I showed him to a cool dugout to have a sleep as he will probably be up all night. I fully intended to have one myself but found the Daily Telegraph correspondent waiting for me. So off we went again in my jeep. Off up the hills and round the companies. I sweated buckets – and so did he – but I had been doing it since 6 a.m. And now it's nice and cool and the stars are shining and the crickets are cricketing and I am looking at my picture of you.

24th July 1952

We had General Van Fleet, the Corps Commander, General Jim and Brig Abdy Ricketts here this morning. The General made a little American type speech, shook hands with the company commanders and told a few jokes over a cup of tea. We had a small guard dressed in the kilt, which impressed him, and was considered 'a nice touch' by the Brigadier. Don't imagine things are hot in this area. We do a bit of shelling and long range shooting but not much comes back. Half a dozen minor casualties from splinters, bright moonlight nights and the enemy keeping well back. The 'talks' also seem to have taken a brighter turn in the last few days and we are all enjoying ourselves and keeping very well.

25th July 1952

I had a lovely swim and some *iced* beer this morning. We had been up and down plenty of hills – streaming with sweat, clothes quite sodden – when I decided to call on one Blundell-Brown, in the 5 DGs. It was heavenly. On Friday I am to take two other officers there for a swim and drinks and dinner. He is such a nice fellow. Its too hot to have a sleep this afternoon, so I am sitting in my Command Post dug-out writing. I had a nice long letter from Rhoddy by the same post. Golly I am hot, the blotting paper is soaking and it is no use mopping as one requires a dry hankie every 5 minutes.

Malta
21st July 1952

My dear David

I hope you aren't having too bloody a time, but I fear with the rain and everything it must be pretty grim. One cannot get any idea from the papers what the fighting is like, and from people who have been there one gets very conflicting reports. The various periods passed through were so different, I suppose. I don't know what they are sending you for reinforcements. If they come direct from Fort George I fear they will be pretty green. I have to retrain mine from the beginning as they can't even drill on arrival. We did at least teach them that when we ran Fort George. Incidentally, some 56 of my young regulars (just about 50% of my regular intake since November 1951) have never come to me, so perhaps they are going to you. I think they should pass through a Battalion first, for your sake. I have been paying 10/- a head to anyone bringing in a regular recruit from our 2nd Bn funds, but we can't go on doing that if the men are to be posted anywhere.

Our future is not so good. We go off on an exercise to Tripoli near the end of August, and in mid September we go to Tel-El-Kebir in the Canal Zone. It is the worst bloody place I know and not even within striking distance of the water. Have to live on rations, and of course, do without women. It really is extraordinary how the British are supposed to do without women. Personally I find sex starvation very ageing. Five months in Tobruk made me into quite a grumble pigeon – I am now several years younger and much brighter generally.

There was a pause of half an hour here. When I started the letter it was a respite to working out landing tables for a combined ops exercise for which I have recently re-grouped and retrained the Bn. Now I am suddenly asked to switch it all back four months because of a flap about our operational role. They keep doing this sort of thing – quite delighted when one manages after super-human efforts to produce the answer, but as soon as the flap dies down they waste no time in giving you a rocket for your education or your transport maintenance which had to be sacrificed to the emergency. It is the people in the War Office and G.H.Q.s who really do the damage. Those types never take a chance on anything, so they issue all the orders for everything, all the time. We poor devils have to make our own appreciations as to what not to do, without the material at the High Ups disposal on which to base a judgement. However, if one passed on half the cock that comes down the line, there wouldn't be any battalions in the Army, let alone bns with any spirit. Apart from Army

98

*matters, Malta is quite good fun. I love the under water harpooning, I
dine out every night, and forget all about the Army from luncheon time
till 5.30am the next morning. Of course the overdraft is huge, but what
the hell.*

*I do hope they get you a truce going soon and that you and the
'Forty-twa' get out of that bloody place before the awful winter. I believe
service there counts double, so that should help to get you back to the wee
ones sooner than normal. Best of luck, old boy, and look after yourself.*

Yours ever,
   Rhoddy.

26th July 1952

Poor Alec Renny-Tailyour was killed on a patrol last night – no,
the night before last. I wrote to his mother this evening. Oh, what a
difficult and unpleasant task. I felt that I wouldn't say too much in
the first letter. Perhaps his father will ask for fuller details. It was all
so sad because he was killed by a piece of one of our own shells. He
called for the fire himself and was not where he should have been.
I told him on no account to call down fire unless he was 500 yards
back from the target and he really had no need of it at all. I didn't of
course put this in my letter. The splinter cut the artery in his leg and
he died from loss of blood before they got him back into our lines.
He looked so well and happy and enthusiastic when he went out.
He appeared to be very keen and sure of making a success of it.

General Jim came up with my Brigadier to see me today and
had a long talk. He has been on leave in Japan for a few days
and wanted to know about everything we had been doing. He
was very friendly and seemed pleased with what I told him. A
few hours later I met him again and my Corps Commander, at a
buffet luncheon with Princess Pat's Canadian LI.

The Corps Commander told me all about the battle which is
taking place on 'Old Baldy' on a neighbouring sector of the front.
The French had done well. They are older men, mostly reservists.
I met lots of people and picked up plenty of useful information. It
is pouring with rain again tonight, but by working day and night
shifts, we have just managed to get into our new command post
in time. It is very comfortable and will withstand a direct hit from
any shell that might come our way.

28th July 1952

I came back yesterday from a long reconnaissance in the back
area – had a hot bath at our forward base and came back very
hungry for lunch, which was hot ham. I went for a two hour

sleep afterwards and woke up in no shape at all. Within an hour I was being violently sick every few minutes and running to the thunder-box between. By dinner-time I was quite exhausted and couldn't have cared what happened. Then the others started getting it. This morning we were a very sorry lot and the Doctor running around with a bottle to help. He nearly put 16 M & B down my throat, but fortunately I asked what they were! And I have told him time and again that he mustn't give them to me. Anyway, all is nearly right again now I must have a real strafe over the kitchen. I put Peter Buchanan in charge of it, but I expect he has never inspected it once. Geordie Chalmer had a crash in his Jeep this afternoon and has gone off to hospital with a broken collar-bone and bruised ribs.

You will have read in the papers about the new Imjin River Bridge. They wanted our Pipers to play at the ceremony, but thank goodness that was called off at the last minute as the American Engineers who had built it, had put up huge and ostentatious notice boards 'Conquerors of Imjin' and all that kind of thing. So the General said it would be just a private affair.

The shelling has slackened off to almost nothing. I hope the Chinamen are as wet as we are and that their deep trenches are full of water.

31st July 1952

Yesterday some General visited us when I was out going round my companies and very much depressed everyone with news of a new crisis in England. We haven't got a receiving wireless set yet, so we are very much in the dark as to world affairs. We are buying one from the American PX Stores.

One of the Imjin bridges was washed away yesterday. I gather a lot of officers had to run for it very fast just at the last minute! The river is enormous. I am going back this afternoon to see the Brigadier, so I shall have a look at the new bridge at the same time.

1st August 1952

My dear Rhoddy

Many thanks for your letter. As you say, one gets very different accounts of conditions out here. It varies very much in different sectors of the front and from month to month. Quite near neighbours of mine are doing really deep patrols in and behind the enemy lines. In my bit we can't go more than 500 yards without getting a bloody nose. For months before we arrived here the Leicesters' trenches never received a shell. Since our second day we have had quite a bit of stick. The Leicesters' trenches were waist deep and they sat on the hilltops sun-bathing all day. We are well down and now all linked up by communication trenches, and floundering about in steamy mud. Our dug-outs were constructed in the Spring and headcover just resting on sandbags. Naturally with the wet they are falling in. We are getting plenty of good timber to reconstruct them but hardly any waterproof paper to make them rain proof. Thank God it's warm so one doesn't mind being wet so much. The men are taking it very well and as usual their spirits rise as the rain falls more heavily. The sappers have done wonders on the roads and they are standing up to the strain very well, but all impassable forward of my Comd Post for a day or two at a time – even to tanks – so everything then has to go up on porter-backs. The line is absolutely static and we are wired and mined onto the very top of each hill. This was done before the enemy started using artillery and now we just can't get off the tops and so are wonderful targets. One of my companies I thin out by 1/3 each day to avoid casualties and make the other men spend the day in various communication trenches instead of in these badly made dug-outs which are just death-traps.

Sometimes we are ordered to go out and capture a prisoner. No-one ever gets one, but we often lose one or two to them and others killed and wounded in the attempt. I can't think why we want a prisoner. The map is covered with red anyway and I can't think why anyone should want to know their units. We can fly at will over their lines so should not be surprised by any large offensive. The Chinese have to sit back on reverse slopes. Any trench on our side of the sky-line is a fair target for a 20pdr shell. The tanks do our sniping for us very well indeed. It's at night that they get the better of us. They are extremely good, very silent, very patient and very quick to react. I need not tell you what we are like! You put it all very clearly in your letter. I am trying to induce the enemy to come to me instead of going out to find him. It worked for the first time last night but we came off second best. However, we did get a Chinaman but he died before we could get the 'I' boys to him. The same happened last week too. I got a helicopter for him, but he just wouldn't keep alive long enough. You see if only I can get one alive-o, it may save us having to do more of these costly little operations. Isn't it extraordinary that we can't get one, even by good luck instead of good management? They pick their dead and wounded as quick as lightning and on several occasions they have fired at and killed their own wounded as our patrol carry them away.

How right you were when you wrote to me 'Discipline and patrolling are the two most important things'. Thank heaven we aren't heavily engaged, so I may have time to train some NCOs before they are killed. They are such good fellows, but so young and so ignorant. I am lucky to have four good Company Commanders and four good 2s i/c but it is hard for them to teach their subalterns and N.C.O.s while coping with everything else – shell and mortar reps and construction of trenches, administration and dozens of visitors.

Well that's the kind of form. We go into the line for about six weeks at a time. Except for the casualties it is better in than out they tell me. One flops round the flaming country digging reserve positions which are promptly filled in by rain. You get a sector fairly near completion and then you are rushed off to do a bit which the Canadians have failed to work on. They only like the easy job of wiring. They have wired my next place up to such an extent that I have no choice of where to dig, except on the top of the hills.

Now and then one can get away for an hour or two for a good party and jolly good parties they are too, but no 'Bint' of course. It's just a change from the telephone and the wireless and a good excuse for drinking and eating well. They are nearly always 'Fork Buffets', but last week I did have a jolly good dinner with KDGs. Dry Martinis, white wine and Brandy, and liqueurs to end up with. They had quite a good cook. The rations are truly wonderful and you can get hams and turkeys over and above the rations for parties – I don't yet know how, but it is more or less recognised as all above board, I think.

Sorry to hear that you are on the move again but I expect it will stop the O.D. getting much larger. No, Korea doesn't count double foreign service I fear. My only hope is that peace will come and there won't be room for all of us in the Far East.

All the best,
  Yours ever,
    David

2nd August 1952

I had a long talk alone with Pat after dinner this evening when everyone had gone. He is very happy and as you know I couldn't wish for a better or nicer companion.

We had a number of casualties this morning very early but we got one Chinese and drove the others off. Unfortunately he died before I could get him back to the Intelligence people. This happened last week too. I even got a helicopter for him, but it was too late. So, we never found out his unit, division, Army, etc. I am trying hard to keep them out of real trouble till they have had a chance to learn a little and I feel that the General is trying to help in this too. Geordie Chalmer will be away for two months with cracked ribs and collar bone. That's a subaltern short, not counting Rowley Tarleton and I have lost some Sgts and Cpls too – wounded. In another week we shall be out of the line and will get a bit of a rest.

3rd August 1952

I am writing to you as I sit in my Command Post at 10.30pm The nightly programme is being fired – guns, machine-guns and two kinds of mortars. Angus Rowan Hamilton has just rung me up to say that one of his Outposts has just heard movements in the bushes. Peter Buchanan is sitting at the other table answering the telephone calls and I sit and listen with one eye on the map. There are a few shells and mortar bombs coming in, but nothing to worry about as everyone is in their dug-outs.

I had a nice letter from Denis R-H today. He was off to the War Office and expecting to be sent to the Canadian or Indian Staff College. He told me the story about Betty Innes's BW brooch which a policeman saw a farm woman wearing. Betty had sent it to a jumble sale in a vase, not remembering where she had hidden it. Denis said that Berowald now has to sell a tractor to repay the Insurance Company!!!

Today I had some poor news. I am shortly to lose Pat Douglas. They want him to go to command the Divisional Battle School in Japan. I know he will do it better than anyone else in Korea and he will be a temporary Lt Colonel, and of course Maudie will be delighted. I shall appoint Raas McRae in his place.

The Celibate Life
4th August 1952

This morning I am writing in my caravan and enjoying the early morning sun. Do you remember that lovely morning in our caravan beside the loch on Skye? Do you remember walking into that icy water and how you laughed at me when you saw the dire effect it had? What a lovely morning and we had a very late breakfast!

Sometimes I miss you very much. Thank goodness I am always kept so busy that the torture of our separation does not often get me down. There is no doubt that some people like Rhoddy, have much more trouble in this matter than others. Peter Buchanan is often like a mad bull. He shouts at the Adjutant and tears strips off the MTO. I have to keep him on a short rein. He is a fine Support Coy commander.

As I was writing this, Peter came out of the CP with a towel round his waist and his chilump chie. He proceeded to do what we all have to do, and carry out our ablutions in full view. There was much soaping and sponging and sloshing of water, then toothbrushing. Peter was duty officer all night and now he is going to relax in the sun. He put down a blanket and a pillow and I got on with my work.

Sometime later I looked up. Peter was obviously very fast asleep. The gentle caress of the sun had wafted him away to the arms of his loved one. That was obvious. Sitting on a wooden bench outside the CP was a young officer smoking a cigarette. He too had noticed what I had observed,and was amusing himself lobbing pebbles in the direction of Peter's towel. Eventually a large pebble landed on Peter's tummy and he awoke with a start, looking confused and very cross. Noticing the knowing grin on the subaltern's face, Peter burst into a verbal explosion which was countered by ribald laughter – all very amusing to me as an undetected observer of this brief moment of this all too human life.

6th August 1952

Pat Douglas has just driven off. I shall miss him very much and I know he is very sorry to leave us. Still, he will get promotion and make a name for himself and the Regiment. I expect I shall have to provide a good many of his staff which isn't going to be at all easy, as with casualties I am already very short.

We had a much quieter day yesterday, thank goodness. Gradually I am getting things more to my liking. One week I have a go at the signals, a few days later the RAP then the transport. It takes time.

Pat will be in Kure tonight, sleeping in a house with bath and clean sheets. General Jim promised me that he would return to me. Malcolm Wallace will be a major again, which is good for him. He is such a nice fellow and very good at his job.

8th August 1952

I have had a sad day here. We lost that charming boy, David Nicoll in a mine-field. He had been round it before. Early this morning did it all again with the Brigade Major and a Sapper officer, noting where the fence had been broken by shell fire. Later he went out with a party of men to mend the perimeter fence and he, poor lad, made a mistake and walked into it. His mother and father and sister were at Crail that day and I think he has a younger brother. He was so nice and so happy. He really seemed to love being out here.

It's quite odd to think that we shall be sleeping peacefully in only two days' time. Nic and my Gunner are sitting beside me in the dug-out as I write. Nic very busy sorting files and tearing up paper. I trained him well at Perth!! The Gunner is writing sheets and sheets of a letter, but I don't know anything about his private life. I must now write a Confidential Report for Pat. Thank goodness I can only find nice things to say about him.

Lots of people write to me saying that they have posted comforts or books. I don't know who they are from Adam, but have to reply of course. Today I had a young American officer who walked in and asked me if he might take my photo for some Highland Society in America. He had driven miles at his father's request.

In Reserve

11th August 1952

Well we are out of the line and had no casualties the last two days. So much has happened, I forget whether I told you about poor David Nicoll's death in a mine-field. It really was terribly sad to go that way.

We have got some nice places to swim near us here so that it is how we shall spend the afternoons, the worst part of the day. It really is cracking hot and no shade whatever. I tried to write to you last night but there were too many bugs round my light and falling all over the paper. So I went to bed at 9.30pm for a change and started writing at 6am in the cool of the morning. There was a heavy mist, but now it is 8am and that's all gone and my caravan is getting too hot.

We are starting an Accordion Band for sing-songs and I have sent to Japan for the instruments. If Pat can find them, the Padre who is visiting the wounded next week may be able to bring them back.

13th August 1952

We had a very hot 12th August and no shooting! I spent two hours in the afternoon lying in the water, thinking of everyone at home and what they would be saying to each other. The men were all having a great time ragging and splashing and diving. They have done very well and all seem to be in good form despite heat, very hard work and considerable discomfort. There is little let-up in the back area except for Sunday. We are busy mending and replacing clothes, cleaning weapons and training. It's too hot to sleep in the afternoons or to work, so we all retire to the river or some nearby pool – it's good fun. Masses of visitors for me all the time which upsets my work, but I have found time to speak to each Company in turn, some at dawn, some at sundown. Tonight I go with the other COs to dine at Bde HQ. Many requests for our Pipes and Drums in the back areas or for farewell parties, such as General Jim's on 1st September. I do wish he wasn't going. He is such a good friend to us. The Peace Talks have again been put off for a whole week. It seems that they will never agree. The night after we came out of the line, our old positions were attacked by fairly strong enemy patrols. I rather wish we had still been there. It would have given the men a show after enduring shelling, the wet and so much digging. As I write, there is great Piping and Bugling going on. The Drum Major looks ten years younger and so does Nobby Clark. Speak of the Devil and he appears – with three letters, yours, my mother's and Didee Shene's – a great morning!!

I miss Pat a lot, but drink far less without him to sit talking to.

Early to bed and early to rise. I can't even read under my net 'cos there are little hard-backed fellows who come through it.

15th August 1952

My right arm is quite bad with prickly heat and I have nice clean linen to lay it on while I write. The heat broke this evening – a lovely thunder storm and no mosquitos and already my arm has healed quite a lot. Tomorrow we go off in a gay party up a mountain at 6am – cook our breakfast on the top and do a little work. We shall be back here before the worst of the heat and then the river for the afternoon! I have such fun in the river. All kinds of chaps come and talk to me and I learn what they feel about things. I feel rather like Alec Brodie without my pips – and not even any trousers!

[This is a well-know story in the Regiment. When Alec Brodie was a Subaltern, he thought he should try to find out what the men thought about things. So one morning he took off his 'pips' and went to the men's communal latrine. He thought that no-one would recognise him without his badges of rank and opened the conversation in his very remarkable upper-class voice with the public school-boy slang 'What's the grub like here?' his neighbour jumped up and ran off shouting 'Mr Brodie's gone mad'.]

I have got the cinema up here now and I went last night for the first time since I have been in Korea. It was a very good film, but a very sad one – all about us it seemed. The man next to me kept offering me beer which I refused, but he smoked lots of my cigarettes! My canvas caravan is in a deep hole tonight with its engine to the morning sun, so from now on I shall be cooler in the early morning and I don't intend to get up earlier than 7.30 after tomorrow. I shall read in bed. And in two days or so I shall have a grass roof built right over it so that it may even be sufferable in the afternoon – when it's cloudy. Don't worry about me. I sleep well despite shelling and everything. Hard physical work suits me and I have few worries with all my good chaps to help me.

17th August 1952

I got the lovely Silkelon handkerchiefs from mother today – far too good for this country I feel, but very nice all the same. We have four Korean women who wash for the officers – and in particular for the CO, so I hope they won't be spoilt. Nobby is very worried about these women. We send a guard with them when they go to the river, to protect them from Americans and Canadians. He wants me to sack them, but as long as there is no trouble, I rather like to keep them, just to show that *our* men can be trusted despite everything!

We are just waiting for 3-4 inches of rain which is supposed to fall tonight. First it was going to break at 9pm – now we expect it at 3am. I shall just stay in bed I think till it stops! At the moment we are all just dripping with sweat and the crickets and the frogs are making violent noises, waiting for the skies to fall. The sky is dancing with distant lightning. Claud Moir gave a very nice little party this evening and Ian Critchley and Peter Lindsay dropped in here for dinner afterwards. I have one of my new hankies under my hand but it is soaked through already.

Next Sunday we give a big party with Pipers and all. General Jim came for Church Parade this morning – just sitting on the ground in the blazing sun. Peter Buchanan played the organ and they all sang very well. Officers and men come miles to hear Padre Tom Nicoll, even when we are in the front line. They think he's great – me too! I had my first draft today AND the rain has started this minute what a relief!! A cool wind is blowing now and everyone is hurrying to tie down tents and things.

Malta
18th August 1952

My dear David,

I don't like the sound of your hill-top positions. They are contrary to all accepted teaching. I can only imagine the system developed as a result of experience showing our tps. were incapable of retaking commanding ground once it was lost.

It must be miserable in the rain and I do hope you managed to get really good cover from the weather before the cold winter sets in. Thank heaven the rations are O.K. – ours are lousy and I feared you would be on that desperate thing called tinned equivalent.

We have just returned from a flap over the Egyptian situation. It came to nothing and never looked like doing so to any ordinary mortal. All we did was to sit in our transport, The Charlton Star, in Tobruk Harbour, together with the rest of the Naval Task Force. We sat there for three weeks. I must say the food on board was quite good and so was the accommodation, but the boring-ness! Of course I had to sit at the Captain's Table, and what with his conversation and that of the professional OC Tps I was driven nearly mad. I used to leave the table on the verge of screaming. I dare say you would welcome such little troubles and consider such an existence a paradise. I remember when I was very tired during the war, saying to myself that I would never grumble again so long as I could get into a fleabag every night and have a bit of a candle for light. Driving or marching up to the line at night one used to imagine the people one saw settling down to rest in ruined houses belonged to some special privileged class that never did a damn thing but eat and sleep – they were probably the poor sods that had taken the place the day before.

Anyhow, here I am back again amongst what all of you and most people in the Far and Middle East would count as flesh pots. It is very hot and our camp is ankle deep in swirling dust, but we can escape. There are two or three restaurants, friends with flats, polo of a sort, all kinds of other games, and the sea. Above all the sea. It is like pea soup and not very refreshing, but still it is blue and full of fish which one can watch or spear according to taste. We go to Tek in September which will be awful, but some poor buggers in our Division have been there since last November.

We have the 6th (American) Fleet in here now. They have a whole Assault Division in transports with them. They never seem to go ashore or take exercise, but perhaps they are content with crap throwing, ice creams and coca cola. I sent a deputy to one of their parties last night – the poor fellow said it was like a Turkish bath. They saw a very bad film which was followed by a cold supper and one coca cola. Not my sort of party.

Better do some work now. I think it is splendid the way you are bearing up under beastly conditions. Don't let the brass hats get you down and take great care of yourself.

Yours ever,
    Rhoddy.

                                                        19th August 1952
Dear General Neil

Many thanks for your letter of 9th August. Our first batch of reinforcements has just arrived – and badly needed they were. In a week's time we shall be nearly up to strength in men, but very short of NCOs. We just can't find suitable fellows to make up to Corporal and we are already short of some Sergeants. What is more, there are calls for instructors for Pat Douglas's Battle School on the way. We shall have to find replacements for the NCOs hitherto found by the Welsh and the Norfolks. Is there any chance of some volunteers from ERE or 2nd Bn? There is promotion waiting for them.

We have taken much advice from other units and have discussed Comforts a great deal among ourselves and we have come to the following conclusions: (1) We all like nice hand-knitted socks and they save the men having to pay for new ones. We have been assured time and time again that the winter clothing is so good that we do not need a great many other woollen comforts. (It was different during mobile operations in the time of the A & SH.) Now we have heated dug-outs and only sometimes need scarves and gloves. Everyone likes to have a nice pullover but they are NOT necessary and we feel that people at home should not bust themselves to provide great numbers of these things. We have quite a stock left to us by KOSBs and Leicesters.

We have got a cinema projector and we get good films – a change of film every second day. When we are in the line the cinema is kept at A Ech. 10 or 15 men per company get back there every day for both cinema and rest. When we are out – or nearly out of the line, as now, we bring up the cinema to the Command Post area and many more men are able to see it without the use of much transport. Companies would naturally like to have it in their own areas now and again, or a night when two neighbouring Companies could share it, but this is not possible because the roads to Company Areas are too rough and the machine would soon be broken up. A second projector would be very much appreciated, but a luxury.

I am buying the instruments for a Harmonica Band. This is a very real need for sing-songs etc and not having our own Band with us, perhaps the Comforts Fund could help with the cost of this, if they do not decide to buy the cinema projector.

The men are all very appreciative of shaving soap, ordinary soap, tooth brushes, razor blades and so forth. Some hair oil wouldn't be a bad idea either. They are in the river so much and their young heads have so much hair which stands straight up on end. Other things they need are boot brushes, blacking (very hard to get here), hair brushes and combs, nail brushes, nail files and nail scissors.

There remains I think, only one other type of commodity – books and papers. We do get the local American army news sheet and quite a generous supply of Sunday papers through 'Education'. Sandy Barnett sent me three or four parcels of books and I shared them out when visiting Companies. They were all delighted. We have, of course, got our Company Library Boxes as the main source of supply, but they often require refurbishing owing to damage by rain or normal losses.

I have just got in from a patrol exercise, Angus R.H. v Malcolm Wallace. It was good. The Brigadier was with me till midnight and I think much impressed with the keenness of our new men. Behind us were real battles every half hour or so – bombing, tracer, flares and a good deal of small arms fire on the Marine Div sector.

Yours ever,
    David

                                                        22nd August 1952

My Dear General Neil
    I left out one important suggestion for consideration of the Comforts Fund. Free Mail. The Leicesters stamped all letters from the battalion out of their Lord Mayor's Fund and I know this was very much appreciated. I

have decided to give every man three free Christmas Cards with stamps. I would also like every man to have a free EFM telegram once in a while. There is one draw-back to this which I have taken up with the postal authorities out here. You can't have an EFM delivered in a Greetings envelope and men are loathe to use this service for obvious reasons. It is apparently a matter which would have to go to the PMG or be taken up by an MP. The Greetings Cable costs twice as much.

Everything seems to be going well. The men are in great heart and working hard. Claud Moir's Company did a very good patrol exercise last night and I was much impressed by Adam Gurdon's handling of a full scale fighting patrol. He is a grand lad. Angus Irwin's Company are busy firing their weapons. They have to go back into the line for a week or two while there is an adjustment of inter battalion boundaries. Angus R.H. has his company on wheels, moving up to occupy a blocking position and Malcolm Wallace is doing a night field firing exercise. I fly off to HMS Newcastle this afternoon with my Brigadier, to dine sleep and return tomorrow morning. On Sunday we have officers of all sorts – American and Dominion to Retreat and drinks. On Monday General Jim is borrowing our P & D to do honour to the American Marine Div and I am to dine there. Nobby Clark – the Senior QM in the Div – is having his B Echelon inspected today. Raas Macrae is representing me.

Yours ever,
  David

24th August 1952

What a day – it has simply pelted with rain for 48 hours and I have been floundering around in it visiting my Companies, taking round the 'Scotsman's' press representative and finally the Brigadier. I ended up by coming home in a boat!! We are now totally cut off from everyone by road. The river rose to 42 *feet* today and our last bridge may be broken down tonight, it was quivering very much when I was there four hours ago and if you crossed, you had to wear a life jacket. The tanks are a little up-stream of the bridge, firing at any large pieces of timber to break them up before they strike the piers. The Sapper Officer there had pulled out 2 dead Chinamen, one donkey, two horses and lots of snakes. My men have been having a lovely time killing rats and snakes as they swim for the shore. I am told that the bag of rats while I was away amounted to over sixty. 'Scotsman' correspondent just couldn't understand how everyone was in such good spirits. He stayed to lunch and nearly stayed too long. We got him out by pushing his jeep, just before the road was finally closed. And so our Retreat party, which was to have been this evening, was most definitely cancelled. I am just wondering if there will be any bridge tomorrow, to take the Pipes and Drums to Div HQ to play for the General.

27th August 1952

The floods are going down now and the big bridge has not been washed away. All the others are out of use. In this area we have been entirely cut off from everyone except by boat. We borrowed an amphibious lorry from the Marines and this took round the rations to the various companies. The RSM and the Drum Major have been in charge of the boats and thoroughly enjoying it. We killed 60 rats the first day as they swam for the shore and 40 the next morning which were perched on a piece of the broken bridge – lots of snakes too! You can imagine the Jock's excitement. In the evening we went to the rescue of 3 Australians who had been out on a deep patrol the other side of the river for 2 days. They couldn't get back because the river was so wide and fast and they were being machine gunned and mortared. First a light plane dropped life jackets to them. Then they jumped into the water and were rapidly swept towards our lines. A Marine patrol brought them in and handed them over to John Moncrieff who ferried them back over the river in the amphibian. John got swept off it by a telephone cable but they got him a life jacket and picked him up again. He did a very good job of work.

31st August 1952

I had a long letter from Rhoddy, now back in Malta, but apparently soon to go to Egypt. It was a grand present for the Battalion – that £600, and great news about the cinema projector. I have shared out the money to the various companies and groups and they will each form a small committee to decide on what comforts to spend it. These committees will each write their thanks, and that way I hope to keep the men in touch with their benefactors.

I am having a success with a new method of teaching the men to patrol and the Section Commanders how to command the patrols. Claud Moir put my ideas into effect most efficiently, in fact he couldn't have produced a better show. The Brigadier came to watch it and was most impressed. Claud is first class all round. I think he is producing better results than anyone.

We had a very jolly party yesterday evening. General Jim came to hear some piping. I had four pipers on the hill opposite our little grass-roofed Mess. They looked fine against the sunset. I also asked the Brig and Col John Orlebar (CO Norfolks). There were a few other guests too, but mostly ourselves. Gen Jim and John O

111

stayed to dinner and we had some iced champagne! I asked the General if he would allow us to give him a farewell parade when he comes to say good-bye. Tonight I go to a party with the KSLI and take Angus R.H. and David Arbuthnott with me.

It's such a curious war, isn't it. I must say the parties keep me from getting bored or too serious and I learn a lot of good tips by meeting so many people.

I asked Nobby where he got all the ice when we gave a party. 'Well Colonel, you know the Americans have a very efficient cadaver disposal service to the United States. They have a lot of spare ice when the front is quiet!'

In a few minutes I must drive off in my Jeep to see Malcolm W and then to call on John Orlebar to discuss some 'shop' which we couldn't do at last night's party. It's raining again and a high wind but very warm. My prickly-heat arm is nearly cured.

3rd September 1952

Once again it is simply pouring – really pouring. I expect we shall be cut off again by the morning. General Jim has just been to bid us farewell, bringing Brig Abdy Ricketts with him. We were only able to muster a small party of all ranks in my reed-thatched dining room but we had four pipers in the kilt to play him away through the mud – his own Regimental march!

I am meant to be dining with our Gunner Regiment, commanded by a very charming man called Jock Slade-Powell, but I doubt if I can reach them and may not be able to return till my boats are working again.

You asked me about my Brigadier. His conferences are the longest things I have ever known. A mad keen soldier who thinks of nothing else beside the Army and his old school. He spoils any party by stopping everyone talking and making some poor fellow sing or perform – very sixth form! Fortunately John Orlebar knows every verse of every Gilbert & Sullivan, so it's always he who has to provide the entertainment. Ricketts is a hard man to discuss things with in an easy way, because he doesn't listen very much, but when one can get through his slow and deliberate flow of words, he will listen. I know that when he makes no reply, you have made your point. He lets you know that he agrees some hours or days later!!

5th September 1952

I have sacked my batman, a Scotsman called Mutrie. He was too stupid and too dull for words and always made me feel gloomy when I looked at him. Now I have an Englishman called Bullock who is also the caravan driver and he looks after me much better and *likes* doing it and has a little conversation too. The rain has slackened, but the river is still rising and will be all round us tomorrow I fear. Tonight, for the first time, we had to put a jersey over our shirts for dinner. It's quite warm again now but there was a coolness in the wind when it was blowing strongly. My Command Post is sprouting dry rot fungus everywhere and will fall down soon, so I am going to build a new one as soon as the rain stops. We cut the fungus off sometimes but it has grown again by the following morning. Angus Irwin is staying with me for a few days – meanwhile Larry Trotter is commanding his company.

4th September 1952

My dear Rhoddy,

Once again it is pissing with rain and in a few hours I shall be on boat supply once more. General Jim Cassels got through the mud in his jeep to bid us farewell. He goes home via Australia, New Zealand and Canada – a pretty good bash after all his farewell parties here – and then takes over 1 Corps. You know him I think. He has been very pleasant to us and we shall miss him.

I have got a new technique for teaching men shooting on night patrols and to use some initiative. It is great fun and they love it. I used to do it in Jungle training. We can't get the British soldiers quick enough on the trigger and so the Chinese get the initiative. I really think this will do it. It's quite simple – The route is marked by broad tape. Sections don't have to stick rigidly to the tape but it leads them of course to the neighbourhood of the targets. Along the route I have men hidden (sounds very dangerous) making various sounds, tins, a burst of fire, digging. There are also a few trip flares and booby traps to find and negotiate. It is all very simple to set up and requires only one officer to conduct. Each patrol takes from 40 to 60 minutes.

My Brigadier was most impressed and was completely taken in by the casualty blown up on a mine – so were the rest of the patrol and their reactions were remarkable! I told the Brig that I had a Jeep Ambulance at hand for such unfortunate accidents!

The men all want to do more of it, but they'll have fresh ground this week. My 'Mines and Booby-traps Confidence Course', which I cribbed from the American Marines, is now being reproduced by the Sappers. I bet they don't shift it to new ground every few days – that is the whole thing. We were all out in the rain last night, before it became too heavy and the big patrols were ever so much better. Two subalterns really showed some ability, so we may be much better next time we go in.

The Americans have got a new nylon stretcher for use by patrols. It weighs a few ounces and with jointed alloy poles only 4½lbs. Without poles you need six men to carry one casualty, but with the poles only two men. *The poles one has to improvise as they aren't issued. The material is so strong that you can drag a casualty along the road on it, if there only happens to be one man for the job, and it doesn't tear or wear through.*

I was flown down to dine and sleep a night on the Newcastle. All too much of a rush to enjoy myself. Only had 15 minutes for a bath and had to leave at 8 am in the morning.

I met some of the other COs – Hal Dean of the Welsh – John Orlebar of the Norfolks – Bill Barlow of KSLI. He is the best soldier I believe. The 'new boy' is Stephens of the Royal Fusiliers. I like Jack Slade-Powell who commands the Gunners and I am meant to be dining with him tonight, but it doesn't look as though I shall be able to get out – or if out then not back. Must ring up the Marines and borrow their 'Duck' again. I love seeing the Drum Major in charge of it!

I must tell you a simple story which amused me very much. We all wash publicly in the river whenever we can, otherwise just in the open on the positions. An officer one evening became rather annoyed because a soldier just stood in front of him and stared. He said, 'Have you never seen a cock before?' To which the man replied, 'Yes, but never a commissioned one.'

Yours ever
  David

                                          5th September 1952
My Dear General Neil

Have I any chance of getting a young regular to replace Alec Renny-Tailyour? I seem to have so many of the older ones, who in these days expect to be at least second-in-command of companies, if not actually commanding – Macdonald, Trotter, Denniston, Lennox and now Severn and Buchanan. I am not complaining, but my weakness is with good and trained platoon commanders. Stormont Darling is one of the best; I lose him in a few months. Adam Gurdon is doing well. Geordie Chalmer is still away and missing this most valuable period in which to train his men and get patrol experience himself. Peter Carthew is such a charming boy and is trying very hard, but still lacks confidence in himself. I do hope we can get him a better Company Commander. Peter Buchanan is so volatile and knows the answer to every question. I gather he is very overbearing to Adjt, MTO, etc and frequently causes unnecessary friction. There is no other cause of friction. They all get on terribly well together. Macdonald-Gaunt is shaping very well. I hope to get him back from Bde. HQ when the new Commander arrives, but I shall no doubt have to send someone in his place. Claud Moir is quite first class in my opinion.

Yours ever,
  David

1. Installation of the Governor, Edinburgh Castle, 2nd Bn The Black Watch.
   The author carries the Keys.

2. CO of the 2nd Battalion, Colonel Frankie Chalmer and officers of his
   Machine Gun Company. Malcolm Wolfe Murray, George Rusk, CO,
   Michael Young and myself.

An exceedingly good team of officers and certainly one of the nicest messes I have ever lived in. The spirit is excellent.

Officers 2nd Bn The Black Watch Palestine Sept 1939.

4. The Australian Contingent, Palestine.

3. (*opposite*)   2nd Bn The Black Watch Sept 1939. Lt Col Neil McMicking and his officers.

5. A Company headquarters team, just before our Somaliland battle.

6. Tobruk. CO 2nd Battalion, Lt Col George Rusk (Rusky), and the author his adjutant. Our headquarters were called the 'Villa Deliah': it had previously been the brothel for the Tobruk garrison.

7. Chindits embark.

8. Black Watch Chindits on
the march.

9. Monsoon.

10. 'Here come the 42nd.
    Here come the Forty Twa'.

11. Our mother, Constance Janet Campbell.

12. Captain Rhoddy Rose DSO MC, Highland Light Infantry.

13. Captain Angus Rose,
The Argyll and
Sutherland Highlanders.

14. Legionnaire Neil Rose,
Medaille Militaire, Croix
de Guerre et palme.

15. My wedding at Brechin to Lady Jean Ramsay. Brigadier Bernard Fergusson was best man.

16. Jean, April 1945.

18. My warrant officers, the 'backbone of the regiment', Korea 1952.

17. (*opposite*) The Officers of the 1st Battalion The Black Watch, with our beloved Colonel-in-Chief Her Majesty Queen Elizabeth, The Queen Mother, at Crail, just before setting off for Korea.

19. A continuous procession of top brass: here is General Collins of the US Army.

20. Here is the Quartermaster General, General Robertson, and our own General West.

21. Our Brigadier, John Kendrew.

22. Angus Irwin, in his dugout.

23. Layout of the battalion: 2nd battle of the Hook.

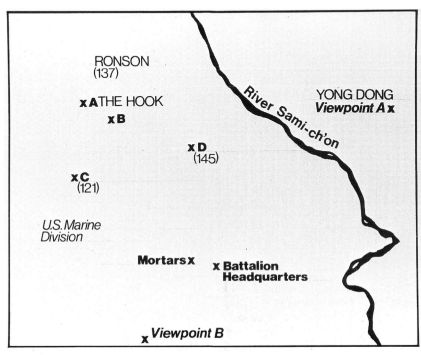

RONSON
(137)

x A THE HOOK
x B

x D
(145)

x C
(121)

U.S. Marine
Division

River Sami-ch'on

YONG DONG
Viewpoint A x

Mortars x   x Battalion
             Headquarters

x Viewpoint B

24. The Hook Position: 1952.

25. The Hook Position: Now.

26. Our padre Tom Nicol MC conducted a fine Memorial Service for those killed in Korea, at the Pusan War Cemetery.

27. The firing party fire a salute for the fallen.

28. My beautiful daughter
Mary.

29. My son Hugh, an expert
shot.

7th September 1952

Last night I dined with John Orlebar and he had the band of the KSLI to play during dinner. As I told you before, he sings all the Gilbert & Sullivan, so there were lots of those well known tunes and then towards the end of dinner they started playing South Pacific! I couldn't restrain myself and everyone laughed a lot and John said 'I have never seen anyone enjoy music so much.' After dinner we sat round and heard a lot of dirty stories. Very few were funny and I got very bored. Jock Slade-Powell and Peter Moore were the other guests. Early this morning I was at the Air Strip to see General Jim away. He inspected a mixed guard of all Commonwealth countries, flew over the front line to watch a last bombardment and then turned for Pusan. Yesterday he shouted to me as we passed on the road and introduced me to General Mike West who will no doubt be visiting us next week. He looked a nice enough chap. The American Marines on our left are having a pretty tough time

12th September 1952

Don't imagine any horrors because of all the training. I am trying to get them up to a standard so that there will be no unnecessary loss of lives. That's all there is to it. They are so young and so unimaginative that they can't foresee what may happen to them and it is up to us the stir up their minds so that when their time comes, they will be well prepared. I have got all the Company Commanders working on the right lines now, so I am taking things more easily and in a week or so shall fly to Japan to visit the Battle School and the Hospitals.

I am supposed to be going out snipe shooting this evening with Geof Blundell-Brown and to bath and dine with him afterwards. It is very hot just now and I must say I don't feel much like it, but sure I shall enjoy it when the time comes. Angus Irwin says one of his subalterns is hopeless. It's taken him too long to find it out. Mustn't worry, must I. It all works out in the end.

14th September 1952

I went to the Church Service and then I discovered that I had forgotten all about the Welch Regiment's party. I had a great time and a good laugh with Hal Deane and John Orlebar. John got caught out yesterday. They had over 300 shells in their area in half an hour and no slit trenches to get into! They haven't shelled so far back before. They have only got 10 days to go before they sail, so they should take better care of themselves. It is much cooler now and I have taken a second blanket into use at night. My arm is nearly better, but I still have to keep a bandage on it to keep it clean and free from irritation or it swells up again. I have been fitted for my winter clothing. You would have laughed if you had seen the party of 'out-sizes'. All the specially short and particularly tall men in the battalion, who had to be fitted individually.

17th September 1952

I had such a jolly morning, which had quite made up for the last two days when I started to feel bored for the first time. I went out shooting with Geof Blundell-Brown at 9am. Of course it is really too early to shoot pheasants, but we shall miss nearly all the shooting as we shall be in the line again in October. I got 6 and we are having them for dinner tonight – 'Spatchcock a la Korea'. Geof had no luck and the other boy, Michael someone, couldn't kill them dead and lost several. It was getting hot by 11 o'clock when we went into my camp called 'A echelon' for cold beer. Tomorrow he comes here to shoot with me and the bag will be all his. After the shooting, I watched my young NCO's Cadre which Raas and Ian Critchley are running. It was very well done indeed. I am so pleased with them and am starting another one for another 30 men next Monday. I have never seen such a change in men in such a short time. They now look hard, smart and self-confident. I have collected a good officer from Hong Kong. He turned up last night and is just the chap I need - a fully trained MT Officer. So now I can use Ian Critchley whole time on training NCOs and when he leaves for home I shall not be without a MTO.

19th September 1952

Something has again gone wrong with the mails from England. What a gap it makes in my life. I do so much love getting your letters every other day. Perhaps tomorrow I shall have 3 to make up for yesterday.

All continues well here. A new subaltern arrived today and a job for David Campbell. He is to be head of the Press Section out here as a Lt Colonel, and I know he will do it very well. He was with the 'Times' for a year and he knows all the other press chaps. Isn't it curious how easy it is to become a Lt Colonel as long as you are no good as a soldier? Good luck to him!

I hear from my Padre that Rhoddy's Padre has arrived here with the Royal Fusiliers. He asked my Padre if 'Colonel David ever went to church. Colonel Rhoddy came once – when the King died – but he never came again!'

Jean Rowan-Hamilton has written to say that they have all asked for you to be President of the Comforts Fund.

20th September 1952

My dear David

Thank you for your interesting letter about your patrol training. I am glad that you are at last getting a spell out of the line to work-up, though the weather must be hell. We have moved again. It makes our seventh camp in ten months. The High Ups live in Cuckoo Land and can't understand why we have no time to train. I am now eight Sgts down with not a single Cpl fit to promote. Just to help me we now have been put on manoeuvres, so I will get nothing done till mid-November by which time I will probably be beyond cure. The Depot have demanded 2 officers, 3 sergeants and seven corporals (the latter to be qualified instructors). If I had such things I would, of course, have made them Sgts. In the last six months we have lost 5 WOs, 4 C/ Sergeants, 12 Sergeants, and 186 ORs. Such casualties would be serious in war where one does get some NCO replacements. All we have had is less than 100 recruits who don't of course help the NCO set. I lost all my drivers and now have only 4 fully mustered, with the rest down in only six weeks experience. The High Ups are very pained to find our tpt is not all that it should be. My new tpt here is even worse. Hardly any of it goes, and the Buffs, from whom we took it over, told us the only way to get spare parts is to steal them. Through the normal channels everything takes five months. My question, which no-one will answer, 'when the Army is obviously at breaking point why have manoeuvres?' But we could have had the instructors had we been allowed to concentrate on making them, instead of farting around on bloody silly manoeuvres. The Generals must have manoeuvres as otherwise they have nothing to do. They don't like doing nothing because they can't show off and they won't go on leave because their wives would make them wash up.

Well I am sorry to have left Malta though it was hellish expensive, we being the only Regiment there. We gave, before leaving, a searchlight tattoo for some 350 guests, and a cocktail party with real drinks instead of the usual hair-wash, for over 200. In addition, I gave a cake and wine party at the Phoenecia (after the Tattoo) for about 40 Admirals, Captains, Commanders and their wives, pretties and so on. It was a very hot night so they knocked off 9 magnums of champagne. The cake was specially made with our badge in the middle and the names of the flagships, and especially friendly ships round the edge. There was also caviare and chicken sandwiches, so I was lucky to get away with a bill of £53. We have managed to smuggle in enough duty free drink here to last us till Christmas, and I am flying back to Malta in two days time to wind up and try and smuggle in some more. Drink is the only solace here. What a bloody place it is – Tel el Kebir.

The Officers Quarters of this camp are awful. I have one room in a tin shed with sacking over the windows and a wash basin stand made of old *packing cases. Nice treatment for a Lt Col of 15 years service. I am having a gun flown out but we are not allowed on Farouk's shoot and when that isn't shot, the duck are not to be found elsewhere. I can't think what we are doing here. A whole Brigade to guard a bloody ordnance dump! They had Mauritius Guard Coys before, but they, of course, just went into partnership with the goblin thieves. I am sure it would be cheaper to give the stores to the Egyptians and pull out. They say it will cost us one million just to repair the roads.*

All the best, Yours ever,
    Rhoddy.

20th September 1952

I have had a lovely day. I walked round all my Companies very early in the morning – and I shot a pigeon on the way home – I had two hours sleep in the afternoon, when it was raining very hard, and I had Turkey and chestnut stuffing for dinner. And I carved the turkey and now we are having an issue of rum, because everyone needs it.

I have written a long letter to my mother. She wrote at length about you and the children and her flat and everything – you know how it all goes. She simply loved seeing you all – and so she should – I wish I could do the same! Oh, what months lie ahead. However, I am getting on well with it all.

I had General West all yesterday morning and we seem to talk the same language. The day before that, I was at a party given by the 1st Royal Australian Regt when I was called to the telephone. He was standing just beside me as I spoke and it was all about the shelling we had that morning. I thought it was nearly over when I left, but Nic then had to ring me up and say that one Bofers gunner had been killed and five men wounded just as I left. The General wanted to know all about it and then invited himself to visit us – without the Brigadier – the next day. It all went very well. We had some good laughs too. The General jumped down into a Mortar pit and his steel helmet flew off. He said 'I gave orders for wearing these bloody things, so I suppose I can't complain.' He is a grand chap. Of course, no-one wears them when he or the Brigadier isn't in evidence. We carry them on our shoulders, but wear the Balmoral on our heads.

There have been great battles as you will have read in the papers and thousands of Chinese killed, but nothing on our bit of the front. The Chinese have been attacking 'to keep up the morale of their army'. It certainly can't have been successful in this respect! Their losses have been very severe and they have gained no ground in the long run. They have naturally chosen the weak parts of the front for their attacks. The Americans and the ROCs don't dig, mine and wire like we do. They don't keep their units in the front line for long periods, so no-one does any work. The result is that their trenches are shallow, their wire practically non existent and no-one would know where the mines were, even if they were put down. So we have been left in peace while the rest of the front on our right and left was aflame?

I was very sorry to hear yesterday from RSM Scott that RSM (now QM) Gibb's boy, who I got a job, has been killed on a motor cycle. Will you write? He was such a nice lad and they loved him so much.

Sunday 21st September 1952

I am so cross with myself that you didn't get a single letter in a week. Can't think what I was doing. I got two from you late last night and read them in bed before I went to sleep and again this morning before breakfast.

John Orlebar gives his farewell party today and he says his next battle is to get all his families to Hong-Kong before Christmas. Only he, his QM and RSM are guaranteed a quarter. The others can't even apply till they have found accommodation and had it approved. On top of that, the CO has to certify that the family in question can afford to pay the rent. Can you beat it?

22nd September 1952

I have just heard the most wonderful news. When we leave Korea we won't be going to beastly hot Hong-Kong, but to the Middle East. And perhaps, who knows, we might go to Cyprus after horrid Korea. I read in the papers that they are going to spend millions there on quarters and barracks. Let us hope some of the work is done in time for us. We will be near enough home to have people out to stay and to fly home for a holiday. I'm thrilled! It might be such fun – the bathing, sun and in Cyprus snow.

The weather is lovely here now: not too hot in the daytime and a jersey in the evening. Tomorrow the General comes to visit us and watch training. I got 3 new subalterns today and all seemed good chaps, better than some I have.

23rd September 1952

I had been plodding round the hills in the dark to see my men in appalling circumstances. Not a single grumble and a smile and happy word from every man. Up to the ankles in mud, lying on

119

soft wet ground, but still in good heart. The rain has stopped. I only wish I could have delayed the move for 24 hours. It was unimportant, I tried but I failed. The staff cannot, or will not understand what the men have to put up with. Thank God they are all young.

28th September 1952

I am spending two nights in the mountains of Japan with Pat Douglas. I motored down to Seoul and spent the night there, flying to Pusan the following morning – and from there to Iwacuni in Japan. Brig Batten was on the same plane so I came across the Inland Sea in his very nice motor cruiser, instead of driving round the bumpy coast road – very good sandwiches and beer served on the trip! Pat came down in his jeep to pick me up in Kure and we had a great buck about everything. He is doing a fine job here. He has revised all the training, is getting the transport and such-like things properly organised and is getting part of the Camp rebuilt. I don't think he will come back to me while we are in Korea. It would really be a waste if he did. Today, Sunday, we are going to have a look at Hiroshima and perhaps call on the 'Ocean' for drinks on our way back. Tomorrow I watch training and the next day visit hospitals etc and get out my winter woollies and those thick over-boots which you gave me. They will be just the thing next month. I shall be back with the battalion on the 1st and then a few days and we will be back in the line – not at all a bad sector this time.

Pat is a lucky old so-and-so. He lives in great comfort here – two baths a day, a Jap girl to do his washing and breakfast and a batman-driver. The only thing he lacks is pleasant companions. They really are very odd, his staff and students! But he can always retire to his own 'wee hoose' when he gets fed up with them. Last night I took Pat to call on Captain Evans (Rhoddy's great Tobruk and Malta friend) on 'Ocean'. He was charming and most hospitable and gave us such a good dinner. He couldn't say too much about Rhoddy and his battalion and he said that he felt sure Rhoddy would get another job when his time is up.

I am off now to watch some night training – my own ideas which have been taken up by the School!!

30th September 1952

My dear Rhoddy,

It's nice to tell someone about what one sees, so here is another letter. The Marines did magnificently but to my mind, not perhaps very professionally. To illustrate. Their third counter attack on the HOOK went in after dawn. The Coy Comd gave out over his wireless 'We go in one zero minutes. Five – four – three' etc. and as they rose up, down came all the enemy guns on them. Poor fellows, they lost 19 killed and 34 wounded in a few minutes – some grenade throwing at the end of the spin and then digging the Chinks out of the bunkers where they had barricaded themselves. The Chinese took a heavy knock. The Marines were doing what they call 'policing' - cleaning up – all the next day. The Chinese likewise, trying to drag away their bodies and both sides shelling.

The American casualties in one battalion plus one Coy of another were 70 killed, 20 missing, 350 wounded. Chinese picked 225 dead, half a dozen prisoners. A Marine who escaped from the Chinese during the battle said that the scenes behind their front at a Medical Aid Post were indescribable. Our gunners were helping the yanks. Together we fired over 30,000 shells + mortar bombs and there must have been 15 or 20 air strikes. The Chinese fired 20,000 shells and they employed 12,000 porters to carry the ammunition forward at night. It's staggering.

And now it is pouring with rain and tonight we are relieved by the DLI. We always change over at full moon and it always rains at full moon. We then have two days and a night in our A Ech area before we relieve the Marines.

I must tell you a funny story about our American Corps Comd. He came up to my OP to watch the Marine battle. He had no Staff Officer, no map or field glasses. Met by our General and the usual crowd. Raised the borrowed field glasses and looked to the South 'Mighty fine' he said. General Jim indicated that he should look to the West, which he did. 'And there they go, rifles in hand.' 'No,' says Jim, 'I made the same stupid mistake. I think you will find that those things are rocks.' 'So they are,' says the big man. He then let out a deep sigh and said, 'I don't mind losing a bit of OPLR but when the Chinese get to the MLR I say NO. The Marines will stay!'

I have got some of my men rebuilding our old trenches round here, so that we shall have a bit of depth. Last year we had it in good defensive shape but now what used to be our forward companies are all in enemy hands and they have dug their guns into the hills and shoot out of tunnels which are hard to find and hard to hit.

I have persuaded my Brigadier to let me have a second Mortar Pl (each of 4 mortars) at the expense of MMGs. I hope to get rid of the MMGs completely in a short time. They are to my mind a waste of valuable NCOs and men in this type of country.

Well I wonder if the enemy will have another crack at the HOOK or whether he got enough stick the last time. He is still said to be moving large forces about in the hills in front of us.

Who is going to get command after you? Bill Bradford is getting our 2nd Bn when Neville has done his time. Must go and get breakfast now.

Yours ever,
David.

In the line again

5th October 1952

Dear General Neil

We are well settled in our new area. We had a fine night for the take-over and no shooting and the whole position is so much nicer than our last one. This time we have two reserve companies instead of everyone being in the shop window. Also we have no tanks to attract additional shell-fire. The dug-outs are good but daylight movement, except on foot, is not possible, without inviting trouble. Claud Moir and Angus Irwin are forward, Angus R.H. and Malcolm are back and supply the big patrols or ambushes. Claud was having fun this morning trying, without success so far, to silence some MMG and rifle snipers about 700 yards from his forward platoon. I saw the MMG snipers when I was up here on recce three days ago with the DLI Commanding Officer. He didn't seem in the least interested, but we find that it pays to shoot at every single chinaman who ventures onto the forward slope.

The battalion is in fine form. They worked magnificently in reserve and the whole standard of training, smartness and team work, improved by leaps and bounds. We ended up with a series of Company Camp-fire Concerts which were greatly enjoyed by officers and men of other regiments by invitation. The Pipes and Drums did fine work assisted by the Accordion Band. I have been running NCO cadres at A Echelon and now have nearly forty good young L/Corporals. There were a lot of volunteers for the second cadre, despite the long hours and very hard work. Raas ran them very well, assisted by Ian Critchley. He is such a nice chap, Raas, and very efficient in his quiet way. He is a great help to me in every way, but I do miss Pat's company. I went to the Base for three days before we came into the line and stayed with Pat at the Battle School.

Yours ever
David.

6th October 1952

We have taken over a much nicer sector this time and everyone is very pleased with it. Two of the Companies are well back and can get some rest and comfort in the day-time. The last place we

122

had every company was in the shop window, as it were. The dug-outs and trenches are much better, and we have no tanks sitting on the hill-tops to draw enemy shell-fire. Yesterday, our first day, we only received 60 shells in the whole area and the casualties were one sleeping-bag which turned into a cloud of feathers, and two men who were 'walking wounded' and may be back in a week.

The Brigadier paid a visit and went round Claud Moir's and Angus R.H.'s Companies this morning. Next week I expect that we shall have to do the honours for the American Commander of their Home Forces, who is coming to my OP to watch a big Artillery Demonstration – a demonstration of the flexibility of British artillery fire, compared to the lack of flexibility in the American Army. It should be fun. They will all come in helicopters. Everyone seems to be in such good form; it's a pleasure to go round and see them all. Malcolm Wallace leaves me on 15th and spends a few days with Pat Douglas before sailing, so you will be seeing him in November. Don't tell *anyone*, but General Neil wrote to me and said that I would be made substantive Lt Col this year – if all goes well. I shot a small buck and we are to eat it for lunch.

8th October 1952

What a lovely evening after a pleasant day! I had three letters from you, one from Bill Bradford, Jack Monteith and my mother. And now I reply to you first, the others can wait.

For two mornings I have got up at 5am to look at my forward positions. I drive up in the dark in my jeep, send the jeep away and walk back for breakfast between 10 and 11am. All vehicles have to be back before about 8am or they draw shell-fire. Till that hour the rising sun blinds the enemy Observation Posts. It's a nice walk and I carry a shotgun for the odd pheasant who happens to get up beside the path. Sappers, Gunners and Staff come along after 11am and then I usually have someone to lunch – the Colonel of the 'Vingt Douze' 22nd Canadian Regt. one day, the CRE today and so on. In the afternoon I do paper-work, in the evening the harassing fire plan for the night and final orders for patrols and then if no patrol battle starts up, I write again. Tomorrow I have no early start so I am going to write late into the night.

They are making my dug-out quite comfortable for me – I even have a wooden floor and electric light. The caravan has been pulled to pieces and they are going to build me a nicer one on a trailer instead of with an engine.

9th October 1952

I wasn't able to write to you yesterday after all. It was one of those non-stop days from before light till nearly midnight. Things were not going right in my back areas – David Campbell again – so I had to rush down there and stir things up. In the afternoon I was walking over the hills, visiting various platoons which one cannot drive to because the paths are in full view of the enemy. They don't see you in the scrub if you walk, but would shell a jeep. I got very hot doing it and eventually got to a platoon of Angus R.H. with a large tear in my trousers from barbed wire. A nice private soldier came up to me while I was resting and insisted on giving me a bottle of lovely cold beer.

At 6am this morning I set off again with the Brigadier and Nic to visit Angus Irwin. We watched a mobile section of mortars in helicopters going into action and firing their harassing task at an enemy position which they can't reach from their normal area, and then we went back to the machine guns and saw them doing a long range shoot. A moment or two with Malcolm and then back here for coffee and egg, bacon and fried bread. The Brigadier was delighted with it all. I had words with him last week. Complained about the shocking condition of my men's tents and said that they were quite inadequate. Pointed out that the back areas were lavishly supplied with good tentage and never had to move, whereas our men were always moving, often wet and cold and only got a miserable little 'Pup Tent' when they went into reserve and are supposed to be getting ready for their next eight weeks at the 'sharp end'. This morning he told me that he had reconsidered all that I had said and had put it to the other Brigadiers and that they had all agreed with my contention.

The matter has now been taken up with the Division Head-quarters and the Gunners, Sappers and so forth will be made to disgorge some of their tents in the infantry's favour. You can imagine how pleased I am – but I didn't show it, just said, 'Thank you very much'! I had another little victory too. When we took over from the Leicesters everything was in a terrible state of disorganisation. Thousands of mortar bombs were unsafe to move, hundreds unsafe to fire. The same is true to a lesser degree in this position and this morning I showed the Brigadier the dump of ammunition which has become useless through mishandling and neglect. He was horrified and said how was it to be prevented. I suggested that his ammunition examiner should go round units *before* things went wrong and not only when he was sent for

124

to condemn what *had* gone wrong. Also some other technical suggestions as to the method of stacking, etc. It all went down well and in good humour and breakfast was really quite jolly. There is one other drum I am beating and I think I may win this too. We go into Reserve and the first thing we always have to do is to pitch camp. I say that the camp should be standing waiting for us.

11th October 1952

Today, for the first time, there's been a cold dry wind from the North West. It was a lovely sunny day but one had to stay in the sun to keep warm. I had our American cooker moved to the dining-room-cum-sitting room dug-out, which keeps us lovely and warm. The food is cooked outside and brought in and put in the oven to keep hot.

Most mornings I get up at 5.30am and go off to see my Companies. I take a gun with me just in case I see a pheasant and this morning I got one – one shot, one bird. Everything continues quiet on our bit of the front, but very noisy all round. We do our best to keep them quiet by giving them everything we have got when they show their noses.

13th October 1952

I shall hear from you tonight, but I think I had better write this morning or you will have another long gap between letters. I couldn't find time the previous day because we had to mount a big bombardment in support of an action on our left. Nothing much came of it.

There has been some quite heavy fighting on our right and the Chinese have suffered a lot of casualties. During the last two days things have quietened down and I hope will become stabilised again. They seem to treat this division with great respect. Night after night we send out ambushes and patrols but they haven't yet come out to meet them. The French-Canadians on our right have had several little battles and have come off second-best, as far as I can make out.

The new General comes to see me at 6.00am tomorrow morning and returns to my Command Post for breakfast! So far I have only met him for a moment on the roadside with General Jim and at a cocktail party.

John Moncrieff has just come to tell me that there will be a big Air Strike in front of us on a hill called WINSTON at 11 o'clock – in five minutes – 1000lb bombs: what a shindy! I must climb the hill and have a look.

125

Intelligence

In several places in my diary you may have noticed a comment such as 'The full report will not be available till later'. Intelligence is not only about the enemy. These many parties during the Korean campaign were my main source of intelligence. Sometimes it was the Corps Commander himself, more often it was a CO in a neighbouring brigade. I made it my business to know everything that was going on. It is very important to keep your finger on the pulse of other units on your left and right and even more important to know the dependability of troops around you when there is a crisis.

I made a study of every Chinese attack or raid that I could find out about. The result of their bombardment was always the same. Land lines were cut, wireless aerials were shot away. No one knew what was happening for at least an hour. Our Command control was stunned. I was determined to overcome this problem and developed a communication system based on *ground* aerials. This, of course, greatly reduced the range of sets, but we could overcome that difficulty by issuing more sets. It was vital to know what was happening at the sharp end so that action could be taken to contain the attack or to mount counter attacks.

Words of Wisdom – from Rhoddy

Rhoddy and I were of one mind about soldiering – although we had never served in the same theatre – and so was Angus.

16th October 1952

My dear David

With all this fighting going on in Korea, you have been very much in my thoughts. I hope it hasn't been too bloody awful.

I fear I am very unpopular with the General as I refuse to admit that manoeuvres every three months is just the thing for a Battalion that has done seven moves and three embarkation 'stand tos' in eleven months. I am asking for my objections to be placed on record. British Army training ceases at the start line, but battles are won or lost on the dirty side of it. We can't shoot, we can't patrol, we can't lift or lay mines, or de-booby trap, or carry out raids. We have no idea of offensive defence, or the handling of the mobile reserve of fire power, and we never will until we are given 8 months of the year for the C.O.s disposal and suitable ground on which to train, and proper equipment (our own and enemy) with which to experiment. *Here, of course, we have miles of bloody ground. The sort of thing we need to do is your patrol training thing with endless variations and elaborations. But before anything else, we must make NCOs, and if* we are not given time to do that in the next year, I truly believe there will be no instructors left. That is the point from which there will be no return.

This last two years of command has been very trying. My time is up in April but they are not relieving me till July. I will get the sack or win my own way by then. I imagine I am not likely to get promoted as I have never been recommended for a Brigade. I don't know what I will do, just leave it all to chance. Ronnie Bramwell Davis has been made a General, and Ned Percival (who is practically illiterate) up-graded from Colonel (Boys' School Arborfield) to Brigadier and Deputy Commander Lowland District. Freddy Noble is MS Scottish Command – wonderful job which he can dispose of in 3 mornings a week. Alec Salmon, a great yes man, with no war experience since 1939, takes over from me. Actually he did command the Irish Fusiliers in 1946 for about a year, and they were so bad he couldn't really have helped making them a bit better.

I suppose I shouldn't complain with you out there about to face that hellish winter and being shelled and bombed and flooded out. Poor old Dum. I am sure you are putting up a terrific show and when it is all over you will have a great feeling that you have really done the Forty Twa proud. You will be heaped with honours and become a Boy Brigadier with a right to tell the Babu-officers where they get off. Perhaps you will be able to get some sanity into the Army. It is time we had some practical soldiers in high places, and Korea experience in very rightly something that cuts ice these days.

Write when you have time. Your letters interest me enormously and I often pass bits of them to my Brigadier who is very interested too. He says he hopes to meet the author one day. A nice man called Lipscombe. At Sandhurst with me but I didn't know him. Dog, gun, and dreary old family type – nice but no good on a party. Look after yourself carefully and wrap up well.

Yours ever
  Rhoddy.

17th October 1952

We had a great evening yesterday – a farewell party for Malcolm Wallace. Somehow or other we crowded 12 people into the little dug-out *and* three of my Mountain Band. I gave them all Champagne cocktails to start with and we had the band and singing, both during and after dinner. Of course it wasn't a late night and several of us were on duty afterwards.

I had two letters from you during the dinner party and one, which I am quite unable to read, from your Aunt Cecile. Honestly, I can only make out the odd word in six. Will post it to you in case there is anything I should know about, but I think it is mostly history.

We got the winter clothing today and only just in time. Everything was white with frost early this morning.

You must tell Hugh that I have had a battle with rats. Now that I don't any longer sleep in the caravan, I have a very low camp-bed. I suppose the cold weather drove the rats in for shelter, they were scuttling about all round me – under my bed and I think sometimes over it. Then they would scramble along the beams and send down a shower of earth from the sandbags. I hurled shoes at them with no result, they just went round and round. So I turned on the light and left it on and went off to sleep thinking that would drive them away. When I woke up there was a rat looking straight at me, so I struck out at him with my fist but only bashed my knuckles. Now I have some very good rat poison, which really does work.

25th October 1952

I had such a good evening at Div Headquarters with Pat Douglas. The General asked me to dinner and I sat on his left. He was charming and most amusing and so were all the others. Pat has got his way over his staff and I am sending him Larry Trotter as Company Commander. Larry has done very well as second in command of a company. He has set the pace for all the others and will set a very high standard at the Battle School too. I can get him back when I need him.

I think after more than two months' work I have managed to get Ian Critchley one of the Territorial Adjutancies in Perthshire. This is his second foreign tour without a home service job and he only came out because Pat C-P didn't give him a chance to do anything else. I shall be very sorry to lose him but I am sure Pinkie is longing to have him back!!

It is not yet very cold and I am comfortable in my dug-out. I only have one trouble in my life out here and that is a very pig headed Brigadier, but he will be going in less than a month so what does it matter. He tries to interfere in anything like the Ian Critchley business and prevent my plans working out, but the General and David McConnel know the form.

25th October 1952

I have an excellent sector this time and *very* few casualties so far. I am now indulging in broadcasting propaganda across to them – with the aid of experts of course. Sometimes they shoot back – sometimes we hear their Political Officers shouting at their own men not to listen. It gives everyone something to think about. The patrols take out sheets with messages painted on them in Chinese and crawl up close to their positions in the dark and plant the sheets on sticks in front of their trenches. This gives the men a sense of achievement because in the morning they can show their friends just where they went the night before and can be proud of themselves – quite apart from any propaganda value their messages may have on the enemy.

I am shooting again tomorrow. The young pheasants were very good tonight and so I have asked a big crowd for 9am tomorrow. I wonder who will turn up?

It's getting quite cold, but winter kit is at hand and you need not bother about me. Nobby Clark sent me six pairs of socks today, but two of them were too small so I gave them to my driver, Dillon, who has just returned from hospital. He is such a jolly fellow. My new batman is fun too – a man from the City of Leicester. He will be carrying the game in the morning.

25th October 1952

My dear General Neil

I was delighted to hear that you were able to place Ian Critchley. The WO sent a telegram through Div asking if he could be made available. My Brigadier, without reference to me, replied that it was unlikely, but a copy of his reply was sent to me yesterday and I was able to stop it before transmission to UK. I am expecting David Severn, as you know, who is an admirable replacement and will be here before Ian departs.

It is very kind of you to congratulate me on things out here. I think I can say that we are a very happy team from top to bottom. We have not yet had a real test, but if it comes and when it comes, I have full confidence in all Rifle Coy Comds and in the Bn HQ Staff and in the men. There are a few weak links – as there are bound to be in a National Service army, but I am sure they will be carried through any test by the others around them. I would like Andy Watson if Neville could be persuaded to part.

Yours ever,
   David.

Warned for a vital task

At one of these convivial parties, the General called me aside. He told me that in the near future the Commonwealth Division was to side step to the left and take over a vital sector of the front from the American Marines. This feature, which I was soon to know so well as 'The Hook', was absolutely vital to the whole front. 'You are to get to know the Marines,' he said, 'and I want you to carry out a very thorough reconnaissance of the whole position.'

The 146th Birthday Party

I made contact with the US Marines and asked for permission to go frequently round their position, to get to know the problems. Their Colonel wanted to make a bit of a splash for their 146th Birthday Anniversary. Would I lend them my Pipes and Drums? This was a splendid opportunity for me to get to know them all at a stroke. I arrived at the appointed hour in my jeep with Company Commanders and some staff in tail. There was my host, a huge fellow, waiting for us. I shook him warmly by the hand and proceeded to introduce my officers. He said something about an Honour Guard. Looking over my shoulder, I saw a line of rather sheepish young officers, obviously waiting to be inspected. 'Oh no, no, no,' I exploded on the spur of the moment, 'You can't do this to me. I am no Ronald Coleman or Stewart Grainger.' One of the young men in the line I knew from a reconnaissance on the position. I called out 'Hey there Buddie' and seized him by the hand and pulled him out of the line and thumped him on the back. The parade, to my great relief, burst out laughing and we all ended up hand shaking and thumping each other. Needless to say, the rest of the day was absolutely informal with lots of laughter and much leg pulling. They are wonderful chaps. (We did not, of course, tell them that we were already well past our 200th Anniversary.)

In the days that followed, I made many extended tours of the 'Hook' and made friends amongst their young officers and some of the men. One young soldier told me with pride, that he could do his Stag (Sentry Duty) and fire his rifle from his bunk! I made no reply, but the more I saw of that position, the more I realised that it was a death trap for the men that were expected to fight there. Their 'Hoochies' as they called them, were very comfortable and well water-proofed, but they were half above ground. Any shell would penetrate the roof; it was proof only against splinters.

What on earth was I to do the night that I took over the position? It would take days to rectify the situation. My men, like the Marines, would not understand when they were told to abandon comfortable quarters for a hole in the ground. Should I tell the General my forebodings? Better not, until I was in possession. The only person I could tell was my brother Rhoddy.

KOREA: TO WAR ONCE MORE (1952)

25th October 1952

My dear Rhoddy

Till two days ago the Division has been right out of all this heavy fighting you have been reading about.

The Americans have all kinds of funny ideas which are no doubt forced upon them by their curious organisation – constant rotation of officers and men, rotation to and from the US and rotation in the line too. No-one even seems to be in any one place for more than a few days.

Their defensive tactics are based on lines of defence. OP Line of Resistance backed up by a Main Line of Resistance. The former is a chain of Platoon positions which are in no way mutually supporting and the latter is literally a communication trench which goes like a snake over hill and dale. What is so awful, I have got to take over a sector of this MLR in a short time and the OPLR has already been lost by them. There are no fire trenches. They just have slits in their dug-outs which are built up, not down, off the big communication trench. I am wondering what I am going to do the first night or two – and the Chinese are only 200 yards away.

The Chinese staged a simply wonderful raid on one of our Canadian battalions two night ago. They practice their men in the back areas for weeks before doing these things (we lay them on in 24 hours, without rehearsal, advice from expert planners or anything). There was no surprise as to the area of the impending attack. He shelled it without much result for three days. He gained his surprise by his plan. The battalion was 'standing to' and other Brigadiers and COs were telephoning best wishes for a good success. Suddenly six searchlights in parallel shone up into the sky at 6 pm. (This was reported later by Air OP.) On this signal 100 guns concentrated their fire on one Coy position. A salvo was fired at each neighbouring battalion Command Post. Infantry, who must have been lying close to the positions since dawn, sprang forward and the Coy which was not then being shelled was quickly over-run. Communications were all cut by the shelling. Wireless sets at the sharp end were all buried in the bunkers. DF didn't come down. SOS wasn't even pre-arranged I am almost certain. Div and Corps Arty opened up on counter battery and fired over 5000 shells. Counter attack was ordered but attacking Coy had first to be relieved by a Coy in reserve battalion area. CA eventually went in at 0300 and no Chinese were there to receive it! Another 3000 mortar bombs, etc, had been expended. Casualties: ours 14 killed, 21 missing, 30 something wounded and evacuated, 15 wounded and at duty. The Chinese? We don't yet know, but quite a lot, 5 or 6 were on the wire. Their patrols were heard dragging bodies away last night and artillery was put down on them. A few have been seen from the air in scrub. It was a battalion strength raid and they may have lost well over a hundred, but who can tell? They outwitted us anyway and what are a few bodies to them?

The other day I was asked to name an officer for the American DSO which was being offered round the place. I said we hadn't done anything yet, why not offer it to the Welsh or some other battalion who has been out here a long time. They, of course, had turned it down before it came to me!

Yours ever,
David.

27th October 1952

My dear Rhoddy,

I am writing you another letter while I have the opportunity, as I shall probably be in rather a whirl for a week or two. I was to have done final recce of our new sector early this morning, but now the Chinese are there and the Marines haven't got it back yet. Thank God it didn't happen the night of our relief! I have been round it once or twice and felt quite sure that it was indefensible. The gallant Marines were not showing any aggressive spirit either. Chinese were walking about un-shot at, the Marines all looked tired and most of them seem to have been relieved or were waiting to be relieved that day or the next. The CO was swamped with paper – promotions for gallantry in the field in quintriplicate, etc. Two coy counter attacks have failed, another goes in later this morning. Much shelling and bombing going on all the time. I do hope they don't throw in the B W to retake the ground the Yanks have lost, but if we must, we must. I watch it all from a very good OP.

I had a 'strawberry' from a very unexpected quarter yesterday – no less a person than the Div Catering Officer!! This fine fellow knows every single Coy cook-house in the Div and visits them no matter what is happening at the sharp end and on foot of course. He said my cooking set up was far the best. I have everyone on fresh rations, the fwd chaps with platoon cook-house dug-outs. They are used as 'warmeries' when the ambushes and patrols come in. The Marines go onto C7 tinned rations all the time in the line and then have to be withdrawn frequently for feeding up. I suppose they are so democratic that no-one is allowed to cook for anyone else, unless he is a professional cook.

I hear that Ronnie Bramwell Davis is to follow George Johnson, my brother-in-law, as Chief of Staff in Edinburgh and George Collingwood has got Lowlands Div. Why not get into the M.S. crowd yourself or do you want another Military Attache' job?

Yours ever,
David

George Johnson, Scots Guards, was the most successful soldier

132

in our family. He commanded the Guards Armoured Division and took the surrender of Brussels.

28th October 1952

The sun shines and we are all quite gay. We have had a bit of a rest and hardly any shelling. We go out in a day or two, but straight in again into not so good a spot – nothing more than an adjustment in the line, but we shall have to work very hard when we get there to put it in good order.

I get up so early that I usually go to bed at ten and then I feel fine at 4 or 5am. The Company Commanders are mostly up at night and sleeping by dawn so I usually see them in the evening. I only have to be up all night when there are 'things' going on. Raas Mcrae is a good help. He works out everything in great detail – something that I am so bad at doing. And Nic does the same, so I couldn't be more fortunate.

CHAPTER SIX
The Hook

First Battle on the Hook

I watched the Marines' battle on the Hook for several days. It was an awesome sight.

The whole feature was covered most of the time by a cloud of cordite. Sometimes there was a burst of yellow flame from a napalm projector. Periodically the American 'Persuaders' (their 8" guns and air strikes) added more noise to the constant bombardment. I had never seen anything like it before. I couldn't make much sense of it, not knowing what orders had been given. What was I going to do the first night? Could I bring patrols up from a reserve company? Had the Chinese suffered enough or would they persevere the night I took over? If we must counterattack, we must. I would do it in daylight with smoke and tanks. There were no minefields to worry about and if I could see the whole battlefield, I could prevent the enemy from sending in reinforcements.

4th November 1952

The Marines seemed to be fighting well, but are suffering very heavy casualties. They must be killing a lot of Chinese with this enormous bombardment. From now on we will be seeing a lot of the Marines, they will be on our immediate left.

In one of your letters you asked lots of questions about General West. He is very amusing, very direct and a grand fellow, with strong opinions. I should say he was a better Divisional General than General Jim and just as much fun. What is more, I think he likes me, at least often he speaks to me at any gathering.

What was to be my plan for the Hook position?

6th November 1952

For days I had been chewing over this dreadful problem and I do not deny that I had put up some strong pleas for guidance. I had a long hard think last night and quite suddenly my plan came to me. I knew just what I was going to say to the Corps Commander in the morning and had a wonderful sleep.

My interview with the Corps Commander went like this:

'Colonel, you have a tough assignment. How are you going to set about it?'

'Sir, you can't bomb the Chinese out of their tunnels. I am going to dig tunnels. There is nothing left of the old fortifications. We start from scratch.'

'I want Korean labour and our Sappers. If my men are to fight after several days of bombardment, they must be able to sleep. If the Chinese attack in great numbers, I must be able to use artillery on our own position, then mop up. We can do this if we have tunnels.'

'Colonel, I agree to your plan and if you meet any difficulties, you have direct access to me.'

I went off with Brigadier Ricketts to show the plan on the ground. The CRE wanted two days to draw 'blueprints' of the tunnels, but I said no to that. I would put down tapes on the ground. Work was to start at once and go on in shifts round the clock. The harder the men worked the sooner they would get out of the shell-fire. I am being given every priority with labour and material, and everyone is very pleased about it – including me!

The Relief or the Marines
7th November 1952

I had a nice morning with my new Brigadier, Joe Kendrew. He walked round each company and talked freely to Officers and men. He bombarded me with questions in the Mess, my Company Commanders all present, so the unanimity of our views was clear. I think everyone took to him.

I am now established on the 'Hook'. The Marines had a very rough time; they have really been through the mill. They were just itching to go, and made no bones about it. The CO said to me, and one or two of my officers overheard it, 'I give you 24 hours' - not quite the thing to say to the incoming commander. I bit my lip and let it pass.

I am very busy and so can only write a hurried note tonight. All goes well and we are getting every help we could wish for – masses of men dig and remake the line. We had a little outpost battle our second night, but held our ground at some cost. If we can keep them off for a few more days we shall be strong again. The Americans are grand fellows and very co-operative. I have masses of reinforcements available and in a few days will be well over strength and will be able to discard some weak links – there *are* some weak links I am sorry to say, but we won't have to put up with them much longer. (This comment refers to two men whom I had to court martial for refusing to go on patrol. I spoke to them myself on the telephone, but they were obdurate.)

We had our first light fall of snow this morning and I am now wearing those lovely over-boots you gave me, and my feet are as warm as toast.

I have a very fine young Sapper officer in charge of the work, George Cooper. He is most enthusiastic and a very pleasant fellow to work with. (In later life he was to become a full General.)

I am so tired, I must stop even before the end of one page. I have been walking and talking for ages it seems. So many people come here and some have to be won over.

10th November 1952

I started at 6am going round 'C' Company, then I did Angus R.H. on the Hook, then breakfast, then several men for punishment, then a 'smoke' expert, then hours of piping and dancing and talking to Marines – then my Company Commanders to dinner.

Last night we had an unhappy accident with a mine. Two days before that we had a small battle and lost, among others, a nice young officer called MacGuigan. It all seems to flow along. Night melts into day; day into night. Sometimes I am bored for an hour or two, then all rush and squiff again. Thank God for the letters. They make life worthwhile. I shall be in my sleeping-bag in a few minutes and before I have had time to think of you, I shall be up and about again.

11th November 1952

Today it is pouring with rain and very beastly, which is holding up the work. Tomorrow General West comes at 6.30am to inspect progress. I do hope it is a better day for him. One slithers about even on the flat, and the hills are almost impossible. We have to go forward at that frightful hour because it is usually the quietest time of the day. Anyway, one gets a good appetite for breakfast!

My Sapper officer is terrific. He is setting up an organisation to mass produce cement beams to support the overhead cover, which is important to keep down casualties. (In the months ahead he was to do a wonderful job, for which the Black Watch and other regiments who fought on the Hook must be truly grateful.)

Now I must go off and get into my nice warm sleeping-bag. I have the telephone beside me and a light, and I never mind being woken up. It is better than hanging about waiting for things to happen.

The rain depresses both sides considerably and stops much of the shelling and nearly all of the bombing. The roads get into an impossible state, so we stop the tanks moving about as much as possible. The 'rocket ripples' go off just the same. Golly, what a noise they make. I am always glad I am not a Chinaman! Young Smart from Brechin is with me and doing very well. I had him in to lunch today. Two officers have had to go off. One with broken eardrums from a shell burst, the other with a broken bone in his hand.

14th November 1952

Your letters arrived in the middle of a small battle we were having, so I didn't really read them much till now. One of our outposts was heavily raided by 50 Chinese and I am afraid they got the best of it. We lost a nice subaltern called MacGuigan, 7 men killed and 10 wounded. The Chinese had casualties too, but were able to drag them away. We spent the night gathering in our wounded and by early this morning there was only one missing. I am afraid he is a prisoner. Tremendous shell-fire was put down in case the raid was part of a bigger attack. This morning there are 1000lb bomb air strikes on the Chinese positions in my area. Some of them must find a mark however deeply the enemy is dug in.

Just as I was going to bed at 4am, the whole thing started up again. We all bundled back to the CP, some with just a blanket round them. I called down my defensive fire and then we waited for confirmation of where the attack was coming in. Peter Buchanan arrived with a rather small towel round his ample figure. He stood in front of my table, legs astride a telephone to each ear, shouting his orders to the Base Plate. His towel fell to the ground – to reveal the whole 15 stone of his manhood. 'Help . . . someone . . . *please,*' called Peter. We laughed, fit to burst.

It was a false alarm! The Americans were putting in a raid on 'Betty Grable' and had forgotten to inform us. However, no harm done and better to be too quick than caught napping. At 6.30am I set forth to visit Angus R.H. and his men who had been in the trouble and then at 9am Claud Moir, followed by the CO and Company Commanders of PPCLI at 9.30 for Counter Attack reconnaissance. Brigadier at 11am, American Brigadier at 2pm, posting 4 young officers to their Companies till 3.30 – and now to bed.

15th November 1952

Dear General Neil

I think I did tell you that we were taking over a sector of the line from the American Marines after their battle on the HOOK. We are getting on very well with refortification. We have been given top priority in the Div for everything – almost unlimited artillery ammunition, all the timber that can be cut and dressed for dug-outs, two troops of Sappers and many Korean labourers. I am driving tunnels through the rock on the HOOK itself, so that if they attack again in force, we can fire the artillery on our own position to kill the majority before we have to mop up. General West and the CRE came up early yesterday morning to see progress and hear my plan. Afterwards he had a late breakfast with some of us. He seemed to be very pleased with everything and made us all laugh a great deal. He is a fine commander – very quick, very decisive and has a delightful sense of humour.

We are building up a great friendship with the Marines on our left. They are grand chaps – no swagger, keen to help in every way and mad about the 'Scotties'. Some of us attended their 146th Birthday and we had the Pipes and Drums and the Dancers out for them. It was a most delightful afternoon – lots of leg-pulling on both sides – formality went to the wind.

B Coy had two grand opportunities to give the Chinese a real bashing, but I am sorry to say that they bungled them both. When I was going round the trenches, I got the impression that their morale had fallen very low and yesterday at some risk I decided to relieve the whole company and put in Angus Irwin. We had a real success tonight as a result. Alec Rattray's patrol spotted a large Chinese fighting patrol approaching our position (as they had done on two previous occasions). He fired his lights and withdrew as pre-arranged. Down came the artillery – Out went Rattray again within a minute – Heard yells and squeals, returned to the HOOK and we repeated the dose – and now he is out again keeping a good watch. Wireless communications and everything worked splendidly and the whole battalion will be as pleased as punch. I won't bore you with all the details of the two earlier failures, but they were very frustrating after so much preparation.

Claud Moir's Company did a very good patrol last night. Richard Haw was in command. The night before, on a recce patrol, he had found the Chinese constructing more caves from which they mounted their big attack on the HOOK. It was a rush job to get a patrol planned and mounted for the following night with a party of Sappers to blow up the caves. Moir's arrangements were splendid and everything went according to plan, despite the patrol bumping two enemy sentries on the way. It was a long and arduous job and it isn't yet finished, as we hadn't enough explosive to do all the caves that night.

As I was writing this, the enemy again came at the HOOK. Alec RT again called down fire, then he heard movement close on his left and threw some grenades. I have now recalled him and he is back in the main position so that we can be free to 'spray it about a bit'. I wonder if it will develop into something bigger. *Rattray is now back and his men in the tunnels. He himself is being de-briefed by Angus. The front trench has just been blown in by three shells but no casualties. Only the sentries are now above ground. Angus and Alec RT and Donald Black, his other Subaltern, are all as cool as cucumbers and working excellently.*

The battle of patrols continues nightly and so far with good success. Last night we caught some of them in the beam of a tank search-light. The HOOK gets daily more destroyed. The trenches which we dug to 6½ feet are now in places back to 3 feet – but hardly any casualties due to the tunnels. C/Sgt Ramsay was killed yesterday – crushed under his vehicle, poor fellow. The road gave way after rain.

Yours ever
  David

It did develop into something bigger. The battle had started.

The Battle
I was determined that my battle was not to be a re-run of the disastrous affair, which I had watched with so many misgivings during the first week of November. The cost in lives of those counter attacks was really terrible.

As our battle developed I quite suddenly realised that I was in a very strong position. My inter communication radio network was so good that I knew what every section was doing and how they were responding to the demands made on them by their Company Commander. We must hold every dug out, every tunnel. We would reinforce when we could: we would fight each trench and counter attack if only for 50 yards. At all costs we must hold. Better to hold what we knew we had, than to counter attack into the unknown.

That is how the battle developed. Spare men who had lost touch were collected and used as reinforcements for weak platoons. The Pipes and Drums and sections of the MMGs were brought forward to fill the gaps.

There was one Company which was not yet under attack. This was Claud Moir's Company. Dare I extract men from here and leave his territory under a skeleton defence? This was really a pretty drastic thing to undertake in the dark and it certainly had never been contemplated or discussed before hand. Can you imagine getting an order in the middle of the night, when all hell was being let loose only a few hundred yards to your left front, 'Pull out every man you can spare and go to the aid of Angus on the Hook'. Claud Moir did that without a question or a word of remonstrance. One platoon he moved there and then on foot across country, but the others he pulled back and put into trucks and motored them round in the dark. It was brilliantly executed.

The Chinese were milling around everywhere. I had given them several doses of 'Air Burst' but there was quite a lot of hand to hand fighting. In Appendix A at the end of this book you can read of each event which I knew of at my Command Post and the orders I gave to implement the defence. We were going to hold what we had and reinforce wherever we could.

We were all keyed up to a high pitch but well under control. My Support Company Commander was firing incredible quantities of mortar bombs. We had a platoon of 81mm and a 3" mortar platoon. He was working closely with my Gunner so that their targets were co-ordinated.

There was just one person in my Command Post who was apparently quite oblivious to what was happening. The Brigade Commander was sound asleep in the large wooden chair, which the pioneers had made for the comfort of the Duty Officer. I gave the Adjutant a wink. We should let the BM know where he was in case they were looking for him. He disappeared some time during the night, without a word spoken.

As the night progressed we had some very anxious moments. My reserves were now all used up, so now it was a question of slogging it out. I called for a Sit Rep from Angus Irwin at 0415 hours.

CO, 'Hold On.'

OC Company, 'That is what I hoped you would say.'

It was now up to me and my wonderful Gunner Reg Port to interdict the Hook from all reinforcement. We knew most of the routes they used and the likely FUPs (Forming Up Points). We must play it fast and loose. Every trick in the Gunner's book. Star shells, air burst, stonks here, stonks there. We were not going to put down great belts of Defensive Fire. If you read the Appendix you will find some surprising intercepts which prove that what we were doing was working. The Chinese were really getting that dreadful thing, shell fire when you are in the open and on the move. Our last job was to cut off the Chinese who were still on the Hook, as they went away with their dead and wounded.

That is the story of the 2nd Battle on the Hook, as best as I can tell it. I believe The Black Watch were twice saved from heavy casualties. The first time it was because the Chinese struck the night before we were due to take over those dreadful 'Hoochies' and which were totally destroyed by the enemy bombardment. That was good luck.

The second time was the result of putting Angus Irwin's A Company in the forward position which was crucial to the success of our battle. Morale was of the highest and the determination to hold our position of the Hook unshakable.

17th November 1952

My gunner, Reg Port told me that an enemy intercept had given Bde HQ two hours warning of the attack, but they had failed to pass it on. I rang up the Bde Commander and repeated the story and asked him to find out if it was true. He rang me back at 10pm and said that it was true 'but he really didn't see what difference it would have made'. I replied that I did not think 75 wounded Jocks would agree with him and neither did I. Would he take me to see the General.

I was absolutely furious. Failing to pass on this intelligence was criminal.

Confrontation
18th November 1952

The next morning nothing happened. I was expecting to get a call from the GI or the AQ, David McConnel, telling me when I was to see General West. I waited for a full hour and then I rang him. No, an appointment had not been requested. What was it about? I told him of my Gunner's complaint and the Brigadier's reply. We are in touch by radio. He is on the Reserve Position. Be here at 11 o'clock.

I had more to say than the first cause of complaint. Now was the time to have it out.

22nd November 1952

My dear David

Today's papers produced the first reliable account of your action at the Hook. It was chiefly your account to the Press. In case it arrives garbled I sent you the following telegram today:

'Officer Comdg 1 Black Watch.

Well done Black Watch. All ranks at home send congratulations on your magnificent action at The Hook. We anxiously await full report.

Neil McMicking Colonel.'

I sent The Queen Mother an account of your first action at The Hook when McGuigan was killed. I will follow it up with your news when it arrives.

I hope it will give you an opportunity for putting in names of those who have done well. It may not be out of place for me to tell you that in August, September and October 1914 the 1st Bn never put in anyone's names for decorations because they considered everyone had done equally and exceptionally well. They had, of course, to change their ideas as the war went on. Then in Palestine, I did not put people in for what we all

*considered mild and small actions until suddenly other Regiments, who
had had nothing like the exciting times we had had, started appearing in
the daily press and the London Gazettes!*

*Your letter to me about the first action at the Hook and dated 7th
November and then the accounts of the 2nd large action in press read
extremely well, ie hard training then extensive and hard work, pressed
hard by you, on the defences and then a big success as a result. Do send
me as full reports as you can as I would like David Sutherland to 'use'
them at the RMA Sandhurst, Buchanan at Eaton Hall and myself and
Jack at dinners in the Regiment's area!*

Very many congratulations
Yours
*   Neil*

Some of my brother's letters are quite unsuitable for general
publication, but they were a wonderful tonic for me when the
going was rough – for which I bless him. This one is a classic and
I am sure the reader will enjoy it. It made me laugh for hours.

Cuckoo-Land or MELF 26
11th November 1952
My Dear David,

*Thank you very much for your last (as ever) most interesting letter
dated I forget what, and issued in three slim volumes. I've left it in my
office where I shall probably finish this letter tomorrow.*

*Well, anyhow, not having your letter to refer to at this time, I may as
well see if I can find anything to say about myself. First of all your guess
is wrong – it is not the housemaid's ink, it is my servant's. Serve him right
for leaving the lid off mine which has turned into a sort of Atholl Brose
during the month we have been away in the wilderness, the wilderness
of jagged hills to the south of where we all had such fun when you and
Jean, Susie and Douglas, Nini and I were young (-ish only in my case)
on the Gulf of Suez.*

*The time when Hugh (my son of 3 months) had squitters at my fête
champêtre on Green Island and the Jewess's face went green, white,
Magenta and Americans Nanny's bum went blerth – blerth -berl belter
– belur every time the LCT juddered on a wave, and when Susie got
screwed off the bog by holding onto the steering gear and you shouted 'I
see you down the ventilator'. This doesn't seem to have much to do with
my news, but there it is. Anyhow it was away to the South of all that
where we were. I always think of South Egypt as North because one looks
at the map with the Mediterranean at the bottom – very confusing, but
I digress again. So my news is that we have been on manoeuvres away*

*to the South of all that, though I think of it as North. So there you are –
compared to just fooling about in Korea you are to gather my life is pretty
stern and rugged. I can't tell you much about what happened as the G.O.C.
commanded all my companies himself and some of the platoons. I once had
a front of ten miles, and while halfway round my visiting got made acting
Brigadier as well. However, I got my own back for that, as while halfway
back again I got put in the bag by the 3rd Grens. It was the only night on
which I got a decent sleep and was fortunately doing my rounds with a
well stocked jeep and trailer. It was a little galling to find out that at the
mid day following no one had noticed the absence of the acting Brigadier,
and my release coincided with the return of the real Brigadier who gave me
permission to consider myself demoted. Sgt McGourty was sympathetic
and gave me the last egg for my luncheon. Since then I've lived on bully
beef, and that still goes on as I suppose no one has told the Q boys the
exercise is over. This is a serious matter as Neguib (Egyptian President)
has made so many laws that no one will sell anything, and rations is all
we have to live on. Even the French Club had no prawns yesterday.*

*Well now what else about the manoeuvres? Let me see. I think our side
won because they had tanks, though the other side say they were all killed
by the air the first day. That seems probable to me, also my Bn which was
sitting on them. Indeed I think my Bn got wiped out every day for the
first three days. Anyhow we all went round and round every mulberry
bush and I imagine the Generals had babies under most of them. In the
end I think our side all came to life at the same time and the other side
got swept back on their admin area, probably because the umpires were
asleep or just couldn't stand it any more. The exercise closed one night
just as the other side seemed to be due some kind of resurrection – just
in time to save my Bn doing a moon light out flanking movement on a
track that wasn't there. That sort of thing happened all the time because
David, 'Speed was the essence of something' - I forget exactly what – but
something hellish important. With this in mind one had to send out recce
to find out something and then chuck the Bn after it before that something
had been found out. Often one was then told to stop doing it and begin
all over again. The best day was five changes of plan before luncheon.
One false start I stopped with great difficulty. I was on ahead of a recce
company, following the line of a nulla, wadhi, alghad or ravine or dry river
bed, while the Adjt was supposed to be following with the rest. Well just as
I got the wash out the Adjutant sat on the exhaust pipe of his dingo and
went dashing madly down a track to give me (as he thought) several miles
ahead, the news. At the same moment the main body started to disappear
down another dry water course and at the same time the wireless packed
in. There was every prospect of a reunion at Brighton, but fortunately
my one accomplishment came to my aid – I whistled on my fingers and
waved a silly little red flag which caused everybody, umpires, spectators,*

actors, exercise dead, P.O.W.s, friend and foe to shout halt for a mile in every direction. (I couldn't shout myself as I had lost my voice from drinking whisky before breakfast.) So you see the Boer War methods are the best. We halted and so were available to be buggered around some more. Never dissipate your reserve David – it is all you have left to bugger up. Very funny you say – yes, but provided 'they' don't try it on us in a real war.

I wonder if you'll have time or the inclination to read all this drivel. I am assuming you are short of reading material of any kind. It is my only excuse.

Well now we are back in Tel El Kebir with two companies on guard, one on the range, and the other in the Adjutant General's imagination. It's to be manoeuvres again in February, but in the meantime someone has had a bright idea . . . we can fill up the time by doing education. When will we get down to the study of war from the start line onwards? Boy Scouts can be taught to manoeuvre but it needs a skilled man to fight.

I am now living to two rooms with H & C attached, having managed to turn out the previous occupants, the ten niggers I told you about. While we were out, some women moved into the next hut. I haven't seen them yet but I've heard them laugh . . . or rather larf. I've no taste for sleeping with constipated hyenas, so I must remain chaste. It's a dull way to live. I lost my Maltese girlfriend just before we moved. She was carried off by her husband, poor fellow. Well now I really have got no more news. I hope to go home on leave in March and I hand over Command in July to Alec Salmon, a wet type with a Bishop's daughter for a wife.

I do hope the sector of the MLR you had to take over from the Yanks turned out better than you feared. You must have done a good job with the BW to get your section so firm, and your observation, patrolling and fire discipline so well organised. No one could have started on active service with a Bn so little trained, experienced or united as yours. To have welded it together and trained it in the line does you great credit and you should not spurn any honour that comes your way.

Best of luck old boy and let me know how you get on.
Yours ever,
    Rhoddy

23rd November 1952

My dear Rhoddy
    Perhaps you will have heard before you got this that my battle came off and we gave them a good trouncing. It has been a hectic few days as you can imagine – generals, press, staff, reinforcements and reorganisation. I am still in the line, but with two Coys PPCLI under Command, while

two of mine are re-equipping at A Ech. The men are very proud of themselves and rightly so. Every officer and man did his stuff – no heroics but damned well and efficiently. I am very proud of them. I had some pretty bad moments. It was an awful decision to bring down Air Burst on my own position – several times – but it worked. A fine Coy Commander, who was right on the ball and had every man under cover. It shook the Chinks good and proper. I had no reserve at all and had to leave one whole Coy FDL almost completely vacant half the night so that I could reinforce the Coy on the Hook. Anyway it came off. I do hope the press don't make a balls of it. It is so long since this Division has had a show, they may well overdo it, but believe me, I have done my best to play the soft pedal.

DF still going down nightly. The Chinese are so keen on collecting their dead – how many more they must lose in doing it! I've sold my Tunnels anyway! They weren't half completed of course – solid rock, but it gave me enough confidence to fire the air burst and they saved many casualties. Four officers wounded, one killed. He went in with the bayonet. 16 missing, probably prisoners, 10 dead, 60 or 70 wounded, many not badly.

Yours ever
    David

26th November 1952

All went well with my interview with the General. It was a great strain having to put my case over strongly, but respectfully. I was with him and the Brigadier for a whole hour and he ended up by saying, 'I think your complaints on the whole are fully justified.'

I had not been back here more than an hour before the first results of my interview started to take effect. One of the things I asked for was a proper camp for the men when they come out of the line – the tents to be pitched and ready for them, with heating, stoves, etc. 'Where did I want my camp?' was the Staff Officer's question. I pointed out that it was not **my** camp but the Brigade's camp and it was up to the Brigade Staff to collect the Seconds-in-Command of all battalions and work out where the tents were to be pitched – to suit us all as our turn came round for a period in reserve. I don't think I shall have any more trouble after this. I told the General several things about which he had heard nothing – the frightful and dangerous state of the ammunition for example – mortar bombs falling short on our own men and that kind of thing.

Well so much for that. The air is cleared, the evening is quiet and the hard grind of daily work goes on. I am busy writing up citations for medals – dozens of them! I am so proud of my officers and men. So many did so well that it is difficult to draw the line anywhere. Raas is being a great help, but my day is from long before dawn till long after dark.I am much more comfortable now that I am in a dug-out with a heater. I had a bath yesterday beside the fire – what luxury.

28th November 1952

I had a most successful day. Everything has worked out perfectly. We had the first **real** conference of COs at Brigade Head-quarters as a result of my interview with the General. We all said freely what we wanted to say. Ricketts listened for the first time and we carried everything unanimously. I was then asked to talk about my battle, which I did very briefly, and to say what lessons there were to be learnt – and a lot of suggestions are going to be put forward to the General. After that I had to go off to poor Roger Doig's funeral. We only managed to find his body yesterday. After that I had a lovely hot bath at my base camp, then rushed back here to see a draft of fine young chaps who have come to join us, and then I read my confidential report, which was a very pleasant surprise after all the struggles of the last few days. It really was a good one – said I had a real flair for training men and carrying everyone along with my enthusiasm, and ended up saying that I had just fought a most successful defensive battle, etc. And so I am happy because I know it will please you and I shall be a proper Colonel soon, with a bigger pension. They won't give me full Lt Colonel's pay yet as I am still too young, and there was no recommendation for promotion.

General Eisenhower arrives tomorrow or the next day and each battalion is sending off 10 men to meet him, wherever he lands. Of course everyone in the world is wondering if he will be able to do anything. Wouldn't it be lovely if we could all go into winter quarters and sail away in the spring instead of waiting till July? I am afraid I have my doubts.

I don't think that any of the three young subalterns were badly wounded, but Angus R.H. got a nasty one in the foot. I suppose he may be flown home or go in a ship in a month or so.

30th November 1952

My first quiet morning for a month. I am busy at my desk, doing Honours and Awards – lots of them, and taking a short rest.

Thank you for your wire. I had others from McMicking, Neville Blair, and a General who commanded us in Tobruk and was at the Annual Dinner in London, General Someone of the 7th Armoured

Division, who said they were proud to have had 1st Battalion with them in Germany.

4th December 1952

My dear Rhoddy

What a lot has happened to me in the last few weeks. It has been pretty hectic as you can imagine. Very many thanks for your telegram. I published it in Orders so that your men who are with us would know that their old friends were thinking of them. Cpl Fallon was very angry that he missed the battle. He is still very lame, or rather has a stiff knee which makes him limp. He was getting into trouble in hospital so I sent him up to the Battle School to help Pat Douglas (my 2 i/c) who is now Commanding it. Pat couldn't find him a proper job so he returned him to me long before he was fit. I put him in charge of the daily leave parties to A Ech, which he did very well, and he was still there when the battle broke. He was furious the next morning when he heard the news and gave the guard commander the hell of a row for not wakening him up. And I would lay any odds that he would have been in the thick of it if only he had known, knee or no knee.

The battle went very well. It was twice in the balance, but everyone did their stuff magnificently, NS Officers, Sergeants, Corporals and Private soldiers. I am mighty proud of them all. Each Section tunnel had a wireless set with ground aerials and they worked all through the night. It was a real comfort to know that there was justification for reinforcing in the dark. We weren't quite strong enough to chase what was left of them at first light. Everyone was tired out. However, we killed large numbers of the little buggers and were picking up bits of them for days afterwards. Their evacuation of killed and wounded is wonderful. They have teams working on it from the very start, who just walk through the shell-fire, unarmed. We had a wounded Corporal who watched it going on all through the night.

We came out of the line two days ago and that very day winter arrived with full force and great suddenness. Last night it was zero, but we have got wonderful winter garments and sleeping bags, so things aren't too bad. Anyway the sun shines. And now I have a new Brigadier and a first class one – Joe Kendrew, a very fine rugby football player. He walked round all my companies yesterday and made a fine impression. And tonight he told me that he was going to change our date for returning to the line so that we could have New Year in the Bde Res Area! 'And I don't care what the Kings have to say about it,' he said.

In his predecessor's last week with the Brigade I had to ask him to take me before the General. His Brigade HQ had sat on an enemy intercept forewarning us of the attack by two hours. I only heard about it through my Gunner the following morning and didn't really believe the story, but

I repeated it to the brigadier and asked him to make enquiries. Late that night he telephoned me and said that it was true, 'but he really didn't see what difference it would have made'. I said '75 wounded Jocks wouldn't agree with you, and neither do I'. With the whole Div artillery and American stuff also at my disposal, I should have been able to break it up. Well I had an hour with the general and I said everything I wanted to say and that I have been fighting my Brigade HQ for, during the past four months. I said that my men must be in heated tents the day they come out of the line and if need be, the tents would have to be taken off Sappers, Gunners and so forth, who all live in considerable comfort all the year round. I am damned if I see why the chaps who do the fighting should shiver in Pup-tents when they are in reserve. I asked for Bulldozers to cut terraces in the hill-sides and that the whole thing should be done under Brigade orders, and not flung at the unit as is always the case. (My 2i/c was on the Siteing Board of course.) I won't bore you with all the other things, but the General said that my complaints were in the main justified – and I fell out, leaving him with the brigadier. I don't think that anything was done about it, but in my opinion, the BM or IO should have received at least a severe reprimand for neglecting to pass that signal.

Everything worked out OK in the two days which remained before we came into reserve, I don't think anything has ever happened more quickly in Korea. I shudder to think of the conditions if the men had come out to pup-tents in that blistering cold. As it was, they just lay down and slept the clock round. Next week more heaters arrive so that there will be two per squad tent and then we shall be OK for Christmas. The other thing I have got speeded up is Courts Martial. I managed to get a case with sentence of 2 years, promulgated in 7 days. The form before that was 60 days – sometimes, on quite trivial charges. We had a L/Cpl up for drunk and striking, which took 56 days.

Well, best of luck. I know this will cross with one from you and I look forward to having the usual laugh.

    Yours ever
    David

In Reserve once more
5th December 1952

It was zero here last night, but with the right clothes I haven't been uncomfortable yet! My sleeping-bag is grand. An American one, which zips up the front and if you give it an extra tug, it all unzips and you can jump out quickly. Now that I am in Reserve, I lie in till late breakfast and read all my papers and make notes before I get up.

I am so happy with my new Brigadier. I had to do a Court of Inquiry today on a Company Commander in another battalion, who got drunk and went out on patrol with one other officer and got captured. His companion got back, badly wounded. I showed the evidence to Joe Kendrew and he took it all off me, said his staff would do all the typing and that sort of thing, so everything is going my way. Aren't I the luckiest man in the world?

Last night we had a jolly evening. For the first time in six months I had all the officers together for dinner. After dinner I happened to pick up the telephone when it rang. It was someone from the Sergeants' Mess, saying that they hadn't any gin and could the Mess Cpl let them have a bottle. So I asked the whole Sgts' Mess to come up and it was a great success – everyone very happy and friendly. Oh, they are a fine bunch of chaps, every one of them.

8th December 1952

I have got a Valor stove in my caravan now and I have had the floor covered, so I am nice and cosy at night – and I have electric lights worked off a battery that is recharged by day, so I can read in comfort in my sleeping-bag – even early in the morning. The last three days have been very hard work, getting all the honours and awards completed, visiting all over the place, conferences, etc, so this morning I had breakfast in bed and had a good doze afterwards. Then I went to lunch at Divisional Headquarters with General West, which was fun and a change. Tomorrow I have to meet the Quarter Master General for ¾ hour and present my Company Commanders.

'The Skins' (5 DGs) leave tomorrow and despite the cold I shall send the Pipes and Drums to play them off. They have been such good friends. One of them said so many nice things to me last night about my men. He said they all noticed what a friendly spirit our chaps have. They always get a cheery 'good morning' as well as a salute from men in the Black Watch.

Everyone is still talking about our battle and the General is putting out a paper about it. Brigadier Joe Kendrew made me go through it with him from start to finish yesterday evening. And I have got all the decorations I asked for. They will be published on Friday out here. Money flows in every day for the men. Another £800 from Comforts Fund – £38 from Pitlochry - £200 from my old home, Taynuilt in Argyll, £15 from here and there. It is wonderful and all easily and well spent. The cinema is going in great style. We built a big hut out of wattle and daub, with ten large heaters in it. It seats 100 and there are always two shows a day, often three. The Comfort Fund projector plus an Army one, allows it to run continuously without breaks between films.

Some of the men lost all their private possessions in the battle;

cameras, notepaper, oil lamps, etc., but I am so rich I shall be able to compensate them for most of it. They deserve every bit of it. I think it is wonderful the spirit they show, in very hard conditions.

8th December 1952

I had your letter of 30th November tonight – by that date you hadn't heard from me since the battle. I can't think what can have happened, but I dare say one or two nights melted together. By now you must have heard, but I don't believe I had much to say when it was all over!

Raas and John Moncrieff have gone off to Kure to visit the wounded. I couldn't go because of the QMG's visit but I will try to go at Christmas time.

I hear that poor John Smart may have to go home as the wound in his arm has damaged a nerve. I hope he won't be a permanent cripple. Angus R.H. is very confident, but I gather that his leg is broken in three places. I do hope he will be OK in the end.

9th December 1952

I am having a rest now. I read a book all the afternoon and there were lots of things I should have been doing, but I just said I wouldn't. It has been such a hectic time and sooner or later one must have a rest.

I had such very nice letters yesterday. One from Neville Blair and the nicest letter I have ever had from an acquaintance, that chap Bill Swannell who was my mule officer in Burma.

28th November 1952

Dear Col

I have been wanting to write to you for a long time, David, after following your activities with great keenness. I would like to have sent you all the press cuttings but I dare say you have them already.

I knew the BW would show up with flying colours more so when I knew you were Commanding. I consider I know you very well and I know you would never give in until you are carried off, only too well I remember the time you stayed in Burma for two weeks with your wound, when you could have been evacuated. How proud I am to have been privileged to have served under your command.

I would have given anything to have been there with you. By your photograph in the 'Red Hackle' Periodicals, Daily and Sunday papers – in fact any reading matter one picks up, when the B W are mentioned, you look still the same, not aged one bit, still that smile and fair moustache. Good luck to you, David, I say. You may, or may not, know that I am back in the Army in Q (Movs). It's a bit different to 'The Watch', but I love to read the 'Hackle' from cover to cover. I sit and live over the past every time I read it – it's a wonderful feeling. You must be very busy doing such an important job. The eyes of the Country are on you.

My love to the Regiment. God bless you, David, may he give you wisdom and guidance to go on to greater things during your arduous task.

Yours,
   Bill Swannell

Visit of the QMG
Today we had the Quarter Master General, Robertson. He was absolutely charming to me and to all the officers and spoke so kindly to us about our battle, and how wonderful our wounded were in hospital, and how refreshing it was to find young men with new ideas, and men who would fight with determination and courage for their Regiment, without any very inspiring 'cause'. I introduced the RSM and he took down his wife's address and said that he would write to her – wasn't that a grand thing? The Sergeants' Mess will be full of it.

He only asked me one surprising question. 'How long do you think a battalion should do in Korea?' I said, 'Well Sir, I have seen some battalions leave *very* tired at the end of a year'.

14th December 1952
I am off to sea with the American Marines for four days – a busman's holiday but a change. For two days the mail has been held up by bad weather your end, but I shall try to have it flown out to me by helicopter. I just can't do without it!

There is a very beastly battle going on to our east. The Koreans are having heavy casualties. I only hope they are inflicting more on the Chinese. They certainly should be, the quantity of shells and bombs that are being expended. Apparently the Koreans go forward very well, but they won't stay in their trenches when they get there.

21st December 1952
It is a lovely sunny Sunday morning and my cold is much better so I was able to enjoy the Christmas Carols. The big Mess Tent was filled and the men sang very well – particularly some of the Welsh chaps we got when we first came out here. Padre Tom Nicoll was in great form and preached well. He asked me to read Hebrews 2 from Moffat. 'What is man that thou art mindful of him'. Have you read Joab's conversion to Christianity? I read the first half of

it in the Picture Post – of all papers! And look forward to the next issue. Thought it was very good.

I am now going off to luncheon with the 1st Royal Tank Regiment who relieved the 5th DGs and will finish this when I return – it wasn't lunch, but just Rum Punch Cocktails – quite fun. I spent the afternoon reading on my bed – nice and warm, but coughing a lot.

21st December 1952

You must not be hurt that you haven't been shown the Queen Mum's letter. You have been a long way away and nobody has been able to keep track of your movements. I haven't had a copy of it yet and it doesn't bother me a scrap. I hope I hear more before the New Year so that I can tell the men when I go round their dinners.

Another lovely day and I have been working all morning in my caravan with the door wide open, but the stove on. I do hate Valor stoves. They make your eyes smart so in a confined space.

Afterwards I walked the General and Brigadier all over the hills to see the men at work. They were both in very good form. All the men were laughing and working with a will – marching flat out in the very cold air – a joy to see them. It went splendidly.

David Severn and another officer arrived today and I hear that four more subalterns are being flown from England.

26th December 1952

We had a great Carol Service in the morning – terrific singing and a proper choir trained by 'C' Company leading it. The men's dinners were really excellent – the Queen Mother's plum puddings from Chivers couldn't have been better. They all had lots of presents from the Comforts Fund and many other sources, torches, cakes, cigarettes, chocolate and so on. In the afternoon we went down to Tockchon to see off our very good Gunners – a great send off, with a light aeroplane swooping over the Station, bombing the train with rolls of lavatory paper; the Pipes and Drums played them away despite the bitter cold. I drove back from there to our 'B' Echelon, Nobby Clark's camp, and there spent the evening at their sing-song. It was great fun – and returned to find a lovely bunch of letters – Rhoddy, Bill Bradford, Pat Douglas and as usual – the ever loving – and a Ronson lighter-pencil from mother. A lovely Christmas!

So glad to hear that General Keith was nice to you. He said a very nice thing in his speech at that last dinner in Perth. 'One thing I know, your CO won't let you be buggered about by any bloody

Generals.' Don't be hard on General McMicking. He is doing very well for us at the War Office.

27th December 1952

My dear Rhoddy

I have had so many letters in the last week or two – in fact I have heard from everyone I like hearing from. It's great fun. I expect we are both doing much the same sort of thing this week. Everyone seems to be madly funny through the alcoholic cloud. The Martinis get drier and drier, because the ice won't melt, people sing louder and worser as the nights follow each other. I haven't sung 'Toni' yet but only because the band can't play it and I can't sing without a band. South Pacific, which was the last thing I went to in London with Jean, is my craze of the year, but the tunes are very difficult. My 'Mountain Band' knows them all now, but the accordionist usually falls over backwards too early in the evening! Anyway we are having some fun.

Best of everything in 1953.

Yours ever,

David

31st December 1952

This is my last letter of 1952. What a year it has been! Such lovely times at Perth and Finningham till June and then both hectically coping with our different tasks for the rest of the year. May the second half of 1953 be as nice as the first half of 1952.

Yesterday the General came to present the medals and a television team recorded his speech and filmed the parade. It will be shown in England in about ten days time. The men looked quite smart and did their drill well despite very little practise. Brigadier Joe turned up in his jersey and apologised for not being smart enough! The night before he had been giving a talk about things to my officers and said that we were the 'backbone of the Brigade'. We must keep it up to the very end, but it is going to be hard work to maintain the same standard for another six months and we are now starting to lose trained officers and NCOs who are going home, having finished their time.

I am now only waiting to hear what the Queen Mum wrote in her letter to General Neil. Perhaps I may get it in tonight's mail so that I can give her message to the men on New Year's Day. It would be just the thing.

2nd January 1953

The festivities have gone off splendidly. No trouble from any quarter worth mentioning. The Sergeants' Mess was really first class. We had *our* dinner party on New Year's Eve in the Officers'

153

Mess and great fun it was. The next morning we attended the Final of the Inter-Company Football Competition at 11am. At 12.30 we all gathered in the Sergeants' Mess as customary, and then to sally forth to serve the men their dinners.

My word what a spread! Masses of cakes and Scotch Bun, nuts and fruit and great helpings of everything. I had to go round each Company and say a few words and at one Company there were the television people again. I hope I didn't make a mess of it! I hadn't prepared anything. At 3pm I went off to visit the CO of the Princess Pats and at 4pm I was with Trudeau of the French Canadians. These are my neighbours at present. At 5.30pm I called on Brigadier Joe and had a good gossip with him and of course another drink or two. Back to the Mess at 7pm to welcome the Sergeants. We had a first class buffet dinner. The Drummy was a bit unsteady on his feet so we two sat down to ours. Poor old Drummy. He was very sad at leaving but he had the most wonderful send-off. After supper we took it in turn, first an officer then a Sergeant, to sing a song. I couldn't sing because I had lost my voice on the Medal Presentation Parade – so I was lucky. We made the Drummy sing the Ball of Kirriemuir and everyone put in verses when he had done all he knew – oh, what verses came out!!! Deep purple!!! Two very nice officers and three valuable Sergeants were also doing their last day in Korea and I was sorry to lose them. They were all piped away early this morning.

I shall be in a bit of a fix for officers for the next few weeks. The wounded ones aren't back yet and their replacements are being flown out but haven't arrived. It takes about two weeks to fly out by RAF. David Severn arrived from Kenya but promptly went down with pneumonia and the other fellow who was in the same ship split his head open in the swimming bath and was put in hospital. David Campbell went off today to command the Divisional Leave Centre and neither Pat Douglas nor Larry Trotter have yet returned from the Battle School. However, we shall be very strong again by the end of January.

4th January 1953

I think all the young here know that Bruce Hamilton is said to be after Mary Walters. Andy Watson told them. I heard from Bernard tonight – just a short note, and got lots of wires yesterday and the day before.

The 'Kings' left the whole area in the most terrible state. The dug-outs are all covered with soot because they have been burning wicks in tins of diesel oil instead of buying lamps. There are refuse dumps everywhere and after being in the position for three months, the trenches and fortifications are still deplorable. The poor old BW have been told, very nicely by the Brigadier, to put things right – and by Jove, in only two days there is a remarkable difference. This morning were brought in 180 40-gallon petrol barrels, and loads and loads of other salvage, just as one example. Everyone knows what is required of them and they set to with a will. I myself went off with the Brigadier in a light plane to see the Second Korean Corps on the once famous Castle Hill, where the Gloucesters fought their famous battle. We went to examine *their* tunnels and see how they compared with mine. They have been at it for two months, ever since their blood bath, and they have done a vast amount of work, but the entrances weren't fortified – mine have a dog leg and a grenade trap so that the enemy can't shoot down them, but theirs just go straight in and wouldn't be tenable if attacked properly in my opinion. It was a nice change and very interesting. I met many interesting people and travelled in comfort.

5th January 1953

Things going ahead apace here now and everyone much more comfortable. Only the odd shell each day. I have got a new type of stove in my caravan which doesn't make my eyes sting and it can be regulated really low, so that I can leave it on at night without any risk of suffocation.

7th January 1953

I had a good defensive Fire Plan exercise at 3am this morning. Trying to train up my new Gunners, and my word they need it – and now know it! I wonder what the enemy thought about it all on this previously quiet sector?

The sun shines, bulldozers roar, compressors rattle away, everyone is hard at work and pleased with their efforts. Thank goodness for lots of work. It keeps everyone keen and happy. If you sit back, everyone gets bored or takes to the bottle.

I hope by now you have had lots of letters from me. I am sorry about that gap when I went to sea and it was very bad not sending you a wire for Christmas, but I was in a whirl and thought that my letters would all be waiting for you at Brechin.

There was nearly a disaster two days ago. My stove went wrong and the whole caravan was black with soot and had to be washed down, but the photograph of you all survived unspoilt.

8th January 1953

There is nothing much to write about. Life just goes on, visiting companies early in the morning a few days a week, a conference or two, going off to have a bath and so on. This morning there is a thick fog so all the sentries will have to remain out or be relieved.

We shall be sending home one or two officers and Sergeants for the Coronation. It will be a hard job to pick them, but I shall try to find married men who deserve the reward. Probably I shall have to let one or two of the selected ones draw lots, but I am not sure yet.

I hear my Marine friends have had some success near Panmunjom so I shall ask if I may motor over there tomorrow and visit them. It is not good for me to do nothing.

12th January 1953

I had the Brigadier all this morning. He is a nice chap. It was biting cold, but bright sun. Noses, ears and moustaches were all frozen and after our tour round we had, and enjoyed, two very good whisky-Macs. He comes up early tomorrow to do one of the forward companies.

There is nothing whatever to write about really. I went over to the Marines yesterday, who are now in the line near Panmunjom. Charlie Barnett's Battalion had just done rather a good show there, killing quite a number of Chinese, but they are all a bit on edge and not quite knowing what is going to happen next. I must try to think up who else I can get to visit, but this afternoon I am going to read 'No Highway' - another Nevil Shute.

12th January 1953

I have a sad thing to tell you and ask you about. Today I heard that it *might* be Canal Zone and not Tripoli. I wrote a strong letter to General Neil and asked that the correspondence be put on the SECRET list as the effect on morale would be so great, and that I would certainly resign if we went to the Canal after this! I am sure I am right and I hope you agree with me. I must make a big case for my men, and for myself.

15th January 1953

I am determined that the battalion shall not be stationed in the Canal Area after being out here. It just isn't fair. The Canal is probably worse than here. Here we have a job to do. There you are just in a concentration camp. The men must be able to relax and mix with the civilian population after a whole year of work and segregation – me too! The men of all other nations go straight back to their homeland and blow off steam.

19th January 1953

You ask about the changes here. Keith Denniston got Malcolm's company and he does it very well. Scott Macdonald got Angus R.H.'s and does it much better than the former. I have fixed everything with Pat Douglas. He came back just to say farewell. Between you and me, I really prefer Raas. He is harder working and more efficient. Pat is better in Command. In a week or so, we all go out to camp – another upheaval, but a change. And changes make work and work makes the time pass quickly, so I don't mind.

20th January 1953

Nobby's laundry has got into a terrible state. They have stolen or lost most of my lovely coloured handkerchiefs and everything comes back grey, and much dirtier than I send it.

I am now busy writing a paper for the Director of Infantry, General Matthews. He visited me after our battle and wrote the other day and asked me to do this for some conference in March. Nic is looking up all the facts for me but I must try to make it all clear and brief.

22nd January 1953

No, nothing happened to me on 12th when my photo fell down. I went round my forward companies in distinguished company – the Brigadier and the Commander Royal Engineers.

Don't bother to send me expensive handkerchiefs. The Woolworth ones are lovely. They soon get spoilt in the wash or lost. The Comforts are sending us dozens, as you know, and I shall get my share from now on.

We have just got some *real* whisky – 94 Proof! It's quite a different thing to what we have become accustomed in recent years. It's export of course. I do wish you were her to sip it with me. I am drinking it neat because the water is so chlorinated. I'll have a good drink of water alone when I do my teeth.

24th January 1953

What are we going to give Hugh for his Birthday this year? Is he old enough for his first bicycle? It is awful to think there is only another year and a half before he has to go to school. How we shall miss him. And Mary looks so grown up in the last picture.

I am busy now choosing officers and men to send home for the Coronation. Isn't it a pity I can't send myself? I think it will be

Angus Irwin, Neil Lennox and Peter Carthew – but this must be a secret until it is settled, and of course may be upset if there is an offensive before the end of March when they are due to leave. They will form our Advance Party to the Middle East.

25th January 1953

It is Sunday morning and I have just time to write to you before Church. After that I shall be in another state of whirl for 48 hours. Everything always seems to happen all at one time – after lunch a party with PPCLI – drinks and buffet luncheon. You remember they were the chaps who took over from us at the HOOK. This evening, Burns Night supper with the RSM and the few Sergeants he has near the Command Post. Very early tomorrow Colonel de German of the French Battalion with all his Company Commanders. Lunch with the 1st Battalion Australian Regt for Australia Day. Brigade Conference at 5pm.

27th January 1953

Peter Buchanan got into a non-sleeping state out here and I cured him in two nights by keeping him talking (which is only too easy) until quite late at night. Poor you, you have no-one to talk to.

I am surrounded by Frenchmen and some of them are so amusing – I have a nice young officer with a beard, called Poupard! He makes me laugh so much and I him too. He is Foreign Legion and a very fine fellow.

31st January 1953

For 3 or 4 days I have been very busy with the French. Grand fellows and we have made a very happy liaison. Tonight they gave *us* a party. My word, what food – the most delicious dinner – many courses and then some singing. They were all so pleased to be away from their American masters who do not laugh and make fun. My officers make fun so well and are wonderful with strangers. I think that it is natural to the Scots. I have to set the pace at first, but afterwards everything comes naturally and I can sit back and enjoy myself. Colonel de German pinned his Regimental badge onto my coat when we were photographed – he said that never in Korea had they met such hospitality, such good dug-outs, such clean positions. Early tomorrow morning I depart to the rear areas for 6 weeks.

You ask about the other British Regiments. Yesterday the General sacked their 2 i/c and three Coy Comds of one battalion. I don't have any friends there. The other battalion is better, but only have a few good officers. Bob Moran of the 'Dukes' is a friend of mine. He is their 2i/c. We were Under Officers in the same Coy at Sandhurst, but he is very intense. Nic tells me that Colonel Bunbury has an A Mess and a B Mess at his Comd Post. He and his 2i/c, the Adjutant and the IO, the 'bridge four', (the gentlemen) in A Mess. The National Service officers are in B Mess. They are heading for trouble if they are attacked by the Chinese. He might lose his battalion. The Chinese aren't playing bridge.

Neil will be so proud when I send him the 'Petou', the magazine of the French Battalion here. They fought a very fine battle at 'Arrowhead' where great deeds were done. My friend Poupard was the Company Commander who bore the brunt of it and he has told me all about it. They were not so expert as we on the HOOK and so had more casualties, but they were magnificent. Our late Brigadier has said that my battle was 'a classic of its kind and size.'

In Reserve once more

1st February 1953

My dear Rhoddy

We got into reserve today – all three Brigades, for the first time in 18 months. I hope it doesn't mean they are going to fatten us up for an offensive. For a week or more we have been sending back parties to hack away at the rock-hard ground to make flat places for the tents. Well we are here, and for six weeks or so will not have to be all the time on the end of a wireless or telephone and 90% can sleep the night through instead of 60%. This morning when I saw the covering patrols away I felt sure that we should have our first cases of frost bite before they got to this end in their open lorries – but no. They were still laughing when they got here and no ears or noses quite dead. What wonderful chaps! We handed over to the French battalion in the 2nd American Division. They were delighted to find dug-outs on reverse slopes and positions in depth instead of the American MLR – not so the Dutch on the left, who wanted to start digging MLR at once, but I think Jack Frost will stop them doing it. It is 2ft deep now.

We had great fun with the Frogs. They had never been treated with such consideration, had never had mine-fields properly handed over or found as clean an area in more than a year. Our Gunners had to stay in the line as the Div Gunners are supporting a ROK Div and it was out of the question to move all our dumps of 25 pdr for 6 weeks. Anyway only the OPs are really in the line. The others live in considerable comfort. Oh what wonderful cooks the French had! For a Mess of 12 at the CP they had 3 cooks. Everything was rather strong with garlic, but damned good all the same. There were some very odd smells this morning before we got away!

I have found a good cook, whom I sent last week to do 3 days with the Indian Field Ambulance – great dividend and it enabled me to hold my own with the French. He taught them to cook curry and they taught him to make soup – and next week I shall send him back to learn more – even if we have to go onto 'all in strew' for a few days, its worth it! Anyway he cooked for 40 tonight and everything was hot and that is saying something in a very large tent and below zero. I can hear all the officers howling their heads off as I write, which is a sure sign of a good dinner, but I admit we also have some 94 proof 'White Heather'.

Tomorrow the Training Conferences and such like start. It won't be much of a rest for me. But I have a good Brigadier in Joe Kendrew and he thinks the world of the Watch. The General is insisting that I take 100 Korean soldiers into the ranks. I said I would certainly do so if I could have a 4th Sec in each PL: or a 4th PL in each Coy, but he insists that I 'spread' them, 2 men to each section – and I am well over strength! We still hear a lot of gunfire back here – ours I hope. It will be hell if the Americans lose either of our key points, the HOOK or pt 355. Eighteen months ago they lost 355 within a few days and we had to re-fortify the damned thing. Good night.

Yours ever
  David

1st February 1953

Dear General Neil

It was such good news that Bill and Mick have got Brevets and that Neville will be in Scotland for the next 3 years. I wish I could be! I am getting into that very difficult position, not knowing where to send my boy to school. I was offered a vacancy at Belhaven next year, but I have to accept or refuse it within a month – and in a month I shall be in no better position to judge than today, so I have turned it down.

We handed over to the French battalion and it all went very well. They were delighted to find positions with depth instead of the American MLR and they said that they had never found such good dug-outs or such a clean area since they came to Korea. Their gratitude was quite embarrassing. Their Advance Parties came through my CP for three or four days and we did our best to feed and wine them. The last night they said we must be their guests and they gave us a wonderful dinner. Oh what cooks! and plenty of good wine. It was all a very happy affair and we have made many new friends.

Yours sincerely
  David

2nd February 1953

Pat Douglas arrives in a few minutes to say goodbye. We are lunching at Div HQ: He sleeps here tonight and leaves tomorrow. Lucky dog!

5th February 1953

I heard from Jim Hutchison yesterday (MP for Glasgow Central). He apparently wants to take up some of the things I mentioned in my letter to him – mostly things like better cookers, lamps and trench heaters. He told me how they had asked you over to see the TV.

Pat says he has never known the reputation of the Regiment stand so high in the back areas. In the hospital, if they have a man who is very down on his luck, they put a BW soldier on either side of him and that does the trick! He was very impressed with the feeling in the Mess here, the cheerfulness and liveliness of what are usually 'dumb National Service Officers'. They are very ordinary fellows individually, but we have got them to come out of their shells and talk and sing.

We are fairly well settled in now and tomorrow must get down to work again – training new NCOs and young officers mostly.

7th February 1953

I have got my cook to make very nice cabbage salads like the French and the curries get better and better, the roasted meat less over cooked. If only I could get him to make soups like theirs. Anyway, we are all putting on weight madly.

9th February 1953

Well we have started work again today. I am trying hard to train young regulars as future NCOs. Geordie Chalmer is teaching them with Rass MacRae supervising and the Adjutant, RSM and QM at call for special subjects. David Severn is back and quite well again. It doesn't take long to be cured of pneumonia nowadays. General Van Fleet's successor is here today but only the Pipes and Drums and VIPs have to meet him. We had a fire in the Band tent the other day and lost two tenor drums which we are busy trying to replace.

12th February 1953

I am delighted that you sent me Aunt Cecily's address, because today I got yet another letter from her. I can only read the first paragraph which says 'Your ears should have been burning badly recently judging by the way your outstanding military ability was being extolled by someone in "The War Office"'.

I had good news from Rhoddy this evening. It looks as though he will get a Brigade. He was going to command one in Jordan but it didn't fit in with his time of departure from the Battalion. At the moment he is commanding his own Brigade because the Brigadier is in Hospital and he will be doing so during the period of several big exercises leading up to manoeuvres. I do hope he does well. I have been made a substantive Lt Colonel, so that's one hurdle cleared.

Brigadier Joe continues to show us every favour and is always asking me to drive with him or comes to have a chat in my caravan. On Saturday we are giving a Buffet Luncheon party for 150 people. Everyone has to be asked by name – none of this business of the Commanding Officer and 3 – so every officer can have whoever he wants. We got a gallon of concentrated red wine from our French friends and so we are going to have Turks Blood as a cocktail – champagne and red wine, better than Black Velvet. The Pioneers and lots of officers are making our tents nice and we are going to have a huge prawn curry and cold turkey and ham and salads. Australians, English and some Canadians, Americans and French will all be there as well as some staff officers. They are all thrilled about it (our chaps I mean).

Nic is away on a well earned leave to Tokyo. I miss his help but there isn't very much doing at the moment, whereas later on we shall be doing some big exercises. Raas is in very good form and Peter Buchanan doing a good job with the MT.

15th February 1953

We saw 'Scaramouche' too. Each Sunday we have a show in the Mess. The Sergeants have it on a Saturday. The men have it all the rest of the week, two shows nightly, but only one on Saturdays and Sundays. There is no mail tonight so the cinema will pass the time. I am proud that you have heard nice things said about me and particularly so if the origin of the report was Nobby Clark who yesterday had 23 years service. He must have served many COs. The other night he and I were watching the subalterns sky larking at the end of dinner and he said how nice it was to see them all so confident and happy, instead of creeping quietly out of the Mess to their beds.

We had such a gay party yesterday. I was so busy that I didn't get a chance to eat any of the good things but we had buckets of 'Turks blood', which was a novelty out here and was voted by all the greatest success. I had a rest in the afternoon and then had to dine with the 'Dukes' and hit the high spot about 2am – rugger scrums, singing and goodness knows what. The General left before the rough house, which was apparently all my doing, but enjoyed by all. We ended up dancing so hard that we went through the floor!! Today I had yet another party, with 3 Royal Australian Regiment. It wasn't a good one, but we all laughed a lot about yesterdays happenings. Driving back with Cpt Dillon, he told me that the 'diggers' were all asking him about me. He said 'Oh the old man's alright.' They said 'We think he is the outstanding one out here.' I said to Dillon 'You mean the best Battalion.' He said 'No, you Sir.' I mustn't get a swollen head must I! I tell you all these things, just as I would if I came back from Barracks to lunch.

We are going to go through rather a testing time this month and I shall have to try very hard to do well. One exercise after another, each Battalion umpiring another, each Brigade doing enemy against another. That is what happens when you are in reserve. The staff must be kept busy. Nic, my right hand will be back tomorrow and I don't think Raas wants any R&R leave. David Arbuthnott also comes back tomorrow so the signals side, which is so very important, ought to work.

17th February 1953

We have just returned from a fiendishly cold exercise and we seem to have one nearly every other day for the next 10 days. If we aren't being exercised we shall be umpiring or doing enemy for some other unit, which is really worse. I hear that George Green, who was my CO in India has got 152 Brigade at Inverness. Cluny MacPherson who was Commanding it, fell down dead when he was playing squash with his son. Wasn't that awful, and I hear that Pat CP is bad again and in Edinburgh Hospital. I must rush for dinner.

22nd February 1953

I heard from Charlie Anderson this evening. They have apparently bought the house in Mull. Presumably he is thinking of retiring. Said he couldn't stand the pace of Perthshire but had everything in Mull for the children's upbringing. Neither of them much liking Hong Kong but naturally loving being together.

25th February 1953

I have had such a good day. The big exercise went perfectly. All my communications worked like a dream and my Companies went roaring through the breach with tanks and guns in grand co-ordination. The General tried to hold things up, but I heard that he was convinced that the supporting fire and the momentum of the break through really was unstoppable and eventually let us go, with the result that the exercise was finished at 2.30pm instead of at 5 o'clock. The officers and men were all delighted with themselves, and tonight, after a curry dinner, we had the cinema into the mess and had a good laugh at a farce. Yesterday morning I spent two hours signing my name on endless copies of applications for men's families to join us. It amused me, while I was doing this almost automatic action, to see how many had produced children before they were married – and one an Officer! I have a few gay days ahead starting on St David's Day. The Royal 'Vingt Douze' Regt, buffet lunch; the 25 Canadian Inf Bde the next day and dinner with the Durham Light Infantry the next.

27th February 1953

Yesterday it was quite hot and all the paddy fields started to thaw. There was hard frost again at night and this morning there was a heavy mist which I am afraid will interfere with my demonstration of mortar shooting. Neil Lennox and Peter Carthew leave today for the Coronation and about 50 other good men and those who have finished their time. Next month I lose another 80, so there is masses of work to do – signing hundreds of documents, interviewing them all about their future and so on. It is going to be hard work to keep up the standard with chaps like Angus Irwin going away. He leaves by air on about 30th March. Rhoddy Willett who was on his way out was taken off the ship and flown home because his father had died. I suppose he is an only son.

28th February 1953

Just think of it tomorrow is MARCH. Only 4 more months in this country and then perhaps home with you in July. We posted off all the documents for married quarters yesterday. Do you think it will be the Villa Fanny? That would be nice for the children wouldn't it. I have been getting up at 3am and going to bed only for an hour or two each night. One exercise after another and so many conferences! Last night I got back at midnight to find *four* letters from you, and one from Neil.

Poor old Neil isn't very well. He says his heart gives him some trouble. He wrote me such a nice letter. I told him all about the Battalion Française out here and sent him their magazine, which made him very proud as many of the Officers belonged to the Foreign Legion.

It is getting very muddy. It still freezes every night but the sun gets quite hot by 10am and the roads in the camp get very cut up. I must go down to the bath tent beside the stream and have a good soak before my lecture this evening. My hair is full of grit from the last four days driving about in convoys.

4th March 1953

I had a letter from Rhoddy tonight. Doesn't think he is going to get his leave when he hoped, as his Brig and another CO are going to Warminster on the Infantry Commanders Conference. He repeated rather a nice story of a Jordan Officer who was attached to them for an exercise. Rhoddy was questioning him about other Arab armies and when at last he asked about the Lebanese Army, the Jordan Officer replied 'Ah! the Lebanese, they are like women . . . you know, Colonel, just for fun!' Rhoddy, of course, was highly delighted.

He says that the food is so bad in his mess that he no longer goes to dinner, but has soup and fresh orange juice in his rooms – and partly too, I think, to reduce his figure which I understand is now enormous. It is so hard to take any exercise in the desert and Rhoddy never walks if he can help it, even in pleasant surroundings, unless he is carrying a gun.

5th March 1953

I had such a pleasant walk this afternoon along the banks which keep back the river from the paddy fields. There was quite a strong breeze and bright sun and all the little Korean children were out playing hop-skip and marbles. It was very pleasant walking on the smooth mud path and I had a lovely think about all the things we will do and games we will play with our children when we meet again. How very kind of Simon to send us a case of whisky.

We are going to have 'Ivanhoe' as our Mess film this week and one evening we are to be entertained by a very good Canadian Band after dinner. They are giving the men an open air concert in the afternoon when it is still warm enough to sit outside.

10th March 1953

Life is rather gloomy here at present; nothing interesting to do; many new men going and coming; training, training, training. We go back into the line about the 1st April and then time will fly and before we know it, we shall be away over the seas. Yesterday it was really lovely and warm, but today it was overcast. We shall probably get some rain before the spring really starts.

12th March 1953

We were all very glad to hear that the Pipe Major may still get the full use of his hand, but it is rotten luck having to have another bit of his leg off. We have one chap out here who has now had this done 3 times, almost too much to bear. The weather has really broken up badly. We had 24 hours of heavy rain and now we have an inch of snow and slush. Anyway, thank goodness we aren't in the trenches. I am busy trying to write up some more Honours and Awards. They are granting each battalion one gong and two MID for the Coronation list. I am going to put Nobby Clark in for a MBE, Claud Moir and CSM Patterson for the MIDs. We haven't been told how many Coronation Medals we are to get but I expect it will be the usual five. I shall give them to men who have been put in for higher distinctions but haven't got them, so that they can be really proud of their Coronation Medals.

13th March 1953

We had a very jolly evening with the Canadian Military Band to amuse us. The Brig came to the dinner and Colonel Bunny Austin, an Australian CO who was with me at Haifa in the war. Raas asked the Brigade Major and another staff officer from Bde HQ! Tonight I am invited to pay a return visit to Brig Joe who has the departing Canadian and Australian Brigadiers dinning with him. It was such a lovely day. I walked the hills all morning and watched Claud Moir's company firing their weapons and doing mock attack all afternoon. Our return to the line has again been postponed but we are going back to that beastly HOOK for a month.

15th March 1953

My date for substantive Lt Colonel has been back dated to 6th May so I shall end my term in command in May '55. Then heaven knows what they can do with me. I know I am no good as a staff officer. It might be the time to leave.

17th March 1953

I had such a nice letter from Jim Hutchinson (MP) saying that he had shown mine to Anthony Head (Secretary of State), who was 'immensely interested' and was going to take 'ginger action' in some of the matters I mentioned, not a word to anyone of course! Tonight, St Patrick's night, I am going to dine with Patrick O'Donovan of the Sunday Times and afterwards may go on to another party to join two girls! – one from 'Bless the Bride' and one called Joan Seaton – a cabaret artist. They are giving a show in these parts. I introduced them to the General at a buffet luncheon the other day and he did the Boogie-Woogie with one of them, much to everyone's amusement. They are quite good company.

Warned for the Hook
19th March 1953

I have had a long day on the HOOK and a successful one. Such a nice American CO, and he has a much better battalion than any I have met before. We shall get a *very* good hand over there, if they don't have another battle before we arrive. It is *teeming* with rain. Nearly as heavy as in the summer. Tomorrow, and perhaps for days, the roads will be impossible. It's cats and dogs, but much warmer. Thank heaven I did my reconnaissance today instead of slithering and sliding on all fours tomorrow.

26th March 1953

It was very disappointing when they changed the date on which we go back into the line. Raas is in Japan now and I was to have gone next week and would have had such fun buying you a pearl ring which would have been in time for your birthday. Now there is no hope for going till May. Angus Irwin left yesterday so you will be seeing him very soon. I shall miss him greatly.

The front is very noisy again now that the winter is over. I do wish these blooming Russians would agree to call it off. I have seen a good deal of the Korean country people while we have been in reserve. (There are no civilians allowed forward of the Kansas Mountains.) They are charming and happy people. Very tough and with a great sense of humour. One day I was searching the hill side with your field glasses, when I heard some old Korean men beside me laughing. I gave them a turn with the glasses and they were highly delighted – I can't tell you what giggles they got. The Brigadier was with me and took photographs of the incident.

Last night the Brig asked if he might attend my tactical discussion. I have been holding one a week and they are popular. The last one was a great success, 5.30 to 8 and even when I closed it for dinner, they all gathered round the blackboard to continue their arguments. The Brig was delighted.

30th March 1953

I have got a hard period ahead, so make allowances for me if I miss a letter or two. I always try to write as often as I can, but sometimes I have nothing to say, except what is boiling inside and which is better unsaid.

31st March 1953

I may have written you rather a depressed letter last night – I hope not – but after doing much too much thinking for my poor brain, I felt rather low. Was very cheered this morning when the RSM told me that he had heard a broadcast saying that the Russians had agreed to the Mexican Peace proposal and wanted to reopen discussions. I wonder if there is anything in it? I do hope so. It all seems so futile and the poor Marines are having a *very* bloody battle – for the last four days.

2nd April 1953

I am going out with Keith Denniston's Company on a night patrolling exercise. At 6am I go up to show the Brigadier round the HOOK and we probably won't be back till after lunch. He is then coming to our Good Friday service which is at 6.30pm.

John Taylor has got some extraordinary Japanese wooden puzzles which are quite exasperating. They are the same idea as Hugh's Humpty-Dumpty, but terribly difficult. They do make wonderful things in wood.

6th April 1953

All is going well up at the HOOK. Activity has subsided considerably since the 5 days of attacks in the Marine sector, just to the West. They had a very tough time poor fellows, and many casualties, but of course inflicted many more on the Chinese who had to attack them. I watched quite a lot of it from the old HOOK, till visibility was quite blotted out by smoke and dust. Now the papers are all full of more talks at Panmunjom, and it really does look as though things are moving to a settlement with a new Government in Russia. I do hope they are quick so that there is no more needless loss of life. Of course, shelling and bombing goes on till the armistice is signed and nightly patrol actions take place all along the front. From your letter it seems that Angus Irwin had got home by the 26th March! We can't think how he did it, unless in a Comet. It certainly makes me envious hearing of him and Angus R.H. busy testing beds! and Pat!!

We have had two peaceful days and I feel much rested. On Saturday we won the Divisional Football Cup. We only got equal in the last 2 minutes and won the second goal in extra time. The men were shouting their heads off and most of the Officers lost their voices – bonnets were flung in the air. Tonight David Severn has heard that he drew a ticket in the Irish sweepstakes – so he gets about £400 and we shall have Turks Blood for dinner!

7th April 1953

It is Easter Day and a lovely day too. No frost last night and I had a late breakfast in nothing more than a flannel shirt and winter trousers. The birds are singing their heads off and in half an hour we shall be doing the same.

8th April 1953

We are now in a staging area just behind the HOOK. We had a very dusty drive up this afternoon and we take over just before dawn tomorrow. Everyone is in very good heart, despite the fact that they will just be in the open tonight. I have got the Cinema projector up here, so they will have a film in a little time, which will while away the time a bit. Things are fairly quiet in the line and may they remain so.

So glad that you had Mrs Scott again. He and I had a very wild party the other night. We won the Divisional and Brigade football competitions. In the evening the team was invited to the Sergeants Mess and I had to fill the cup. We were all singing our heads off before long – Nobby Clark and the Padre were my supporters

On the Hook again
10th April 1953

All goes well so far. We had rather a lot of shells at the Command Post yesterday but no damage. The patrols did well and we inflicted some casualties on the enemy. There was quite a heavy attack on the Marines to our West at 4am in the morning but I shall not know any details till this afternoon. It is rather nice being back in our small Mess again. The food is much better and it is much more comfortable than living with 40 others. I am getting all the help I could wish for from Brigadier Joe – extra ammunition, sapper labour, extra mortars and tanks. There is only one plan I put forward, which I hear is not yet passed. I want anti personnel mines to be dropped round the Chinese caves from the air. We can't shoot at the mouths of the caves because of the shape of the hill, which is known as 'Warsaw'. In these caves the enemy is quite safe by day and he can sneak out of them in large numbers at night and surprise us. He had his reserves and First Aid Dressing Station in them when he attacked this position before. If we can get the mines we can make the area almost impossible for him – anyway for large numbers.

Aggressive Defence
12th April 1953

Just a hurried line to tell you that all goes well. We had a very difficult and dangerous patrol to do last night and everything went perfectly. We have driven the enemy from the Warsaw feature by using all available weapons in the best way and only this morning we proved it by putting out a whole platoon in a silent sweep to search what remains of the trenches. The Americans who were here before us took 14 killed and 23 wounded doing the same thing – this morning, not a shot fired! I am delighted and the Brig was very pleased. We did have a few casualties and one man killed on the other flank, but this was due to a few unlucky enemy shells I am trying to deal with these guns and mortars tonight. Tony Lithgow arrived today, plus the whisky, so I must try to find time to write to Simon. I met our new American Corps Commander yesterday and the General made me give him a short talk on the HOOK. He is coming up in a helicopter to visit us some day soon.

I said farewell to a very fine lot of men today – 3 Sergeants and about 80 National Servicemen. What fine fellows they looked. I felt very proud of them. Hard at it now trying to bring their successors up to the same standard.

13th April 1953

I am in the pink, despite very long hours of work. Everyone seems so happy and helpful: troubles just melt away. Today I took Tony L all round the positions and told him all the things I wanted him to do – by asking other people what they were doing and showing them what I wanted them to do. We had breakfast at 10.30 – and what a good breakfast! I gave each little company Mess a bottle of Simon's whisky and they were all so pleased. The rest we will use in the Command Post Mess where we have such heavy expenses with entertaining all the visitors. It really is very kind of him. Everything seems quiet tonight. We had rather a flap last night and I was throwing about artillery and mortar bombs all over the place for a bit, but it was all due to new and inexperienced Corporals, I am convinced, I wasn't taking any chances.

16th April 1953

Everything is going along very well. The work progresses at a great pace and early tomorrow morning General Mike comes up with me to the Hook. I have been given all the things I asked. I got a special allotment of ammunition, which is more than enough and a whole troop of sappers to help with the fortifications. Everyone is very pleased with themselves and much in the public eye, with many visitors to have a look at the 'sharp end'. Yesterday we had four Naval Air Pilots from the 'Glory'. We dressed them up in tin hats and armoured waistcoats and took them round the Hook. The enemy threw in a few mortar bombs, not too close, just at the right moment and the sailors were chuffed – stayed to dinner and had too much to drink. I was able to slip away when I had had enough of them. Today we had Daily Mail and News Chronicle among others and we did the same with them. I went over to the Marines this afternoon – our old friends of last autumn. Of course there were many changes since then. The Americans rotate so quickly and poor fellows they had over 400 casualties in the March fighting. My friend Charlie Bennett has gone as an instructor to the Korean Marine School. His successor is called Duncan but wasn't there today. With a name like that, no doubt he will be asking for the Pipes and Drums who are at present filling sand-bags!!

19th April 1953

Another Sunday and nearly two weeks in the line passed. The fortifications are getting on well and the enemy is busy with propaganda broadcasts – 'Don't shoot at us tomorrow and we won't shoot at you'. We take no notice of course. If they want peace they can have it, but we must not allow them to trick us as they did last year. It is today or tomorrow that the first batch of wounded and sick prisoners should be handed over and we are wondering if one or two of ours taken on the Hook may be among them. The common purple azaleas are coming out all over the burnt and battered hillsides and in some sheltered corners I have found tiny violets and minute strawberry plants, also seen some fine old cock pheasants fighting.

The new Comet air service has started and none of us like it. We would rather have old letters four times a week than recent ones only twice. I heard yesterday that yet another Battalion has gone to Kenya. Doesn't look too good for us! Let's hope General Robertson gets a move on with Neguib. Claud Moir and Peter Buchanan are both worried about their prospects of having their families in Tripoli. The Military Secretary has warned me that they will be wanted on the Staff again in December, which doesn't give them 9 months in Tripoli, which is at present the minimum time you must be in a station if your family is to join you.

22nd April 1953

This morning I went round the Coy of the Dukes which is under my command with Brig Joe. The Company Commander is a fellow called Benny Cavenagh – a very pompous but delightful fellow, with a pendulous stomach and no idea whatever of commanding anything. The Brig and I had a good laugh about him on the way back and the Mess were almost hysterical when I repeated some of his most crashing remarks. Last week for several days I was trying to induce him to send out an ambush and he always found some reason not to do so. Eventually when all valid excuses were exhausted he said 'May I postpone it till tomorrow night as I shall be fully employed today with smearing the clothes with anti-mite!' (The mites which give Korean fever). No wonder some regiments aren't very good!

The lice or nits which pass on Korean Fever are a problem. The Americans throw away a lot of their rations: the rats thrive. Healthy rats are hosts to many lice. The British poison rats causing lice to look for new hosts. Better not to use poison, British are not to be defeated by this argument, so they provide cats to eat rats. No one is to feed the cats so that they *must* eat rats. Cats eat only best parts of rats so that nits are still left to find new hosts. *But* poison *does* work. Cats are driven to find new hunting grounds. Chinese do not have any rations to throw away and they pick up every dead Chinese. Cats get very angry and make awful noises all through the night. Standing patrol on 'Ronson' reports Chinese talking in loud voices. CO orders stonk with 'air burst'. Poor cats!

Tomorrow I go to the station to see the Canadian Artillery away with our Pipers playing.

23rd April 1953

There have been no Black Watch men among the returned POWs. The General went down to see them and said that they were in good heart. One of them told the General that many of the American prisoners seemed 'To just curl up and die'. Our men always rally round each other when one of them is down on his luck and it is such a help. I think I told you the story before, of the way they cure this type of man at the Base Hospital. They just put a Black Watch soldier in the bed either side of him – and it works!

Things go on much the same as before. The daily round of shelling enemy strong points, nightly patrols, air strikes, digging and more digging. I get two new Officers today, a Major Morrison and a 2/Lt Blakeney. I have got one boy named Sandy Younger, who was wounded in the Hook battle who still appears to have shell shock. He goes all queer when a patrol is even mentioned. So I will put him into the Mortar Platoon and hope that will put his mind at rest. There are some very lovely clumps of Forsythia out now and several wild cherries. The Padre tells me he has found some Irises.

24th April 1953

We had a bit of a show last night but it went very well. The Chinese staged three raids on the Divisional front and they succeeded in capturing prisoners in the other ones, but we caught their raiding party good and proper with machine guns and artillery and grenades. They managed to carry away their killed and wounded except one, before our patrol was back on the scene of the action, but he died later in the night. However he had some letters on him so we may get an identification when they have been translated. My men did very well. They were bold and steady and suffered no casualties on the patrol. We did however have three lightly wounded from the 5 or 6 hundred enemy shells which came in during the raid – one Officer Ken Forbes, but he may be back again in a week or two. Brigadier very pleased and I am to have lunch with him to discuss it all.

26th April 1953

Things have settled down nicely. The flare up was apparently due to the heavy troop movements in our rear and the Chinese thought they were going to receive a heavy attack. Last night the Brigadier told me that we have had some intercepted enemy wireless messages translated which shows that they were caught good and proper by my mortar and artillery fire and that they asked their commander for permission to withdraw. We caught them again early last night, just by luck, and could hear them shouting and yelling.

I hear most interesting things about the returning wounded from the General and Brigadier who go to see them as they arrive. Our men have little respect for the Americans who they say 'just can't take it' one of our men said 'They seem to expect Coca Cola and Ice cream in a prison camp'. They talk about 'atrocity marches' – only 10 miles a day, and an old man of over 80 did it without complaint. Our men said that they were not bullied and that the propaganda was very childish. So far none of our men show 'even one red hair' as the Brig put it. Do you remember me telling you about the War Office Team who visited us at Crail and said how our men were being converted to communism? I didn't allow them to speak even to the Officers about it and said they were making mountains out of mole hills, just because some private soldier put a few sentences into his letter home, so that he could gain some privilege – cigarettes or extra food.

28th April 1953

Here it rained hard all night and this morning the trenches were very mucky when I went round, but the leaves have burst their buds and in patches the grass is bursting through the brown and fallen weeds.

The talks at Panmunjom are not making a good start. The Americans are not giving way and personally I think they are quite right – but I know that isn't the popular view in England or in our papers. I have been told that our representatives in China know that the Chinese want peace very badly. They are taking a real caning in the front line and further back and they can't make any progress with their blooming 5 year plan. If the Americans are firm I think they will get reasonable terms and we might even get some compensation for all that we have lost in China. No-one wants the war to drag on, but we don't want to sit here for years waiting for it to break out again – or to sail from here to Indo China. We have got bigger guns on the way and soon the Atomic Shell will be available!! That will fix them!! At the moment I am wondering what will happen on May Day. We must be ready.

29th April 1953

We have had very bitter news today – it is to be the bloody Canal Zone for certain. General Bailey came to see me this morning (The Director General of Personnel Administration) – *mal* administration I think! He told me to let it be known and the ill tidings is now going round in the pouring rain. He said that he could give me no assurance that it would only be for a month or two. So there we are! Blast it!! I have written to Jim Hutchinson (MP) and General McMicking and in a little time, I have no doubt that the Press will pay me a visit and I shall not encourage them to soft pedal anything the men say about it. I think it is absolutely monstrous. No other force in the United Nations army would be asked to go to a concentration camp after a year on active service and they all get very high pay. I am afraid mail nights will be sad occasions for many people from now on. They were all getting so excited about seeing their loved ones again.

30th April 1953

Dear General Neil

This morning we received from General Bailey, Director of Personnel Administration, the bitter news that we are definitely going to the Canal Zone when we leave here in July. He told me that I had better let everyone know and he said that he could give no assurance that it would only be for a month or two. In fact, he gave me to understand that it might even be for a year or more, if no satisfactory settlement could be made with Egypt, – and we all know where talking gets us with Egyptians, Persians and Chinese. This will be a serious blow to my men's morale. I am not sure I shall put it out.

We all appreciate the difficulties with which our government is faced. We know that it was the Socialist Government who reduced the strength of the Infantry by half. But we also know that no other country in the

United Nations Force would ask its soldiers to go to the Canal Zone
concentration camp, after more than a year on active service in Korea.
Well paid as they are, they wouldn't take it.

The Americans are negotiating from a position of strength and so none
of us expect peace to come quickly out here. We are preparing a heavy
retaliation plan for the night of May Day, should the Chinese put down
bombardments as they did in 1952. We are also planning for a grand Feu
de Joie for the Queen on the evening of her Coronation, but this will be
fired into the air I trust.

Yours ever,
  David

30th April 1953

It was so nice to hear of your two enjoyable days at the Races.
It arrived at just the right moment when I was feeling worried
and angry. I had such a desperate day of arguments yesterday
and last night a soldier went off his head and nearly killed Alec
Rattray and put 3 bullets into the tin hat of another soldier (his
hat saved him). Then more arguments all morning. I heard, by
chance, that the date for our relief here had been changed without
my knowledge. The Duke of Wellington's CO had 'fixed' it. The
Brig goes on leave tomorrow, so it was very lucky I discovered it
before his departure. The Dukes haven't done a damn thing since
they came to this country and have been in reserve for over 3
months. Every day in the line in this position is a risk for more
loss of life. Any night there may be a big raid. Nearly every night
there is a small probe. We have taken more casualties than anyone
since the Gloucesters – and I don't see why the Dukes shouldn't take
a share for a bit – They have 1200 men, nearly 400 more than us!!

3rd May 1953

I am afraid I have missed a day or two. Things haven't been going
too well, but now everything is fine. My patrol under Sgt Hay was
a great success last night – no casualties and all the information we
wanted obtained, the enemy caves closely examined and no-one
has been able to do it for months. The Americans, poor chaps, tried
so hard to do it and lost so many men in their attempts. May my
luck and my plan just hold for one more week. There still remains
one even harder task, but it doesn't seem so hard after last night.
Last night was Chinese New Year and everyone was expecting
one of the sore points to be attacked. It came on the Canadians in
the sector which I held in January. They took a severe knock I am

175

afraid, but full details are not yet available. The Canadians never seem to be very ready; they don't patrol well at all. Two nights ago at this very point they had 75 yards of their defensive barbed wire removed from under their noses! That should have been a good enough warning, don't you think?

4th May, 1953

A quiet night, except that a Chinese patrol on my Warsaw feature had a battle with itself. I had just gone off to bed and no-one woke me – neither did they mortar the Chinese, to add more confusion, which I should have done.

Today we got into our 'Jungle Green' cotton clothing. So summer is really here. It is still quite cold at night but some hardy ones have started bathing in the afternoons. Only too soon we shall be sweltering once more.

5th May, 1953

I am anxiously waiting, for a report from my patrol. They have been out now for two hours and we can't speak to them on the wireless, for fear of the noise giving them away to the enemy. They are crawling down a long spur to see if the enemy are working on some caves about 400 yards from our lines. This afternoon I shelled the caves with Howitzers and in the evening dropped some 1000lb bombs on them – by mistake! The Americans wouldn't bomb them because they considered them too near to our own lines, so I gave them as the target some more caves which were the other side of Warsaw. Of course they bombed the ones they said they couldn't – and I was delighted! Now young Clasey is on his way – I hope on his way back – to see what he can see. As I write this a report has come in from Tony Lithgow that Crowe can hear Chinese talking on RONSON – what is he to do that won't upset Clasey's patrol. I say 'turn on tank searchlight and fire only small arms if Chinese seen'. Tony say 'Thank you out' and now we wait for a moment – to see whether Chinese are really there or whether it is wild cats making love!! Oh I do wish this patrol would come in soon, but I must just keep fingers crossed and trust that he does it well. Good luck to him! Things hotting up now – mortars to fire soon and perhaps more.

6th May, 1953

I have put in my application for leave. I have no idea what kind of reception it will get, but I feel that I have done more than enough work to deserve it. Mind you I don't think it will be a very long one, but I would do anything to get home to see you even for a few days.

We are having some difficult patrols to do just now. Young Michael Clasey did a very good one two nights ago and brought back some first class information after clawing through 3 belts of barbed wire out and in. Unfortunately two of his men were very badly wounded by a mine when they were nearly home and they both died. Last night Gray was in command of another patrol and his Sergeant, Edmonston (the battalion's goal keeper) did very well and killed some of the Chinese. Gray had bad luck – a bullet through the leg when the action was nearly over. He was able to walk back and I have no doubt that his family will be quite pleased if he is in hospital till we leave!

Only a week to go now and I am doing all I can to keep everyone out of trouble by using fire power instead of men. The Americans did the latter and lost nearly 200 here in 2 months.

3rd Battle on the Hook
8th May, 1953

We have had another battle – not such a heavy one as last time thank God! This time the enemy tried to come in without a preliminary bombardment. He got to within 20 yards of our trenches and there was some hand-to-hand fighting. We put down everything we have got and it all went splendidly from that point of view – but sadly we lost two very fine officers. The battle lasted from 2 am till dawn.

I shudder to think what will be in the Sunday papers. It just so happened that we had the correspondent of the News of the World spending the night with us. He seemed a very nice fellow and I did what I could to induce him to keep his report in good taste. Of course he has got a scoop and no doubt will make the best of it.

Everyone in very fine fettle. I must say I am very tired but very proud of them all. My Brigadier is on leave – thank goodness; it is one less person to talk to. Tonight things are quiet. At the moment I have my old friend Sgt Tim Hay out on Ronson, picking up one dead Chinese and one dead Jock and some equipment which was dropped out there this morning. We have spent the day mending the damage to trenches, getting men to the baths and to have a good sleep. Only four days to go!

I must now write my report to General Neil if I can keep my eyes open for another half hour – but I must, because things are just starting up again. 'Lights on' 'Green Finger flashing to Rome'. That's the jargon. 'Enemy in front of me sending message to their Headquarters'. *Answer* Mortar fire on both and make it hot.

177

10th May, 1953

It is very early in the morning but I won't be able to write to you later because I am off to Div HQ to give a lecture on our battle to the General and all the assembled COs. The Brig came back from leave last night and heard the story in outline and went straight off to the General to tell him what a fine show he considered it to be. He said he had never before known anyone build up such an excellent fire plan or have such control. Wasn't that good? I do hope I can make it all clear to them. It all happens so quickly at the time with information and orders flashing back and forth. There is not time to remember everything, but good old Nic sits there with all the telephones ringing, messages coming in over the wireless – and somehow jots the gist of everything down with accurate times in the margin. The other fellow who has got to speak is the Canadian CO, whose battalion got such a thumping. I am very sorry for him.

Before he left me, the Brig jokingly remarked – 'Well you have got your way at last'. I asked for a conference such as this many months ago, so that we could all take advantage of each other's experiences and ideas. I then said to the Brig, 'Try to persuade the General NOT to take the chair. If you or Brig Alland take the chair, discussion will flow much more freely and the General can be left to sum up at the end'. We'll see what happens! The Brig is going to fight for my leave all he can. It may be only two weeks at home, but just think how lovely it will be!!!

I shall be able to get Tony Lithgow a MC I think, but keep that a secret. He was good but not quite up to Angus Irwin's standard. A little bit excitable but who wouldn't be. He had the hell of a night.

11th May 1953

This is our last day and night here. A bit of a scare last night but nothing came of it. The rain will drive both sides to take shelter. It's going to be a very uncomfortable night for the relief and the roads will be almost impossible tomorrow. However wet it may be, it's not cold and that's a mercy.

11th May 1953

Forwarded to Rhoddy by my mother
Dearest Mother

We have had another battle. Not such a big one this time, but we inflicted great damage on the enemy and they admitted it on their propaganda broadcast the next evening but said 'Look out, we will give you what for in five days time.' I had two very fine young officers killed, one of whom got the MC in the last battle. I have been much complimented in the handling of it and yesterday was asked to speak about it at Divisional HQ to the General and all the other COs. Full success was nearly in my grasp, but my Company Commander failed me and did not carry out my final order. As the dawn broke I ordered forward two strong fighting patrols to sweep the battle field and seize the enemy dead and wounded. One attempt, a weak one, was made and I ordered it again. The Company Commander remonstrated and said it was 'murder'. I ordered it to be done 'at the double' and said that I had the whole Divisional Artillery to lay down a smoke screen if it became too light. Iris Blakeney's son did the northerly sweep, magnificently and without a casualty. The other boy was recalled by his Company Commander just as he was going forward. He could see the Chinese picking up their dead and wounded all over the place and he only had to open fire for a few minutes to have them on the run. Such is fortune, but anyway it went well apart from this.

Tonight it is teeming with rain and everything is very quiet as a result. We were meant to be relieved tomorrow morning by the Duke of Wellington's, but the weather has caused it to be postponed for 24 hours. We shall all be glad of a rest and I hope shortly to be in Tokyo and enjoy some good food and comforts.

Love
David

The discussion at HQ was interesting, but NOT a discussion, as I feared. The COs were all longing to be left alone and allowed to get down to brass tacks, but that was not to be. My talk went well and I made them all roar with laughter by reading out Private Mackenzie's account of his hand-to-hand fight with some Chinese. I have got lots of good stories coming in and will have them printed and circulated as I did the last time.

The CRA Brig Gregson, came to breakfast with me this morning and we had an interesting talk about the Canadian battle and my own. He said that for nearly an hour, the Gunners were completely in the dark during the Canadians show and could do nothing to help. During ours he knew every move from start to finish. We then talked about yesterday's discussion and he is going to try to get the General to fix another one. I pointed out that we didn't want all the Staff Officers present. We want to be able to 'let our hair down' and say what we think.

12th May 1953

My leave is going through. The General thinks it's possible and they hope to be able to get me as far as Paris for nothing – so perhaps you could meet me in Paris! And if it is too hot we could go to the seaside and I shall be entirely in your hands. Won't it be lovely if it all works out like that. I shall not have any clothes, just that one thin suit which I came out in, but that doesn't matter in France in the summer does it? Do you know anyone you could stay with in case I am delayed a day or two?

The sun is out and it is as sticky as a greenhouse after the rain but there is a nice breeze. I have moved my caravan out of its pit to make way for Ramsay Bunbury and after breakfast tomorrow I drive away to the reserve area. And there is a chance that we may even not go back into the line again. When I had my row last week, it was because they were going to leave us yet another week in the line so that Ramsay B could send some more officers on leave. I quite blew up!! I said to hell with their leave, I hadn't had any myself in 11 months and his Regiment hadn't done a job of work yet. And what was more, Scotland had done more than its share – always up front at the sharp end and had suffered more casualties than any other regiment since the Gloucesters. I was very angry. This morning the Brig was very charming and said he hoped to get the fourth battalion in another Brigade to do our last spell – we only have 3 battalions in this Brigade.

14th May, 1953

I am getting through the work in fine style. Everyone is helping. Tomorrow we have to set about the Honours and Awards. Today I nearly finished my report on the battle. I am tired but the old brain is working better than usual and I hope I shall make a success of my report. It makes wonderful reading. Raas has got it at the moment and he is thrilled with it. You can see nearly everything that was happening from minute to minute – and there are some very funny bits too!

Tonight we had a cinema show just in front of my caravan – it was just right – lots of love and opera. They all loved it and seem in such good heart – wonderful chaps. It was a nice break for me and took my mind off things. Then I found three lovely letters waiting for me – you, mother and Pam Wilmot – all full of kind thoughts. Now I feel a million dollars and shall have a glorious sleep. I shall be able to go to Tokyo in a few days time and I know the best man from whom to buy the pearls.

15th May 1953

I delayed my leave till tomorrow so that I should get your mail tonight. It was lovely – 3 letters – and now I shall have to go a whole week without hearing from you. It will be perfectly beastly but I will make up for it by trying to tell you everything I do, and I am getting so excited about the earrings!

I am throwing off all the cares for a week. I do hope all goes well but the Duke's are not very happy or firmly in the saddle on the HOOK. May they learn quickly so that the BW doesn't have to go back and retake it. I was up there this evening in case they should want my advice on anything – and then the Brig arrived and we had a pleasant talk about things over a whisky and soda and I got in a few hints without appearing to stress things too much. I still have my mortars there in support of them and Keith Denniston's company in the quiet bit, so I know everything that is going on – and some of it isn't very satisfactory. They are jumpy and not prepared to make quick decisions or put down enough fire close to their own men.

My wonderful boys. I have such confidence in them all. We see eye to eye and never need to have long conferences. Peter Buchanan said to me tonight – 'The trouble in *that* battalion is that no-one commands. There are four or five majors all giving different orders and the CO kind of swans about in the middle. No-one dares to do anything in case he should be wrong'.

Telling the Story
I sent the following letter to the other battalions, who had not then been in close contact with the enemy, which I hoped would be helpful advice.

The Third Battle on the HOOK   16th May 1953
For several months, all enemy activity had been on and round WARSAW. By the middle of April, we had driven his patrols from this area and the centre of activity had moved to RONSON.

Contacts on RONSON had been frequent and casualties were inflicted on the enemy by our Defensive Fire on several occasions. His patrols were also in the area of GREEN FINGER, much of which is dead ground and there he had the shelter of some caves which had been spotted on air photographs.

On the nights of 4/5 and 5/6 May, our patrols confirmed that the enemy was developing these caves. On 6 May we brought 8" guns to bear on the area with the aid of air observation, and put down very heavy harassing fire that night on all likely Forming Up Points. The night of 6/7 May passed without noteworthy incident but we harassed fairly heavily that night and again on 7/8 May. The raid came in at 0150hrs 8th May.

Lessons we learnt last year

In our November battle we learnt some valuable lessons. The value of guaranteed wireless communications, so excellently organised by Major Irwin. Every section was in touch with Coy and Pl HQ throughout the battle: aerials and sets were secure in the tunnels. Those communications enabled us to go on counter attacking throughout the night, despite enemy penetrations, knowing that our own men were holding out.

Fire Power and Communications

We have had great success by manning all OPs with Bren or Brownings on tripods. The man on duty fires a burst and observes strike so that his range to the selected target is absolutely correct. He then just waits and watches, his binoculars to his eye, his finger on the trigger.

We had little difficulty in sweeping the enemy off WARSAW by the co-ordination of OPs and fire power and it did not take much ammunition to do it. The link up was between the Company Commander, the tank with searchlight, MMGs on neighbouring hills and rifle company OPs. The enemy could be surprised at any moment in the night by either the searchlight or 60mm mortar flares.

Sniperscope

We have also been able to make good use of the night sniperscope (infra red). The RONSON standing patrol had one and the forward trench of the HOOK another. The sniperscope in the forward trench had a tripod mounted Bren gun beside it, laid only on the northerly trench on RONSON, down which the enemy could come without being observed by the standing patrol.

The sniper watched the enemy till they were in the beaten zone of the Bren and then told him to fire. On one occasion, after the Bren had fired, the sniper saw one of the enemy pick up a dead man and put him over his shoulder. The Bren fired again and Pl Comd put a cluster of 2" Mortar bombs all around the enemy patrol.

Telephone Line

During the November battle the line from the HOOK Coy CP to Bn CP was cut by shell fire at the very beginning of the action and all orders and information had to be passed by wireless. This time we had buried the line back from the HOOK and we had contact by telephone all through the night, till an unburied portion was cut behind hill 121 in the morning.

Counter Attack

At the end of that night in November, when we were all very tired and considerably disorganised, Lt Haw on his own initiative went out in front of the position and brought in some of our wounded: the enemy had gone. This brought home to me a well known tactical principle, the importance of the counter attack. If I had thought of it, I could have stood up fighting patrols from the company on hill 121, which could have swept up the RONSON re-entrant and surprised the enemy while he was picking up his dead and wounded. I made up my mind that I should not miss such an opportunity a second time.

The Opportunity

As dawn approached on the morning of 9th May, we got our second chance. There had been no enemy penetration this time and no hand-to-hand fights in our own trenches. Orders were issued for the preparation of fighting patrols to go forward onto GREEN FINGER and RONSON. The enemies' line of withdrawal was being cut by artillery fire and smoke was prepared in case the patrols should require cover in daylight.

The GREEN FINGER patrol met no opposition, but BLAKENEY went boldly out, almost to the paddy and brought back valuable information. For one reason and another the RONSON patrol was recalled by the Coy Comd.

Communication and Control

The pressure on a Coy Comd in a battle like this is terrific. He had twenty stations on his wireless net, through which to get information and to pass orders.

Major Lithgow had some bad luck with his communications. The forward Pl Comd and Pl Sgt were simultaneously killed at 0230hrs by incoming shell fire. This caused Major Lithgow to send the 2i/c forward to re-establish communications, which in turn threw a heavier burden on him, with no one to help in the CP.

Life of Wireless Batteries

At 0235hrs the officer i/c of the RONSON standing patrol was successfully passing back information to the CP. At 0255hrs his set started to fade. This was because he was using his battery for the second night. Because of the shortage of batteries, we had to do this on normal nights and there is no reason why we should not. But it is pretty serious when you get caught out in the middle of a battle. In actual fact 2/Lt Graham was still able to hear his Coy

Comd, but unable to reply. He had to relay through the Pioneer Platoon.

Bayonets

De-briefing of men after contact showed that many men did not fix their bayonets. Had every man done this there were several occasions when a bayonet would have been the best weapon to use.

Prisoners

How many Chinese reported as dead on RONSON were only wounded? We all remember how 2/Lt Younger escaped on Ronson on the night of 18/19 Nov by shamming dead.

Dope

In this de-briefing of subalterns and men who had been in close contact with the enemy my IO came to the following conclusion. All those who saw the enemy on the HOOK, got the impression that they were doped. They rushed about madly in all directions and seemed quite oblivious of all the shells landing around them. They would suddenly stop, no doubt when the effect wore off. These reports are confirmed by the discovery of opium seeds picked out of a captured cigarette packet. There was a most repulsive odour on the position the next morning from dead bodies.

On Leave in Japan
21st May 1953

I am at Elisir, the British leave camp on the outskirts of Tokyo. It seems very nice and quiet and I had such a good breakfast – tomato juice, poached haddock and poached eggs. I have a bed room and sitting room in the senior officers wing and a long bath, all in green, just next door. Yesterday I was in Kure and went round the Hospital. All my men were in very good shape save one – poor Corporal Laird. I am afraid he is done for. They are going to try to fly him home before he dies. He got a shell splinter in his spine just below the neck and he is quite paralysed. It makes one's heart bleed to see such a fine, good looking boy in such a state. He was lying very still and did not appear to be in much pain, but he knows there is no hope. His poor parents.

John Smart dined with me at Kure and ordered cars and a launch to bring me over from the airport. He is a nice lad and very keen to return to the battalion. His hand is nearly better and they all like him at Headquarters where he is acting as the Brigadier's Personal

Assistant. I shall try to get him back just before the battalion sails so that he can get to know them all on the journey.

21st May 1953

I have had quite a pleasant day wandering about the centre of Tokyo: all rather muddling at first and I didn't see anything that I could buy, except an aeroplane with a *real* engine which you fill up with a fountain pen filler, but I know Hugh is still too young for it.

On my way back here I called on Mrs Neville, the wife of the Military Attaché, who came out on the ship with the battalion and has entertained many of the officers when they come on R & R. She was going out to an official dinner party with the Swiss Minister. On Saturday morning she is going to take me shopping in her car and to lunch with him afterwards. Tomorrow evening I go to dine with General Shoesmith, our Chief of Staff at American Headquarters.

I had a lovely dinner here this evening – very good Hors d'oeuvres, Oyster soup, Curried Lambs Tongues and Lobster Thermidor!! And now to bed for a long, long sleep after a few pages of my book 'People of the Deer'. It would be such fun, if only you were here, but it is not long now till July.

22nd May 1953

I have bought the pearls! I do hope they wont be a very bad match for your own. I got two lovely big ones for earrings and then set about trying to match them. I thought a ring with three smaller ones would be nice, but I had to buy four, because they are sold in pairs, and then I bought a pearl star brooch which one day you could give to Mary for her first dance, but I think you will like to wear it till then. When I got back here, I found an invitation waiting for me from the Ambassador to go as his guest to fish at Nikko for two days – so I shall not spend any more money! The Rolls is coming for me at 7.30 on Monday and I am to drive down with him on Wednesday. I fly back at 2 am on Thursday and a light plane will take me up to the Div Air Strip. The next morning we go back into the line, but a nice quiet place for our last month.

I am going to dine with General Shoesmith this evening – shop talk I expect – and to shop for the children tomorrow morning with Mrs Neville. She is a nice person who goes round the hospitals and 'natters' to the men, as she says. Full of chatter and energy. I am getting so fat on lobster and steaks!!

Recalled from Leave
23rd May 1953

All my lovely plans have been boxed up and I am back with the battalion. I went out to dinner with General Shoesmith – a *very* charming man and a very delightful host. He gave me such a wonderful dinner and we had a great chin wag and then he drove me back to Elisir. I was just going to bed when I got a message that I was to return by the fastest possible means – so there was no fishing and no more comfort. There is a great flap on here about an impending attack. I didn't get any sleep last night, rushing about in aeroplanes, so must stop now.

25th May, 1953

Things move very fast these days. I have just heard that we are now to go to Kenya instead of the Canal Zone – nice climate and good sport. I do hope you will be pleased. Really I think the Canal Zone would have made me quit the Army. Let's have a really good governess and perhaps we shall be able to have friends out for the English winter.

Everything is in rather a flap still but I have gathered all my scattered sub-units together and everyone says they are so glad that I came back, because they were being bullied from the moment I left. The camp was in the process of being struck as I drove back. I gave the order 'Stand Fast' and in a few minutes the tents were going up again!! I can't tell you what a state of excitement the Staff had got into and nothing has happened yet.

26th May 1953

My dear General Neil,

We are all simply delighted at the turn of events and are greatly looking forward to Kenya. The news arrived at a most opportune moment. We had been off the Hook for a few days and are all looking forward to a rest in reserve. I went off to Kure to see the wounded. On my first evening while dining with the Base Commander, I was recalled by an Ops immediate! The Ambassador had asked me up to Nikko for a few days trout fishing. I got back to find the battalion spread out all over the place and under various people's command. It was a real flap and went on for 5 days. Now all is settling down again. The new unit on the HOOK had let things get out of control and it looked as though we might be required to counter attack it, – so no-one has had much rest and tomorrow we go back into the line, but in the quiet Yong-Dong sector, 2,000 yards from the enemy and every company can be visited in daylight in a Jeep.

The weather is lovely just now. The hardy ones are already bathing and the hills are all brilliant green.

We have got a very fine looking representative party for the Div Coronation parade. Raas is commanding the whole show and three of us will help as hosts at the luncheon afterwards, when the General entertains the representatives of all the Nations.

The new subalterns who have joined us are a really good lot and all goes well despite the loss on drafting of another 74 very fine men.

The Coronation Medals are being given to WOs and Sgts who, with any luck, should have had an award.

Yours ever
David

26th May, 1953

We are all so terribly excited about Kenya. Everyone is laughing and talking about it and bubbling with plans. Some people have friends and relatives there – David Severn knows everyone and I had a letter from Peter Carthew to say that he is being considered as one of the Governor's ADCs.

The 'HOOK' attacked once more
29th May, 1953

We had a heavy attack again last night but this time we were *not* on the Hook. The Dukes have been there for nearly two weeks. The full news of last night's battle isn't out yet. At one time they had most of the Hook over-run and the Chinese were blowing in the entrances to tunnels. There was a terrific weight of artillery fire put down all round the feature. We had many shells in here, but only one casualty thank goodness.

Today the Chinese have been attacking the Turks on our left in broad daylight and must have taken terrible casualties. I believe the following waves of men came up unarmed and picked up the weapons of the fallen in true Russian style. Today has been quiet with very few enemy shells coming in, but they may well have another go having done so much damage to the fortifications. The Peace Talks start again on Monday.

Don't worry about my journey home. If I get permission to do it, I shall do it in style as an official guest of the Canadian Army – and I can tell you I won't delay an hour longer than necessary in Canada! I would so much like to meet you in France, see the house and fly to Kenya with you. Do hope it all works out that way.

I am so glad that you liked Mrs Raas. You didn't mention her name – and that Christopher is nice too. We *will* have fun in Kenya.

I have got another DSO. We had a few bottles of champagne the other evening to celebrate Tony's daughter and Peter Buchanan's imminent departure to Kenya and then all went to bed. Just as I got into bed the signal came for me from Kure – so back they all came to my caravan – which smelt like nothing on earth in the morning. So I suppose I shall be on the Coronation Parade to receive it. Nice to get it now, instead of months after leaving the theatre.

6th June, 1953

I have just finished two awful days writing up all the terminal awards. What a job it is! The advance party of the Royal Scots has arrived and today or tomorrow I get my last draft in Korea. The Regulars stay with me, but the National Servicemen remain behind with the RS. All this really does give one the end-of-term feeling, but there is still a month to do.

Everything is nice and quiet here but they are still having a lot of trouble on the Hook. Now the Royal Fusiliers have taken it over and are doing much hard work to repair all the damage. I was pleased to hear that all the bunkers we built stood up to even the heaviest guns. They had to blow them up with the big charges which the attacking infantry brought with them. They have had a very hard time, The Dukes and the Royal Fusiliers. I am glad we didn't get let in for a third battle. The 4th Battle on the HOOK is told in 'Fortune Favours the Brave'.

13th June, 1953

The rumour is that there will be an Armistice within 5 days. We then sit here for 12 days and salvage what timber and ammunition we can and then, Oh who cares!! We shall be off and away in no time. It's thrilling, it's wonderful, it's marvellous!!! I have given up all thoughts of going on leave again. I just can't face it. Must save the money for Paris where we can share every pleasure and then HOME! How I am longing to see you all again and may we never again have such a parting.

18th June, 1953

We do live in a world of ups and downs. This afternoon I got a signal from Nairobi saying that our families must *not* leave by the July boat because the new C-in-C would have to make up his mind about the subject of families. Will you please find out when he goes to Kenya ((I thought he was there) and why he can't make up his mind before 17 July. Do give Jim (Sir James Hutchison, MP) a ring and ask him to turn on the heat! Don't delay your packing, or selling of the car. I am sure it will turn out alright in the end. One can fly round the world in 5 days, so why shouldn't he make up his mind in a month?

21st June 1953

At the moment we seem to be in the doldrums. I am terribly tired and also bored. Sometimes I long just to have my meals sent to the caravan, but I don't! And when I get there it isn't too bad. I have been getting those damned headaches again, down the left side of my neck. Anyway, it's only ten days now.

I had a long walk today and ended up at the bath house and had a lovely long soak. 'Bertram' the Korean bath boy is a gem. He makes everyone laugh and he has a wonderful face. If he gets very friendly, he squirts you with cold water and scrubs your back. A great character. The Sweet Chestnut blossom is out now and the trees look as though they are dripping with cream. There are also Tiger Lilies. The Padre had a lovely vase in the 'Church' this morning and we took communion – the guns thundering over head – some enemy shells coming rather too close and I knew it would be up to me to say when to take cover – rather took my mind off things!

23rd June, 1953

So sorry that you have had all that unnecessary trouble trying to find lodgings in Paris. As things are now, I am afraid it is quite out of the question. It wouldn't be fair on Raas. Anyway, it has been a nice dream in the past months and the prospect has given me many pleasant hours.

Still no news from Kenya, but I will hear any day now and will send you a wire. They must give us a bit of a let up some time. I wired to Kenya and told them that we now have 25 officers and 312 regular soldiers who are due 8 weeks leave, 220 National Servicemen who are due 4 weeks etc. etc. I don't think they yet realise that we have been flat out for over a year and must have some consideration some time. I am sure all will be well if we keep plugging on at it.

30th June, 1953

I am trying to get a bit of a rest before I have to face the final week of farewell parties and parades. We had a small success last night and no casualties on our side. I do hope I can keep them out of trouble for the next three days.

Out of the Line for the Last Time
4th July, 1953

We are out of the line and have started handing over our weapons to the Royal Scots. Now I am busy with plans for farewell parades, cocktail parties and speeches. Oh I do loathe the speeches! Our Gunner Battery gave a very nice champagne cocktail party for us and today the Sappers do the same. On Sunday we entertain close on 200 officers at Retreat and the Sergeants about 100 at the same time. On Tuesday the General and Brigadier came to speak to us on Farewell Parade and on Wednesday we get into the train. We go to a camp at Pusan for three days and hold our Memorial Service in the Cemetery there. The Padre has gone off to get the printing done. I get such 'chokers' when I read my address. I do hope I don't make a fool of myself. They are still arguing about my flight to Kenya – whether I go from Tokyo, Pusan or Singapore but I will wire you when I am certain.

I am still hoping that all will turn out well. I am bringing considerable pressure to bear in Nairobi. I gave them all the facts and said that if we didn't get our families, many more officers and men would have to be sent home on leave, which will greatly weaken the battalion.

6th July, 1953

My dear Rhoddy

I am off the bleeding Hook and it was only just in time or we should have had a third battle there. I had to have rather a row with my Brigadier when he suggested that we should remain there yet another week – because the DWR still had some officer on leave, or rather due leave. I ask you! I told him that they had 1200 men and had been reserve for four months.

It did the trick – and they made a pretty average balls of it. My beautiful fortifications which stood up to two days of pounding from the 105s and 122s, were captured by the enemy and blown up with satchell charges. They were having an O group when the attack started! Tanks were hull down and no one gave the order for the DFs, till it was too late. They then fired a box barrage for the rest of the night while the Chinks blew up the position inside the box. Anyway they got it back in the morning but minus many men who were blown up in the bunkers and tunnels.

They were then relieved by the Royal Fusiliers, who have also been in reserve for months. After a week on the 'sore thumb' they are still making little sense. I have done all I can to give people the form – I have even put it on paper, but they just won't get down to it till they have to. They don't need support company commanders for the normal Patrol war so they don't train them. Their lines don't get cut in the patrol war, so they don't bother about wireless communication. And as you know, you can't just say 'Hey Presto' about such things. Anyway they have got to learn the hard way now.

The Royal Scots advance party is here and we'll be off in a month. The Ambassador asked me to go up to Nikko for three days as his guest to catch trout – Rolls and all that to fetch me. Then I was recalled, 'Ops Immediate'.

Anyway I am glad I got back because the battalion had been buggered about from the day I left. When I arrived I found the whole reserve camp being pulled down. I asked the meaning of so much unnecessary activity and was told that the Royal Fusiliers wouldn't take it over and that we were returning to the line.

I soon discovered that the battalion to which I had been recalled – presumably to command – was scattered to the four winds as labour gangs or in blocking positions. It took me all day to collect them again and repitch the camp.

Yours ever,
David

7th July, 1953

There is still hope that you may all join us in Kenya fairly soon. I heard from the Adjutant General's Department last night that they are trying to induce General Erskine to make an exception in our case, as we are eventually to be the permanent garrison battalion, whereas the other two will move on. I am told that he is a charming man and a very fine General. Let's hope that he isn't too hide-bound by rules. My own plans are still rather vague. Yesterday I got orders from W.O. to fly at once to East Africa. It was going to take 15 days! I had to spend 4 days in Malta among other places. The General said that he was going to refuse to comply (a) because of the Memorial Parade in Pusan (b) because he says I must have a rest and not be 'buggered' about any more for a bit. So it looks as though I shall go by ship now, but I may be taken off at Singapore if there happens to be a plane available.

It has been a hectic week. Only a few hours ago has it stopped raining during the past 4 days. We just splosh about in wet clothes. However, the rain hasn't prevented a steady round of parties – Company Smokers, Sergeants Mess, Gunners, Sappers and so on. The General and the Brigadier, Americans, French and all the rest have been about the place saying goodbye and well done to everyone. Now I have the CO of the Royal Scots to cope with – more talking, more drinking and as usual I am getting a throat. In an hour or so is our final Retreat and probably over 100 guests. We had to postpone it on Sunday owing to the downpour, but over 50 people turned up and drank an incredible quantity of gin. I went off to the Sergeants' Mess with the General where we had a curry dinner and a *very* enjoyable evening. We eventually carried him out to his car in a huge wooden chair. The next day, I and all my company commanders met him again at luncheon at Brigade Headquarters.

The boat is three days late owing to a typhoon but I think we shall make up the days by spending less time in the Pusan Camp, which is excellent.

16th June, 53

What wonderful news from you tonight – that all the families will be on the ship sailing on 17th July! Everyone will be thrilled and they will arrive only 3 or 4 days after us.

Conclusions

Many years ago I wrote to the American Marine Corps for a copy of their *History of the Korean War*. It was a great disappointment. There was no commentary about fortifications, the use of barbed wire or minefields. We British have learnt a great deal about fighting defensive wars. We start nearly every war in retreat and then build up our strength while fighting from defensive positions. The American experience has been the opposite. They come in with great numbers of troops, ships and planes to smash the enemy with all their power.

No European nation would have developed the American OPLR and MLR method of defence. It could never withstand repeated assaults on one sector because it is linear, without depth.

The Chinese were very good at night, very quick moving and very quick to react with their weapons. They did not press us during full moon, but they were constantly probing during the wane and the dark period, digging caves, which would be used during future attacks as Forming Up Points or as Advanced Dressing Stations.

The Korean War in 1952–53 was a night war and that was to our disadvantage, with our semi-trained troops. That was our only disadvantage. I think we should have made more use of Artificial Moonlight (searchlights reflected off the clouds). We had the generating capacity and the communications to switch on and off at will. If you can see the battlefield, you need not use thousands of shells and mortar bombs on Defensive Fire, when you are attacked.

When the Marines first fortified the feature which was to become so well known as the 'Hook', they built 150 Block Houses off the MLR for their squads to live in and fight from. They were constructed of magnificent timbers 8″ × 8″. One Marine told me that he could do his 'Stag' (sentry duty) and fire his weapon from his bunk! These dreadful things were suitable protection from marauding Red Indians, but death traps for the poor fellows who were expected to fight from them. Every single one of them had been destroyed by the time I took over the 'Hook'. I had foretold this in a letter to my brother.

The American Army is really a Citizen Army. How can you hope to become 'professional' when your Officers and Men rotate on a points system, even when they are in the front line? This is democracy gone mad. This system of fair shares for all was the cause of very high casualties; there can be no team work this way. These two things together, the MLR and rotation, were in my view the reasons why we did not win the Korean War: it was a draw.

The fortitude of the Chinese, in the face of our complete domination with all weapons, was truly staggering.

CHAPTER SEVEN
Kenya (1953–1954)
The Mau Mau Rebellion

The 1st Battalion in Kenya

Sir Evelyn Baring had recently been transferred from South Africa as Governor of Kenya, but owing to the Mau-Mau emergency, General Sir George Erskine was in command. He was a very senior General. I thought of him as one of the 'old guard', like Field Marshal Wavell and General Ritchie in my Regiment. General Erskine's regiment was the 60th Rifles.

2nd August 1953

I arrived at Mombasa yesterday and came up here to Nakuru by air with Angus Irwin. This morning we flew to Thompson's Falls where two of my companies will arrive this evening. We then motored back through Gilgil where another Company is to live. It's lovely and cool and after a long drought, there has been rain, which has made everything as green as could be. Our quarters are pretty wretched but Angus and his chaps have done wonders to make them better and have extracted some good furniture out of the Staff. We shall even have beds of a kind. My Headquarters is the Agricultural Buildings on the Show Ground, bamboo and straw with floors of cement blocks. We sleep in the bull pens! We also have some tents and a hut has been converted as shower baths. In such a nice climate, it won't be too bad.

I am afraid we are in for a very hard time once we are acclimatized – we work in the mountains in *very* thick bamboo forests – spells of a week or two, then a few days rest in some place like this. The food is wonderful. Last night we had steaks such as I have never eaten and masses of fresh cream on fruit salad – we have to pay for it of course. Today I had lunch at the Country Club – again wonderful meat of all kinds, salads and lovely local cheese. My choice was like Brie.

General Cameron met us at Mombasa and we talked a bit about families. His attitude was, 'I don't think you will want them when you see the conditions. You will very seldom be able to get away to see your families even if they were out here'. He said he would see me about the matter in a few days when I have been seen by Brigadier who is still out in the jungle. They can't have it both ways. Either they grant us leave to fly home in turn, or they grant us leave to come out of the jungle. Angus Irwin says he can let his house without any difficulty.

The altitude is a little trying at first and makes one very sleepy. I must go now and lie down for a bit. The troop train is late which means that I shall be very late to bed tonight and I must be in good humour to meet Brigadiers and Generals tomorrow. All's well as can be without you.

5th August 1953

I *did* write to you before I landed at Singapore and I can't think why you didn't get the letter. I told you all about the Memorial Parade and our farewells in Korea and from Singapore I sent you the pearls in a little toy box for Mary, but they will take weeks by sea.

It really is a hectic life. I seem to drive or fly all day and meet masses of people – farmers, ex-soldiers, police and civilians. All very muddling and very tiring and return in the evening to a horrid little room which leaks all over when it rains – which it seems to do nearly every evening. Today I drove General Erskine for miles on his tour of Police posts. We had the usual *wonderful* lunch, which was paid for from money captured off a Mau-Mau Secretary who was made prisoner the other day!

The General was very pleasant but wouldn't talk about our problems till Monday, when he pays me an official visit. The Brigadier comes tomorrow morning and my head is bursting with so much talk. I simply *must* get home on leave or I shall pack up. I think the altitude here makes one very tired and muddle headed. The Kenya people say that none of them can ever remember names, so perhaps I am no worse than they are, but it is such a mental strain. I would so much like to spend a lovely restful month with you in our home. Kenya without you would drive me off my chump.

Lots of people would put you up and have asked us all to make use of their houses. I would like to come on leave as soon as I have done my utmost for the others and then fly out with all of you when things are more settled. But if the General won't let families come out, I really think I should chuck in my hand in January. (The Second in Command of the Buffs has just done so.) It's just not worth wasting the best years of one's life. Better let old Mick B.B. have a shot at it. What do you think?

I got some civilians in last night to talk to the officers about the

195

Mau-Mau. I thought it would be a good thing for them to hear about it from the people of the country before they get wrong ideas from Junior Police Officers. By chance I apparently picked two very knowledgeable men and they were most interesting. It's a filthy cult – quite revolting. So far nearly all the casualties to the Military have been caused by our *own* weapons – men shooting wildly in the jungle. The Mau-Mau are cowardly and only attack lone farm houses or their own people who have been enrolled as Home Guards and are armed with bows and arrows, spears and sometimes a shot gun. They rob the fields and cattle for food and then retreat into the mountain forests. Now I must bath as I must go out to a meeting.

10th August 1953

All is well! The General has been and gone. I am to fly home quite soon and he is going to *try* to start a regular air service like they have in Egypt. He wants to get the Civil Servants in on it so that it will be cheaper for everyone. As regards families. I *think* they should all be out before Christmas. So everything will be OK soon. Why the hell they couldn't have decided it all months ago, I can't understand. Anyway, things seem to be moving at last and I may arrive any time within a month!! I'll just send you a cable, Whoopee! I feel grand already. 'There is nothing like a dame'.

Just now it rains most evenings and sometimes in the mornings too. Much, much cooler than Korea. In fact you can wear ordinary tweeds at this time of the year and you need blankets at night. I haven't been to Nairobi yet, but I am told that it is a good deal warmer there. I may be going there tomorrow night after our air reconnaissance of the next area which the battalion is to take over. More building to be done – we always seem to be building. Nothing is ever prepared before we get there. Anyway SEE YOU SOON.

GHQ Nairobi

I had an official interview with the General in his office. I gave him a run-down on our domestic problems. We were nearly into our second year of Active Service and many of our Officers, Warrant Officers and NCOs were entitled to claim home posting, should they choose to do so. Without them the Battalion would be in a sorry plight, but all were very willing to stay, if they could be joined by their families.

The General's response was not at all encouraging. There were no quarters available, he said, and others were already on the waiting list. I pointed out that we expected some special consideration after many months of active service, considerable casualties and some anxious times at home. My plea carried no weight with the General. As a last shot I said that I would take over some of the hotels which were empty because of the emergency, if he would authorise the families to be sent out. To this he agreed with an ill grace, saying, 'On your own head be it and don't expect any help from my Staff. Having your families at the Brackenhurst Hotel won't stop me moving your battalion wherever I want to use it.' I said that I felt sure we would find more hotels near enough to where we were to operate.

I haven't encountered this kind of attitude before. I hope my Brigadier will turn out alright.

1st September 1953

It's Sunday and I must go off to read the lesson. I have left my Moffat [bible] at home and it's going to be difficult to read Paul so that they can understand him. The Padre has picked a bit about 'soberness and being at peace among yourselves'! That's part of my present trouble. I have so many men undergoing detention for fighting and drinking and my Companies are so far apart, I spend 5 or 6 hours a day driving – such a waste of time and so tiring.

Rhoddy wrote in a letter some fine advice on discipline, which I quote verbatim.

Words of Wisdom
Dear David

The Jocks always do slosh people, especially RMP. They can only be controlled by their own police and by collective punishments dished out by their CO. The English Generals can't understand this. I found one had to get the man to see that being put on an outside charge was an offence against the Regiment and the CO. I used to tell them that it was everyone's duty to see that drunks did not get into trouble and to let them fall into the hands of the RMP was like leaving a trail of men fallen out on the line of march. I had considerable success with this method.

Yours ever
   Rhoddy

I have spent the last two days giving B Company a hard time. Their administration is all to hell and they were the main cause of the letters to the papers. I ran an officer up in front of the Brigadier and he is now on a special report. I think he had the fright of his life. His Company Commander is also thoroughly shaken. I

197

told him I would not have my Companies run like a volunteer rabble. I inspected all his books and not one single one was in order – nothing checked, nothing signed for. His men unwashed and disorderly, drinking and fighting while he and his 2 i/c were in Nairobi. It'll take time to put it all right.

The day before that I wrote to the Ministerial Enquiry about the food. I do hope Antony Head reads it himself in the original, but I feel that bits will be cut out. I have pulled no punches and I am sure my facts are right. We'll have to wait and see whether there will be an improvement as a result. At the bottom of the trouble is the old story of the Staff living in comfort in Nairobi, having half holidays and weekends and us working round the clock with no recreation. The men can't go to a canteen and buy themselves a supper. If the rations aren't good enough they just go hungry. One of them wrote to the papers that he only got ½ a sausage for breakfast. He was quite correct. That is the ration. Of course he is meant to have a cereal as well, but it is only 2oz of flakes 10 days out of 14, and that just isn't enough, so it all gets eaten in about a week. The other days they issue rice, spaghetti or macaroni as a cereal. I ask you, have British people ever eaten these things for breakfast? Now I must have a blitz on 'A' Company and only hope it isn't as bad as 'B'. Despite everything, I seem to be getting on well with the Brigadier. I am perfectly frank with him and he seems to react well and is doing all he can to help.

Poor Peter Lindsay has had such bad luck. He went off in great form to rejoin his family. The plane had engine trouble and they were all told to go back to their hotels. Peter went early to bed and the others were all whisked off to the landing ground at 4am. No-one woke Peter. He stormed round GHQ and I am told they more or less laughed at him and just said he would have to wait for a week. So Peter went home at his own expense £140!

30th December 1953

My Dear General Neil,

We are probably going to be moved into 49 Bde in January where we shall be with the Northumberland Fusiliers – a very anti-group Battalion with very high proportion of Regulars. We shall be deployed round the top of the Aberdares in an area where the wild beasts are more numerous and more dangerous than the Mau-Mau. Our new Brigadier's name is Taylor, nick named 'Bone Head'. We shall not serve under Harry Thurlow who takes over this Brigade in February.

Brig John Tweedie (A & SH) has been a great help to me and I am sorry that we are not to remain under command of a Scotsman, He naturally understands Jocks and the troubles particular to them – and we have had plenty. I think we should be more selective in our recruiting – I mean the whole Highland Brigade. I know there is a shortage of NS manpower but we are accepting regulars who are quite impossible in either Civilian or Army life. I got rid of a lot in Korea who were near mental cases and I have got rid of 12 more here, who are thugs or jail birds. I put up two more the other day whose Civilian records alone were sufficient – 16 to 18 jobs in a year. There are now 5 or 6 more who are borderline cases and that I hope will be all for a long time. I feel that the intense competition for high recruiting figures must be the cause of these men getting past the selection teams. They have done us so much harm in the eyes of higher authority and have led many good men into serious trouble.

Operations are going very well in our area and the Brigade Commander has been most complimentary. We have got the District Officers and Police working much more closely with us than most other districts apparently. Some of our Platoon Commanders are outstanding as patrol leaders, particularly Hugh Blakeney and Duncan Grassie. I am sure it is not all good luck. I do wish that Hugh would become a regular, but he is going to learn Factor's work at Blair apparently.

Archie John's death was a sad blow. He was obviously enjoying his return to Regimental life. We all feel very deeply for poor Lady Wavell. It was a sad Christmas.

This next month we are to be visited by both Walter Elliot and Antony Head. I want them to see and speak to the men, but the powers that be want them to be taken into the jungle. We must try to do both in the very short time available. I'll write again at the end of January. With every best wishes for 1954.

Yours sincerely,
  David

White Highlands

Our second task was to clear up the Mau-Mau infiltration in the White Highlands, that wonderful farmland adjacent to the Aberdare Forest. Some of the Settlers had Mau-Mau sympathisers in their labour lines. They did not employ all the labour by any means, but they needed large quantities of wood for cooking and water. It was during their excursions for fuel and water that the Mau-Mau lay in wait for them. So we would have to issue instructions restricting foraging parties to certain days of the week and under guard

The Settlers were not the type (like ourselves) to be pushed around by anyone, so we had to devise a method of approach which would win their co-operation. Each Company Commander

199

was to invite the Settlers and their wives in their area to a social gathering. No-one was to be left out. I would, of course, attend the party to get to know them and hear their views. The CO's Fund was able to soften the financial burden, but all the Officers paid a generous share.

There were a few Settlers who kicked up rough over the restrictions, but I had a very good retired Indian Army Brigadier as a District Officer and he could usually insist on co-operation, without recourse to the Governor or C in C.

1st May 1954   *Nairobi*
My dear General Neil,

It was grand to hear that Jack has done so well and is now getting a GI job. I am glad that you have Angus Irwin in mind for the Depot. He is very thorough in everything and very firm with all subordinates. After the Depot, I feel that he should go as an instructor to Sandhurst or Warminster, to make up for his lack of Staff experience. I know he would be keen to do something of the kind.

Raas left late last night and he got a great send off despite all the work we are doing, much of which starts very early in the morning. He was very popular with Officers and Sergeants – always smiling and a charming personality,

I am sure David Arbuthnott will do very well with 4th/5th – and what a pleasant start to his married life!

Jim Stewart is going to be a first class Company Commander on a par with Claud Moir. Adam Gurdon is also a very good officer, years beyond his age. I enclose a 'strawberry' which was sent to me by Brig Beyts DSO MBE MC, our District Officer in the White Highlands, General Hind, has also said some very nice things about our work up there and in Nairobi, but I am sorry to say that we are not in the good books of the C-in-C as regards discipline. His AQ goes direct to him about any and every incident, but we have been strongly defended on this score both by Brig John Tweedie and Brig Bill Taylor. I have still got a few really bad hats who will have to be got rid of.

No more now as we have a very early start on the Asian Quarter tomorrow.

Yours sincerely,
  David.

19th April 1954
Dear David,

On your Bn's departure I would like to express my appreciation of their perseverance and hard endeavour, which have won admiration from all of us, who reside in this unsettled area - This has always been a difficult area both from Military and Political points of view, and success is harder to come by than in the Reserves.

You have certainly maintained the Settlers' morale by the personal interest shown by all your Officers in their affairs, by the sympathetic manner you have helped them in their difficulties. We look forward to your return, and hope the change will make a pleasant break in this uphill struggle.

Yours sincerely,
Billy Beyts

The Strategic Road

As the situation in the White Highlands was brought under control, we were given a third task: to build a road up the Escarpment and through the Aberdare Forest. The purpose of this road was to save the troops and police the long drive through the Kikuyu Reserve to Nairobi.

I was given a labour force of about 3000 Kikuyu for the pick and shovel work. The Government provided funds to feed them, but they were not paid a wage. It was my job to survey the route, organise the work and give protection from the Mau-Mau. The District Officer provided the food.

The work went ahead at a good pace. It was just the kind of job that our Company Commanders were used to organising, making Jeep tracks up the Korean hills and digging the tunnels on the Hook Salient. Our young DO was very enthusiastic to get the very best out of the labour. We formed the labour force into two parties and the two camps would be moved forward every week or so, as the road progressed.

Imagine our dismay when orders were received from Nairobi that all labour was to be released and sent back to their homes, as there were no funds to pay for their food. The DO and I went down to the camp to explain the situation to the Headman and to our surprise, instead of the news being greeted by a mighty cheer, the Headman after some excited discussion came forward and asked if they might carry on with the work. Their wives would bring them potatoes and pocho from their shambas. They liked being in the camps, where they were free from intimidation.

I passed this information to the AQ, who saw the General, who permitted the work to continue, at no cost to the Government. Twice a week the wives would arrive, many with a child at breast and food on their heads. It all became rather a jolly party. Somewhat naturally some of the wives asked if they might remain in the camp overnight. Eventually the whole family would move in. This was how it came about that we started building our first two model villages. The first reason was the need for sanitation. The Kikuyu did not live in villages. Each man had two or three huts, one for himself and one for each wife. Now, in a big camp, it was of course necessary to have deep trench latrines and that alone made it impossible to move camps every week.

My DO had some firm ideas about the proper size and height of a good Kikuyu hut. Its ventilation was important to get rid of the smoke and he considered that they should have a proper door and window. These ideas required galvanised hinges and 6" nails, but having no funds at his disposal he did not see how he could insist on his standards being adopted. I did have a fund, which I could use with discretion, so I paid the bill for the hardware, about £350 if I remember aright, and building proceeded apace.

Our villages were protected by a ditch in which we planted bamboo stakes with sharp and fire hardened points. Each had a small watch tower at the gate. In the centre of the village was an open space, so that the DO and other Government or Welfare Officers could gather everyone together for instructions or discussions. This open space was to be used for games like net ball.

About this time the Minister, Antony Head, paid his official visit to Kenya. I knew Antony Head quite well, as I sometimes met him at Drummond Castle when he came to shoot grouse. I now had to show him part of the White Highlands. Naturally I took him to see the new strategic road up the Escarpment, of which we were all rather proud.

The C in C was with us in my Jeep – quite a load. As we went along, I told Antony Head the story of the Kikuyu wanting to stay and work without any Government reward. The C in C had neither seen the road nor my experimental villages and I felt on tenterhooks, but I pressed on with my story. When we were standing looking at the village Antony Head suddenly said to the General,

'I think there is something in this, why don't we put them all in protected villages and get the Mau-Mau off their backs?' Simple isn't it, when you happen to be a Minister of State! I struck while the iron was hot!

'May I have my £350 pounds back?'

Lord Head laughed and said, 'Yes of course, David.'

Someone else must have received the recognition for what really was my initiative to rehouse the Kikuyus. No mention was made by the C in C in subsequent meetings and nothing concerning it was mentioned in my confidential report: neither was there any recommendation for promotion. C'est la vie.

During the year that followed, one million Kikuyu were indeed rehoused in protected villages, a vast undertaking. I often wonder how much it cost. How did it compare, for instance, with the three million pounds spent on bombing the beautiful Aberdare Forest with RAF bombers? Who could have thought up that ridiculous idea and who had authorised the expenditure? I can't believe that it was Antony Head. He was much too well clued up.

The Wives

Having our wives with us was quite wonderful and, of course, made our contacts with the Settlers much easier and more friendly. In fact, in retrospect, it is hard to see how we could have done without them. They never gave me a moment of trouble and my wife had every one of them as a new friend.

The Settlers' wives were all 'Pistol shooting Mammas', so we taught our wives to shoot. My wife was already an experienced deer stalker, but when the RSM took his ladies' class for instruction, he had some dicey moments.

At one time, my wife and I had a small corrugated house above our camp at Gilgil. It was most appropriately named 'Faut de Mieux'. One evening the Adjutant telephoned to say that a Mau-Mau gang was moving up the valley in our direction. Jean said she would ring back if she could see them and she and Pte Thompson would fire at them if they came close enough. We had practised the children with a drill in case of an emergency. Hugh was to take his sister to their bedroom and lie quietly under their beds. He had his assegai there in case of a real emergency! The native servants had separate quarters, just as if they were with a Settlers' family. Pte Thompson and my wife were well able to deal with raiders should they materialise.

Sometimes when I came home from flying or motoring round my enormous estate, I would give Jean the tip to warn the children. Then she would go round the house from window to window, firing at beer cans. It gave everyone complete confidence. Me too!

One day when I was away from home, as usual, Jean blew a huge rattlesnake in half with her gun. Hugh was rather put out because she had spoilt the skin, but two halves were better than none!

The ominous predictions of General Erskine and his staff proved to be entirely unfounded. We had no single complaint from any wife about the conditions under which they lived. We had a ball of a time.

Farewell to Kenya

This book has grown and grown as it went along. I never intended it to be such a saga, but it has just happened that way. But I must not go on any more about Kenya. 'A Subaltern's Diary' by John Rankin gives a very good account of the life on patrol in various parts of the country, but this was published privately and may only be available from the Regimental Museum.

Before we left Kenya, we gave a Ball in Nairobi. The plan was to have as few 'Official' guests as possible. Invitations were to be for the many personal friends and the young Settlers, who had been so hospitable to the Regiment.

Of course I had to have the two Generals, but we had a large party for many close friends, who had opened their homes to my wife and children and given them the most wonderful time, when I perforce had to be so much on tour.

My wife had a wonderful gown in white slipper satin, embroidered with all kinds of silks and stones. The Officers were of course in the Kilt with white Mess jackets and so were the men of the Colonel's Mountain Band!

After dinner at the famous Muthaiga Club we repaired to the Assembly Rooms. General Erskine and my wife started off the dancing and I partnered Lady Hind. We had not progressed more than half way round the room, when one of my officers came up and said he wanted to speak to me urgently as there was trouble at the door. I took Lady Hind back to her seat and made my apologies.

It transpired that there was a very determined lady, in a gold lamé dress, surrounded by an equally determined posse of the dance committee. She was quite sure that when the CO had been informed of her family name and that her family were close personal friends of my wife's family at Brechin, she would be allowed to come in.

Stalling for time, I asked whether she had a partner. A young man in full Scottish rig stepped forward.

'Have you an invitation?' I asked.

'No,' he said.

'Very well, will you please find a taxi and escort your partner back to the Club.' Of course the story was all round the Ball Room in a few minutes and the party took off like a rocket and was a great success into the 'wee small hours'.

There was more to this story. Apparently someone had overheard the 'gate-crashers' placing a bet of a case of champagne that they would gain entry to the Ball. We drank the champagne the following morning. We needed it!

Our time in Kenya was over. It had been a wonderful experience for all of us. We had occupied and restored order in the Kikuyu Reserve, we had given assistance and security to the Settlers in the White Highlands and we had started a strategic road over the Aberdares. We took away many fond memories of new friendships and the wonderful scenery and climate of that very beautiful country. So we boarded the train for Mombasa and with our wives and families and comrades of many dangerous adventures, we enjoyed a comfortable and lazy journey home to Glasgow.

General Neil McMicking was there to meet us. The Battalion lined the ship's rails and gave me a great send off. My three years in Command were over – and never a dull moment and never a night in barracks.

CHAPTER EIGHT
Home Postings

To Hythe

After some leave and some very good grouse shooting in Glenartney, I was given another job as Lt Colonel, Chief Instructor at the Small Arms School, Hythe. The Commandant was Colonel John Orlebar who had Commanded the Norfolks in Korea. John was to undertake the modernisation of Ranges. He and his staff carried out extensive experiments with automatic falling targets and machinery which would operate a large number of targets with only a few men.

My aim was to change the attitude of the School to its use of fire power, and to bring the reality of war into teaching. I knew it was going to be a tough job. Little had changed since I was there as a student in 1933.

Bisley was the high point of the School's year. Accurate long range firing, taking wind and change of light into careful consideration. This was not the way to train men for modern war or close combat fighting.

One of the first things I developed at Hythe was a Field Firing range with moving targets on sledges. These were activated by men in dug-outs with wire hawsers on pulleys. I felt quite sure that I could prove that if you did not restrict the action of students, but actually encouraged them 'to have a go', you could prove that with most men, there is a natural instinct to hit the target. In my view the teaching at Hythe inhibited this instinct.

General Jim Cassels had left X Corps and had become DMT. He gave me a date when he could come to Hythe, to see how I was getting on. This was my chance to win support for my theory.

I was going to have a competition between Students and Staff Instructors. Why not have a team led by General Jim himself, with a Lt Colonel and some Majors? I explained to the General that there would be just one concession for his team. Each Officer would have a NCO beside him in case of a stoppage.

Six teams took part. Surprise, surprise, the General's team got the highest score. General Jim was a bit put out and muttered to me 'David, you have cooked the books.' I sent for the Captain in charge of the Markers, who confirmed that the

206

scoring was correct. The Students had also outshot the Permanent Staff.

I am ready to bet that no other Director of Military Training has ever got down on his tummy and shot against all comers. General Jim was game for anything.

My appointment at Hythe was extended by a year, as I still had much reorganisation to put through, but I realised that this was 'curtains' for me. My two great friends, Mick Baker and Bill Bradford, both a few months junior to me, had been saved from the 'chopper' by Brevet promotion. Bernard Fergusson and Jack Monteith had both become Brigadiers. I had apparently reached my ceiling. I can't pretend that I was not disappointed. In fact when the Staff at the School asked me to choose a night on which they would 'dine me out', I declined their offer and said it wasn't the kind of party I could enjoy, I would rather just fade away. I may say I was not taken by surprise; I had seen how Colonel Ian Stewart was treated – the man on whose tactics the Jungle Warfare School was founded. He got short shrift.

My elder brother Rhoddy, who had trained from scratch two battalions of the HLI in the War and had taken one of them right through the Low Countries to the heart of Germany, and had then been used again to command the 1st HLI for a full term in Jerusalem and the Middle East, was not recommended for a Brigade.

I too had to fight my corner once or twice and despite compliments from some distinguished Officers on my military ability, I was never recommended for higher rank. I had fought two successful battles in Korea, had given considerable Aid to the Civil Power in Kenya, indeed I had spawned the idea of Protected Villages, which more than anything else, brought the Mau-Mau Rebellion to an end. I then carried out a long over due reorganisation of the Small Arms School. Not a bad record in 5 years of very hard work, but there was to be no reward, no promotion.

Many years after leaving Hythe, my son Hugh went there on a course in preparation for many arduous tours of duty in Northern Ireland. I was very proud when he told me that I was still remembered there as an innovator of shooting and training techniques.

Retirement
I have had a wonderful life in retirement in Perthshire, the home of the Black Watch and the home of our families. My son and I have had years of wonderful sport and great hospitality in Glenartney. In the sixties it was year after year, week after week on the moors, shooting and stalking. Sometimes an evening flighting geese and

duck. My cup simply overflowed. Each year Lord Ancaster would have more or less the same friends to stay and I was privileged to meet them. Antony Head has already been mentioned in this book. There was Jock Colville, who wrote that wonderful account of his life with Winston Churchill during the War, and George Christie of Glyndbourne, Cosmo Crawley, that very fine shot and many other interesting and amusing people.

Some years Hugh and I were allowed to go out to the furthest part of the moor, on the Braco March, to walk up grouse, before our host arrived in the North. One year I took with me my nephew in the Scots Guards. We shot so many grouse that the head keeper, Alistair McIntyre (who served with the Black Watch in Germany) said, 'Any gun who shoots any more carries them himself'. A week later when I met the Laird, I got a rocket, 'David, I did say you could take out some boys, I think young officers in the Scots Guards are a bit much.'

What a wonderful start in life this was for a young man during his years at school and university. Lord Ancaster was my wife's cousin and treated Hugh as another son. I was a bit worried that moving in these very grand and privileged circles might make my boy a bit of a prig. I need not have worried. He had his head well screwed on and the one thing that Lord Ancaster avoided at all costs was ostentation. The house guests at Drummond Castle had simple fare on the moor, a bottle of beer or a bottle of cider. There was never wine or flasks of whisky handed round.

The object was peace and tranquillity. He didn't like a lot of men for loaders. There were plenty of birds in those years. Lord Ancaster would allow anyone to shoot with two guns if they chose to, but with a wife or a mother to load. Hugh did not just become a very good shot. He made deer stalking and the ecology of forest and moorland his abiding interest. He is now an expert in these subjects and is in considerable demand to speak at schools and universities. He is also a professional stalker. He culls the hinds and skins them and prepares the trophies for the taxidermist. The wonderful life of the woods and the moors is his life: a hard life, but very rewarding. It has brought him many friends all over the country and in Europe.

Drummond Castle

Sometimes we were invited to stay for a whole week at Drummond Castle, although our own home was only five miles up the glen surrounded by the Drummond estate. It was to give us a rest from the endless work of running a home with hardly any domestic help.

It was almost like my early life experience at Balmoral Castle when I was a subaltern in the Royal Guard.

At breakfast the sweet scent of violas and roses would sometimes waft up through the French windows. Drummond Castle garden is one of the finest in Scotland.

There were always six or more guests staying in the house and others were often invited to dine. One evening I was placed beside the famous Nancy Astor. She was a very old woman, but still a voluble talker and dominating personality. I was not required to contribute more to the conversation than a few grunts, perfunctory gasps of amazement or nods of agreement. She told me of all the wonderful and wealthy young men who had been in love with her at various periods of her life. In due course she turned her attention to Lord Ancaster on the other side. I started to rack my brains for some not too stupid question to ask her, to get her going on some lighter topic.

The next course was handed round and before I had time to open my mouth, she was off again replaying the same record, so to speak, almost word for word. In those days I was not aware of the problems of old age. Eventually I made a very gauche mistake; I tried to break into her story with a flippant interjection and got a flea in my ear for my pains. 'You naughty, rude young man.' End of story.

One of the guests who, like us, was given a holiday every year, was a very famous professor. He did not indulge in blood sports or anything like that, but had the beautiful house and its lovely library to himself all day long, while we were out on the moor. James Ancaster was a very kind and most considerate man of delightful character and quiet sense of humour. He was rather doubtful that the eminent professor and I would hit it off. Taking me aside before dinner he said, 'You won't contradict him will you, David?'

'No fear of that, James. He isn't aware of my existence, but I do get some quiet amusement listening to his dissertations.' He was at that time much in the public eye over the spoof Hitler diaries. The poor professor pontificated too much and made an awful fool of himself.

James Ancaster was a very charming character, beloved by all his many tenant farmers, gardeners, keepers, stalkers and everyone indeed with whom he came in contact. His principle charity was BLESMA, The British Limbless Ex-Servicemen's Association, established in nearby Crieff. Its doors are now open not only to ex-servicemen, but also to firemen, policemen and the rescue services. He had lost a leg below the knee, when serving with his regiment in France.

'Not a very gallant affair,' he said to me in a typical self-effacing aside. 'One of our own tanks ran over me and lay on my leg for quite a long time. It wasn't very pleasant each time they fired their gun.'

That was his story, but I am sure there was much more to it than that.

Then there is a story about James which I am sure many people who know him will enjoy. We were all standing at the foot of a steep hill with a line of butts stretching up over the skyline. James said in his quiet, rather slow and diffident voice, 'We will take our places in ascending order of decrepitude. I stay here. Andy (Drummond Moray) you go in the next butt; Hugo (Lord Brassey), I think you might just make it to the next one. Now David will you please place the other guns for me and go in the top butt yourself. Put Hugh on the outside in the peat hags.'

What wonderful weeks these were and to know that when we returned to our home on Saturday morning, we would be back again on the moor on Monday morning with a new lot of friends, who arrived at the Castle on Sunday evening. James Ancaster is greatly missed in Glenartney by us all to this day.

I did not realise it at the time – one never does of course – but we were living in the very last days of an era of the wonderful hospitality of the great families of Scotland. In a very few years all of this would come to an end for impecunious officers like myself on the fringe of a society which was disappearing. Sport was to become the preserve of the very rich, who could pay not only for the cartridges, but enormous sums of money for just one day of good shooting or stalking, and probably not even with personal friends, but virtual strangers in a syndicate. I was indeed a very fortunate infantry officer.

In the seventies it was wedding bells and babies. Two wonderful visits to my daughter and her young family in Cyprus to play with the first grandchildren on the beach. In the eighties it was teenage time, water skiing on Loch Earn and canoeing on Loch Tay, sports meetings on the lawn; the garden tractor and bringing in logs. Then long sessions in the evening, playing Slippery Sam, Smutty Peter and Butter the Bread with Grannie. Vast appetites of course. Giant snowman made in the garden right into the winter night. It was the last day of the holiday. What fun it all was. Now in the nineties we have the greatest fun, watching them all turning into young adults. One a good piper, one delightfully musical – all rather artistic – one a powerful hockey player and another a gymnast and one a *very* fast swimmer. All with delightful easy good manners and interesting conversation. We just live for the next visit.

Who is responsible for all this fun and sport? Why Jean, the girl that I married of course – the lass from the House of the Laird of Cockpen – the Earl of Dalhousie.

Farewell.

16th November 1952

Outline of Events 2nd Battle on the HOOK

Serial No	Time	From/To (Company)	Event
1.	1909	D	Report hearing burp gun and SA fire from the area of 2/Lt DOIG's patrol which was on the ridge leading to WARSAW (CT 105108) having been delayed going out owing to shellfire.
2.	1924	A	Report NO contact with either WARSAW patrol or 2/Lt DOIG's patrol.
3.	1942	D	One wounded man returned to 'B' Coy from WARSAW patrol.
4.	1957	A	Coy Standing Patrol in.
5.	2101	A	'A' Coy being attacked. The attack appeared to come from three directions, along the WARSAW ridge, along the RONSON ridge and up the valley to the SOUTH of the HOOK. Enemy arrived in fwd trenches of 1 pl before their own barrage had even lifted.
6.	2102	RA	Own party asked to fire close DF No 4092 which covers the approaches from RONSON (CT 101102).
7.	2103	To A	Recall your patrols. All heads down.
8.	2103	RA	DF 4092 reported shot.
9.	2105	Tks	Ordered to fire on RONSON. They used their searchlights as well but were unable to see any enemy in the smoke and haze.
10.	2109	RA	Repeat DF 4092.
11.	2118	D	Report enemy mor firing from WARSAW.
12.	2120	Bde	Asked to put on YONG DONG (136104) searchlight.
13.	2123	A	No 1 pl report that it appears to be quiet at the moment. SA fire and a few grenades are coming into the pl area.
14.	2127	RA	Offered a ripple of rockets by US Marines. Asked for it to come down on 096104.
15.	2130	D	Report at least 4 mors firing from WARSAW on both sides of the spur at 105106 and a fire on WARSAW.
16.	2137	B	Coy standing patrol at 115103 in with one man wounded.

17.	2140	C	*Sitrep.* Heavy fire on the HOOK. Patrol on RONSON over-run.
18.	2142	A	NO enemy seen and shelling seems to have dropped off. Enemy got as far as RONSON and didn't come any further.
19.	2145	RA	DF 4092 shot.
20.	2145		Bde warned 3 PPCLI to stand up one coy.
21.	2147	A	Enemy on the HOOK. This info was obtained by a messenger who got round the fwd trench to 2/Lt BLACK in his CP and was reported back on the 88 set. Almost immediately after this arty DF (VT) was fired on the HOOK itself.
22.	2150	To A	U target coming down, keep in your caves.
23.	2150	RA	Ripple fired.
24.	2152	C	Reported enemy attacking one pl of 'A' Coy and that shelling on the HOOK has re-started. This shelling was thought to be both enemy and our own.
25.	2201	CO to A	Fire on you stopping now.
26.	2202	RA	HOOK being heavily mortared.
27.	2203	D	Shelling on 'D' Coy increased.
28.	2205	RA	OC 'A' Coy requests VT to continue on the HOOK itself since he discovered that the enemy were still there.
29.	2207	B	Ordered to stand by to be relieved by a Coy of 3PPCLI and to move to 'D' Coy Adm Area when relieving coy of 3 PPCLI arrive.
30.	2214	B	Pls getting ready to move.
31.	2217	CO	Prepare to lift all fire off the HOOK and put a belt of fire round the perimeter of it in order to stop the next wave of enemy attack.
32.	2220	RA	Mike target on 105106 using VT.
33.	2224	C	Report that enemy numbers on the HOOK are considerable.
34.	2225	From A relayed through C	Fire now lifting off the HOOK. Pl going out to have a look. Nothing seen.
35.	2225	A	OC 'A' Coy made use of the lull to send the remains of 2pl under Sgt GAIT to reinforce 1 pl on the HOOK. The P/M being wounded, the Pipes and Drums were put under comd of 2/Lt RATTRAY to reinforce his own pl. 2/Lt RATTRAY's pl then moved up the hill in order to take over the high ground and look after the RIGHT flank of the coy posn since this posn had been vacated by 2 pl on moving forward to the HOOK.
36.	2230	D	NO enemy. Fire decreasing.

37.	2235	A	Lift Vt. No 1 pl going out to have a look. Think that enemy are driven off.
38.	2237	A	Shelling decreasing.
39.	2240	A & C	Request for ambulances. 'C' Coy sending own fwd to 'A' Coy Adm Area.
40.	2244	D	SA fire from WARSAW.
41.	2247		No 1 pl thinks that enemy are forming up for another attack.
42.	2247	3 PPCLI	One Coy 3 PPCLI on it's way to 'B' Coy now. One pl of 'B' Coy moving off to tpt now. The two other pls ready to move.
43.	2255	CO/D	'D' coy to send one pl to reinforce 'A' Coy as soon as shelling has eased.
44.	2255	C	Small amount of shelling on 'C' Coy.
45.	2255	A	Report all pretty quiet.
46.	2258	Bde	Following intercept received:- 'Chinese ordered to move to 164'.
47.	2259	Tks	Tks on 121 have been firing hard for the last 5 mins.
48.	2300	A	HOOK still being shelled.
49.	2304	D	10 pl ready to move. Ordered to go to 'A' Coy CP via the Coy Adm Area.
50.	2305	B	4 pl moved off in tpt.
51.	2312	A	Shelling still continues. We are unable to search area.
52.	2324	D	4 pl of 'B' Coy arrived at 'D' Coy Adm Area. Ordered to proceed to 'A' Coy.
53.	2327	CO	Following code-names arranged for arty fire plan on the HOOK:- BUTTER – VT on the HOOK RESIST – DF to prevent attack coming in on the HOOK.
54.	2331	RA	A ripple of rockets coming in shortly. One more will be coming 30 mins later.
55.	2333	Bde	*Intercept* (a) 'Have captured 12 BOARS'. (b) 'Send special class to 164'. This was interpreted to mean, 'Send Aslt Engrs to the HOOK to deal with tunnels'.
56.	2355	A	*Sitrep* Have a considerable number of X and Y and there is considerable damage to the posn. I am now consolidating.
57.	2337	A	Report PW in 1 pl. these happened to be two Chinamen who came into 1 pl CP and lit a cigarette. They were shot at point blank range and presumed to be lying there wounded. However when the situation eased and light was

214

			produced it was found that they had gone.
58.	2340	RA	Ripple of rockets shot.
59.	2359	B	Coy of 3 PPCLI now moving on foot up to the FDLs.
60.	0001	D	5 men returned from Sgt KERRY's ambush patrol on WARSAW.
61.	0010	A	*Sitrep*
			Coy moving up. A few enemy are still in what is left of the fwd trenches.
62.	0014	D	4 cas in 'D' Coy.
63.	0018	Bde	Bde now informed us that the radio traffic of the enemy HQ operating against us had died down for a period of about two hrs.
64.	0020	Bde	'C' Coy 3 PPCLI moved off to concentration area behind pt 121 (CT 103095).
65.	0020		Relief of 'B' Coy by 'B' Coy 3 PPCLI complete.
66.	0025	RA	'RESIST' shot.
67.	0026	From OC'A' through RA Chunnels	Attack coming in. Chinese in fwd trenches of the HOOK.
68.	0029	CO/A	You must mop up.
69.	0031	B	Asked if there was any indication of the attack coming in from WARSAW.
70.	0032	A	Am being attacked now.
71.	0032	Tks	CO ordered tks to fire at enemy on RONSON.
72.	0045	CO/A	Counter attack force is to remain in deep trenches by you CP area.
			2/Lt SMART's Pl of 'B' Coy (4 pl) was the first pl to arrive and was put into the trench in front of 'A' Coy CP. Soon after this Lt HAW's Pl of 'D' Coy (10 pl) arrived and was told to occupy the high ground formerly occupied by elements of 2 and 3 pls and to bring fire to bear on the HOOK while counter attack was launched until Green Verey light went up.
73.	0048	CO/D & A	Where are the two reinforcements pls.
74.	0052	C	Tks say it is NOT on to go up to the HOOK.
75.	0056	A	Situation somewhat obscure. Are being heavily mortared.
76.	0059	CO/RTR	Tk is to move or rather will move up to the HOOK. The intention of putting a tk up on to the HOOK at the time of the counter attack was to make the men feel that there was some support going in with them. OC 'A' Coy, on hearing that the Tk was coming up, delayed his counter attack. His plan was then to move 4 pl up with the Tk until it reached it's firing posn on top of the HOOK and then swing 4 pl round

			the RIGHT flank in front of the Tk to clear up the HOOK.
77.	0100	D	Two pls of 'B' Coy on their way to the HOOK.
78.	0110	Bde	*Intercept* Enemy calling for reinforcements.
79.	0121	A	Can you see to fight.
80.	0124	Intercept from A Coy	4 pl 'B' Coy instructed to go in with Tk.
81.	0125	A	OC 'A' Coy told Tk comd to drive through the jeep and 15 cwt that were blocking his way to the HOOK.
82.	0130	A	Ordered to stand by a second pl to move on to the HOOK. Told that Aslt/Pr Pl will be coming up to occupy vacated Pl posns.
83.	0132	RA	VT now lifted off HOOK. This was OC 'A' Coy's signal for the counter attack to begin.
84.	0137	Intercept from Tks	Tk hit, driver hurt. This Tk was hit in the drivers compartment by a bazooka. It happened at the very moment that the attack was to go fwd. At the same time three or four LMGs opened up on the Tk from the ridge between 'A' Coy CP and the HOOK. They shot straight down the route of advance.
85.	0147	A	Putting down VT for two mins to deal with enemy on ridge. After that the attack will go in whether the Tk is ready or NOT. Counter attack went in the moment the VT lifted and advanced about 50 yds. It was then held up by fresh LMGs opening up. OC 'A' Coy then ordered 4 pl to open fire to 3 pl (2/Lt RATTRAY's pl reinforced with the Pipes and Drums) who had meanwhile been moved on to the start line. 3 pl then went fwd through 4 pl with covering fire from 10 pl as arranged, and succeeded in reaching the lateral trench across the HOOK. They were there, held up grenades from enemy established on the highest point on the HOOK.
86.	0223	CO/D	Organise a sup of filled LMG magazines and other small arms and send them to 'A' Coy HQ.
87.	0225	C/CP	Green flare seen on top of HOOK.
88.	0236	D	Aslt/Pnr Pl now arrived at 'D' Coy. 12 pl of 'D' Coy to move to 'A' Coy by shortest possible route.
89.	0246	CO/D	Coy 2i/c to remain in present loc and take over Comd of Coy posn forming a Comp Coy. OC 'D'

			Coy to move to 'A' Coy CP and take over comd of reinforcements arriving in the Coy posn.
90.	0247	A	*Sitrep* Elements of 1 pl holding line of crawl trench from 1 pl CP. Other pls are to pass through. The counter attack force is still holding lateral trench and trying to mop up.
91.	0253	RA	Mopping up complete except for one rather stubborn pocket of resistance.
92.	0255	A	All clear behind HOOK CP. Shortly after this 2/Lt BLACK reported that he was being fired at from behind.
93.	0257	D	OC 'D' Coy has left to join 'A' Coy.
94.	0302	Bde	All Chinese radio sets have closed down. This infers (a) Attack has failed/ or (b) Wrls ops have been hit by counter bombardment.
95.	0307	RA	Heavy mortaring on RIGHT fwd pl of 'C' Coy.
96.	0307	D	Sitrep from Capt MACDONALD now OC Composite Coy on 'D' Coy posn. LEFT Pl posn – 11 Pl CENTRE posn – Aslt/Pnr Pl RIGHT posn – Vacant 2/Lt GRAY's pl of 'B' Coy (6pl) was still with 'D' Coy in the Coy Adm Area. This pl was ordered to proceed to the HOOK by shortest route.
		CO	Ordered MMG pl to go fwd as riflemen to fill vacant pl posn in Comp Coy.
97.	0310	C	Coy being heavily mortared.
98.	0311	Bde	*Intercept* Chinese calling frantically for reinforcements.
99.	0327	Intercept from 'A' Coy wrls net	1 to 1A, 'Are you happy, where you are?'. 1A to 1, 'No, never have been'. 1 to 1A, 'Don't be a clown. Out'.
100.	0335	A	OC 'D' Coy now arrived at 'A' Coy CP.
101.	0343	A	OC 'B' Coy now at 'A' Coy Aid Post in Coy Adm Area.
102.	0345	A	Group of enemy on RIGHT of HOOK.
103.	0348	A	*Sitrep* One pl now established on the HOOK. One pl of 'B' Coy reforming and distributing amn. They are being fired at from the RIGHT rear. Lt HAW's pl was ordered to move down from the Coy CP and round the LEFT flank with the task of mopping up and occupying the fwd trenches on the SOUTH side of the HOOK.

			This pl, having got so far fwd, came under considerable MG fire from BETTY GRABLE. (CT 098099).
104.	0354	C	MMG on BETTY GRABLE is being engaged with stens and brownings.
105.	0355	A	OC 1 pl reported that the remainder of 'A' Coy which was now all on the HOOK was being attacked from all sides.
106.	0357	RA	'RESIST' ordered by OC 'A' Coy.
107.	0358	RA	'RESIST' Shot.
108.	0401	RA	Shot on DF 4092 also.
109.	0403	D	'D' Coy CP being shelled.
110.	0415	A	CO called for a Sitrep from OC 'A' Coy. OC 'A' said that he was still battling to get on to the HOOK. One pl was on it's way there and the other pls counter-attacking were suddenly attacked. CO told him to hold on. OC 'A' Coy replied, 'That's what I hoped you would say'.
111.	0423	C	Enemy arty fire has now started from 'C' Coy.
112.	0425	D	12 pl on it's way to the HOOK encountered approximately 20 enemy on the ridge between it and 11 pl posn of 'D' Coy. Pl comd and half the pl reached the HOOK. Sgt ROBERTSON with eleven men, remained 11 pl posn. He was ordered to mop up enemy and get through to the HOOK.
113.	0430	RA	Two bty targets using VT were fired on to 098108.
114.	0431	CO/D	11 pl ordered to shoot down the re-entrant running NORTH from them.
115.	0444	D	Sgt ROBERTSON on trying to reach the HOOK with the remainder of 12 pl was fired on from both sides of the ridge.
116.	0452	A	Sgt ROBERTSON party must NOT go along crawl trench to the HOOK but must make for 'A' Coy Adm Area.
117.	0457	MMG	Ready to move fwd to 'D' Coy as a rifle Pl.
118.	0503	Bde	Intercept from US Marines. Time of origin 0457 hrs. 'To appear bit by bit', and shortly afterwards. 'To appear at once'. CO considered this meant a new attack forming up.
119.	0515	A	2/Lt WALKER on arrival at 'A' Coy with his men was reinforced with what men were available and sent up to 1 pl on the HOOK to assist clearing enemy from there.
120.	0522	A/D	Making progress. Opposition appears slight.
121.	0524	CO 26 Fd Amb	29 cas evac so far.

122.	0526	Intercept from 'A'Coy Wrls net	1A to 1, 'Our own DF is falling short. Can you rectify this?'. 1 to 1A, 'It is NOT our DF'.
123.	0530	CO/C	Send your body armour to 'A' Coy Adm Area.
124.	0534	To D	Send a guide to your Adm Area to meet MMG pl on it's way to you as a rifle pl.
125.	0537	C	OC 'C' Coy 3 PPCLI has arrived at Coy CP and his coy is in the Coy Adm Area.
126.	0550	RA	Firing airburst over WARSAW.
127.	0552	A	Few enemy still on slopes fwd of CP. OC 'A' Coy ordered 6 pl of 'B' Coy to move fwd and safeguard the RIGHT flank to prevent further penetration from WARSAW approach. It was at this time that 2/Lt GRAY and Maj ROWAN-HAMILTON were wounded by one of our own grenades thrown at them by the enemy.
128.	0557	D	CO ordered 11 pl to go out first lt to deal with enemy on ridge between them and the HOOK.
129.	0557	A	Twelve men of 12 pl arrived at the 1 pl CP. 12 pl was to go round the LEFT flank to clear enemy on both sides of it. Just after 12 pl moved off from 1 pl CP to carry out this task, 2/Lt WALKER got wounded.
130.	0558	A	Reported that they need more men. OC requested a Sitrep from 'A' Coy. Sitrep: Situation very confused. Small parties of the enemy have suddenly appeared again all over the place. CO asked: 'Have you any reserve left?' OC 'A' Coy replied: 'NO'. CO said: 'Stick it out'. CO informed Bde Comd that all reserves had now been used.
131.	0600	CP	Bde Comd informed CO that 'C' Coy 3 PPCLI would relieve our men on the HOOK at first lt.
132.	0600	RA	DF 4092 fired.
133.	0602	D	NOT much left of No 3 sec 11 pl.
134.	0610	C	PPCLI counter attack moves to the HOOK.
135.	0615	D	MMG pl arrived in 'D' Coy Adm Area.
136.	0620	D	11 pl patrol ordered to go out as soon as it is light and mop up enemy between 'D' and 'A' Coys.
137.	0620	A	Coy holding it's ground. Still small parties of enemy on fringe of HOOK who have small piles of grenades with them.
138.	0630	RA	Fired a smoke screen between 093106 and 095103.

139.	0643	Intercept of 'A' Coy wrls net	1A to 1, 'Some enemy are throwing grenades down on us'.
			1 to 1A, 'Without being facetious throw some back'.
140.	0653	To D	Report progress of mopping up.
141.	0700	C	One pl of 'C' Coy 3PPCLI on the HOOK, the other pl is just below it. This Coy met NO enemy when they arrived on the posn.
142.	0710		CO and IO went fwd to the HOOK.
143.	0801	A	Evacuation of wounded being carried out. Relief is in progress.
144.	0820	A	Comd on the HOOK passed to 'C' Coy 3PPCLI (to be known as 'Z' Coy).
145.	0933	D	All wounded off the HOOK. Two wounded and two dead removed from WARSAW Ridge. Chinese are still on WARSAW, but are being engaged by PPCLI.
146.	0945	OC 26 Fd Amb.	OC 26 Fd Amb estimates that bn has had over 70 casualties.
147.	0950	RA	Smoke programme as previously arranged being fired in front of WARSAW.
148.	1000	Fwd Control	Reported hearing on Bn Comd 31 set net: 'Chinky, Chinky; Hullo Chinky here'.

APPENDIX B

Address given by Lt. Col. D McN C Rose, DSo at
the Memorial Service
1st Battalion The Black Watch
Royal Highland Regiment
July 1953, Pusan

We are here today for two reasons. To remember our comrades who have died in Korea, and to thank God that so many of us have survived and may now return to a more normal way of life and soon we hope to be re-united with our families.

When we left Crail over a year ago, no-one could tell what lay ahead, but we all fully realised what a great tradition we had to live up to. Now we can look back and we know that we have done well. We have added a page or two to the long and distinguished history of our Regiment.

Twice we have been chosen to hold the vital ground in the Commonwealth Divisional Sector and twice we repelled the enemy's furious assault without giving a yard of ground. There have been long, cold nights of sentry duty and the strain of many patrols: we have been heavily shelled on numerous occasions and there have been days of back-breaking work with pick and shovel. There have also been many gay times with good company and laughter which we will all remember with pleasure.

Today, despite casualties and the steady drain of friends who have gone home, we stand stronger than a year ago and with much valuable experience to help us in the future.

It has been a great experience to have served in the United Nations Army and to have made friends with and fought alongside the soldiers of so many different countries, in addition to our kinsmen in the Commonwealth Division.

One thing that has greatly impressed me is the deep respect and even envy which the Americans have expressed for our Regimental System. They have seen what we know to be of such great value – the continuity which it gives, the importance of having a common background and mutual friends at home, the support of a large community in the Regimental Area.

Three days ago our Brigadier and our Divisional Commander told you all on parade how pleased they were with the good work this Battalion had done. Yesterday I had a letter from General Maxwell Taylor and another from General Wells. The credit is shared by every officer and man of the one thousand seven hundred who have served with the Battalion, whether in Infantry Companies, with Supporting Weapons, Signals, Transport, or in the Administrative departments. Everyone pulled his weight.

All these Officers speak of traditions. Our traditions are not just sentiment. One of our traditions is a really close comradeship between all ranks and the comradeship in this Battalion has not gone unnoticed out here. It has been particularly commented upon amongst our wounded, whose cheerfulness and high morale, their keenness to get back to the Battalion, has been an inspiration to all around them.

To those who do not fully recover, we all send our best wishes for the future. They will not be forgotten I can assure you, but will receive all the help that the Regiment can give through the Black Watch Association.

Those who are still in hospital but will soon be quite fit again will find a real welcome awaiting them when they return to us in Kenya.

To the relatives of the fallen, whose graves here are marked with a Red Hackle, we send our deepest sympathy.

GOD SAVE THE QUEEN